Literary Terms Made Easy

Deciphering the Language of Literature

A Comprehensive Study

Abha Bhardwaj Sharma

Notice

Preface

Literature is more than just words on a page; it's a dance of language, crafted with special techniques that give depth and emotion to a story. However, this beautiful complexity can sometimes feel a bit overwhelming, especially if we're not familiar with the terms used. That's where **"Literary Terms Made Easy: Deciphering the Language of Literature" by Prof. Abha Bhardwaj Sharma** steps in.

Our book is your friendly companion in this vast world of literature. It breaks down the fancy terms and techniques, making them easy to understand, no matter where you are on your reading journey. But we go beyond just definitions. We dive into examples from well-known stories, illustrating how these terms come to life in actual narratives. Imagine literature as a puzzle; each piece, whether it's a metaphor, a pun, or a symbol, fits together to create a complete picture. With this guide, you'll not only see the full picture but also appreciate the beauty of each piece.

In a time when quick tweets and short online videos grab most of our attention, diving deep into literature offers a refreshing escape. This book not only equips you to understand literature better but also inspires a renewed love for timeless stories.

A notable feature of this guide is its comprehensive approach to literary appreciation. Readers are not just introduced to terms; they are shown how these devices function in the broader context of literary criticism. Each term is accompanied by explanations, examples, and insights that aid in deepening the reader's understanding.

What sets "Literary Terms Made Easy" apart from similar books is its universal appeal. Whether you are a seasoned professor, an eager literature student, a casual reader, or even someone preparing for competitive examinations like the UGC NET in English, this book caters to all. For those pursuing academic excellence in English literature, be it at the bachelor's or master's level, Prof. Abha's work is indispensable.

The layout of the book is reader-friendly, with each term clearly defined, explained, and illustrated with examples. This makes it easy for readers to navigate through the terms and find the ones they are looking for.

"Literary Terms Made Easy" is a testament to Prof. Abha Bhardwaj Sharma's expertise and passion for literature. It is a must-have for anyone seeking to enhance their understanding of literary analysis and appreciation. This guide is not just a book; it's a bridge to a deeper, more nuanced appreciation of the literary world.

Let's embark on this journey together, exploring the hidden treasures of literature and celebrating the stories that connect us all.

Our goal is simple: to ensure that literary terms cease to be obstacles and instead become windows—transparent panes through which the beauty and depth of literature shine resplendently.

CONTENT

34. **Dialogue**
35. **Connotation**
36. **Denotation**
37. **Cliche**
38. **Metonymy**
39. **Synecdoche**
40. **Picturesque**
41. **Satire**
42. **Parody**
43. **Burlesque**
44. **Metaphysical Conceit**
45. **Conceit**
46. **Paradox**
47. **Pun**
48. **Repetition**
49. **Style**
50. **Understatement**
51. **Sublime**
52. **Colloquialism**
53. **Epigraph**
54. **Epitaph**
55. **Juxtaposition**
56. **Aphorism**

57. # **MUSICAL DEVICES**
58. **Rhyme**
59. **Rhythm**
60. **Meter**
61. **Alliteration**
62. **Assonance**
63. **Consonance**
64. **Blank Verse**
65. **Free Verse**
66. **Caesura**
67. **Onomatopoeia**

101. Euphony
102. Tmesis
103. Tricolon
104. Syllepsis
105. Periphrasis
106. Aporia
107. Antanaclasis
108. Aposiopesis
109. Catachresis
110. Enthymeme
111. Epistrophe
112. Pleonasm
113. Rhetorical Question
114. Erotema
115.Tautology
116. Deus Ex MAchina
117. Exposition
118. Anthropomorphism
119. Archetype
120. Archaism
121. Euphemism
122. Motif
123. Portmanteau
124. Malapropism

LITERARY DEVICES

LITERARY TERMS

POETIC DEVICES

MUSICAL DEVICES

RHETORICAL DEVICES

"Deciphering the Language of Literature
A Comprehensive Guide"

What is Literature?

Literature, as a term, encompasses a wide spectrum of written and spoken materials. Its vastness can often blur the lines between general written pieces and artistic literary works. To get a clearer picture, it's essential to understand their distinct characteristics and purposes.

Read the two passages

Passage 1

Literature is a big term that covers all sorts of written and spoken stuff. Think of it like a big box where you can find everything from a student's random notes to famous speeches by leaders. This box also has technical guides on how machines work and exciting stories that pull readers into different worlds. Every item in this box has a job: to share some kind of message or info.

Now, let's try to break things down. Some written things are straightforward and clear. They're made to give specific information or instructions. Examples are news articles, school papers, office notes, or guides on how to use a gadget. These are like the 'how-to' or 'just the facts' parts of the literature box.

On the other side, we have the artistic stuff. This is where writers get creative, pouring emotions and deep thoughts into their work. They use special writing tricks like metaphors and tell stories that make readers feel things or see the world in a new way. These can be poems, stories, plays, or novels. The cool thing about these works is that different people might get different meanings from them, and that's okay!

Sometimes, these two types mix a bit. Like, a news article might be so well-written that it reads like a story. Or a story might have lots of real facts in it, making it informative like a report.

In short, literature is a big mix of all kinds of written and spoken materials. Whether it's simple info or creative writing, each has its unique place and purpose.

Passage 2

Literature, in its grand tapestry, weaves tales of human epochs, diverse cultures, and myriad emotions. It's an echoing symphony of voices, transcending time and space, casting a labyrinthine shadow over the definitions of written and spoken word.

Within this expanse, scribbled musings of a dreamer find their place beside a leader's rousing oration; the mechanical heartbeats of technical manuals beat in tandem with the passionate pulses of novels that sail across realms of imagination. Every piece, whether a whisper or a shout, tells a tale, bearing its own essence and intention.

Yet, in this boundless realm, distinctions shimmer. Some writings stand as lighthouses of clarity, beacons of information—newsprint, scholarly articles, and crisp memos. These pieces are the straightforward narrators, shunning the allure of ornate phrases, striving solely to inform, to enlighten with precision.

But then there's the other kind—the poetic souls of literature. These are tales painted with emotions, draped in metaphors, and dancing with allegories. They're not just messages, but melodies— poems, novels, and plays, each a cryptic canvas of human experience, open to myriad interpretations, dazzling in their depth and ambiguity.

And sometimes, these worlds entwine. A piece of journalism takes on the hues of a novella, or a story cloaks itself in facts so real it mirrors an academic discourse.

Analysis

The two passages, while discussing the vast domain of literature, approach the topic from distinct angles that align with the concepts of "general" and "literary."

The first passage uses simpler language and relatable analogies, akin to a "general" understanding of a topic. It talks of literature as a "big box" with varied contents and offers straightforward classifications. This approach aims for clarity and broad understanding, making it accessible to a wider audience, much like general written pieces aim to inform without complexity.

The second passage, on the other hand, adopts a more "literary" style. It delves deeper into the nuances of literature and employs a more sophisticated vocabulary and structure. This passage doesn't just inform but invites reflection on the layered meanings of literature, akin to how literary works prioritise emotion, aesthetic, and introspection. It provides a richer, more detailed exploration, much like literary works themselves which are dense with symbolism, allegory, and emotional depth.

Thus, the first passage's straightforward, accessible style can be seen as representative of general written works, while the second passage's intricate, reflective style mirrors the depth and complexity of artistic literary works.

General And Literary Texts

1. **General texts** are designed predominantly for the common reader. They aim to provide information or instructions in a direct, comprehensible manner. The primary objective is the clear and efficient conveyance of information. As such, they are crafted in straightforward language, have a logical structure, and prioritize accessibility for a broad audience. They might not delve deep into evoking emotional responses or employ intricate language features.

In contrast, **literary texts a**re rich tapestries woven with the intricacies of language. They don't just communicate; they resonate, stimulate, and evoke. Employing an arsenal of literary devices, poetic devices, and specialised literary terms, these texts paint vivid pictures, stirring the senses and emotions of the reader. Sensuousness is central to their fabric, engaging the reader in an immersive experience that appeals not just to the intellect but also to the heart. Beyond the beauty of their language, literary texts are often profound, serving as reflections on the human condition, societal concerns, or deep-seated emotions.

They're not just texts but art forms, where every word is carefully chosen, every metaphor is meticulously crafted, and every narrative twist is designed to provoke thought. Often open to multiple interpretations, they encourage readers to delve deeper, to question, and to derive personal meanings. In the words of the famous adage, a literary text can be seen as "a thing well said," striking a balance between form and content to deliver a potent message in an exquisite package.

2. A general text operates like a well-paved road, guiding its readers without detours or unnecessary complexities. It aims for efficiency, ensuring that readers, regardless of their background or prior knowledge, can traverse the text with ease. Such texts often act as bridges, closing gaps in understanding or providing essential information. They are the reliable tools in our daily lives, the instruction manuals, the news reports, and the factual articles that give us clarity and understanding without demanding deep introspection.

In juxtaposition, a literary text is like an intricate maze or a winding forest trail, offering myriad paths of exploration. The journey it promises is less about reaching a specific destination and more about the experience itself. It invites readers to pause and appreciate the landscape of words, to get lost in its twists and turns, and to find themselves in its narratives. The allegories and metaphors present in literary texts often serve as mirrors, reflecting both the universal truths and the intimate idiosyncrasies of the human spirit. They don't merely state; they suggest, leaving readers with lingering thoughts and emotions long after the last page is turned.

3. A simple text tells a story, straightforwardly leading the reader from the beginning to the end, much like a stream flowing in a predetermined direction. Its narratives are clean and linear, offering satisfaction in clarity and directness. Readers grasp the tale, understand its context, and acknowledge its message. They might appreciate the narrative but move on once the tale concludes, much like leaving a familiar path once traveled.

On the other hand, a literary text is a symphony of words that doesn't just narrate but enchants. It lures readers into a dance, inviting them to feel each note, each crescendo, each poignant pause. Such a text doesn't merely tell; it bewitches, making readers wonder in awe at the magic woven by the author. A truly great literary piece compels its audience to revisit it time and again, discovering new nuances with each read. It becomes a cherished possession, shared with fervor, and discussed with passion. Readers don't just appreciate the narrative; they fall in love with it. And such love often extends to the author, creating a bond that transcends the confines of the pages, making them timeless icons, adored irrespective of the story they tell.

So understanding a literary text demands more than just reading skills; it requires a certain finesse, an appreciation for the subtleties of language, and a passion for delving into the layered meanings of words and phrases. Let's unpack what's necessary:

Literary Sense: This is an intrinsic ability, often developed over time, to feel and comprehend the nuances of a text. Just as one develops a palate for fine wines or gourmet food, a literary sense is cultivated through consistent exposure to various forms of literature.

Knowledge of Literary Devices: Literary devices, such as allegory, allusion, foreshadowing, and more, are tools writers use to convey deeper meanings, elicit emotions, or paint vivid images in the reader's mind. Understanding these devices enriches one's reading experience.

Poetic Terms: Understanding poetry requires one to be familiar with terms like meter, rhyme, enjambment, and caesura. Poetry, in many ways, is a dance of words, and knowing its moves helps one appreciate the rhythm and grace with which it flows.

Puns, Metaphors, and Beyond: These are just the tip of the iceberg. There are similes, personifications, hyperboles, oxymorons, alliterations, and countless other devices. Each offers a unique twist to the narrative, a fresh perspective, or a deeper layer of meaning.

Critical Thinking: Beyond all the technical knowledge, approaching a literary text with an open mind, ready to question, interpret, and analyze, is pivotal. The beauty of literature is that it's open to multiple interpretations, and critical thinking allows readers to derive their own insights.

Advanced Literary Techniques: As literature evolved, especially into the realms of modern and post-modern eras, the techniques employed became even more intricate. Stream of consciousness, metafiction, intertextuality, and unreliable narrators are just some of the innovative methods authors use to challenge conventions and redefine storytelling.

Post-Modern Writings: The post-modern era introduced a wave of experimental literature, often blurring the lines between reality and fiction, author and character, narrative and meta-narrative. To navigate this intricate maze, one needs an understanding of the post-modern ethos, its skepticism, playfulness, and penchant for deconstruction.

Complexities of the Author's Mind: An author's psyche is a reservoir of experiences, beliefs, fears, and dreams. To truly appreciate a literary text, it helps to understand the mind behind it. This doesn't just refer to their biographical details, but also their influences, the zeitgeist of their times, and their personal philosophies.

Cultural, Historical, and Philosophical Context: The setting of a story isn't just its physical location or time period. It's the entire cultural, historical, and philosophical backdrop against which the narrative unfolds. This context provides invaluable insights into the motives, behaviors, and choices of characters within the story.

Our journey through this book is aimed at equipping the reader with a comprehensive understanding of these elements. Consider this handbook your trusty compass, guiding you through the vast, enchanting forest of literary texts. With this guide in hand, not only will you navigate the world of literature with confidence, but you'll also unearth its treasures and revel in its magic, enriching your reading experience manifold.

POETRY

Poetry is a form of literary expression characterised by its use of heightened language, structured rhythm, and carefully chosen words to convey emotions, ideas, and experiences in a unique and artistic way. Unlike prose, which is written in paragraphs and follows conventional grammar and syntax, poetry often employs various techniques and devices to create a distinct aesthetic and emotional impact.

Imagery: The use of vivid and sensory language to create mental images that evoke emotions and experiences.

Figurative Language: The use of metaphors, similes, personification, and other figurative devices to convey meanings beyond the literal.

Rhythm and Meter: Many poems use patterns of stressed and unstressed syllables to create a rhythmic flow. The specific pattern of rhythm is called the meter.

Rhyme: The repetition of similar sounds at the end of lines or within lines. Rhyming patterns can vary, including end rhymes, internal rhymes, and slant rhymes.

Structure: Poems can take on a variety of structures, such as sonnets, haikus, ballads, free verse, and more. Each structure has its own rules or lack thereof, affecting the poem's visual appearance and pacing.

Stanza: A group of lines in a poem, similar to a paragraph in prose. Different stanzas often convey different ideas or shifts in tone.

Theme: The central idea or message explored in a poem. Poets often use imagery, symbols, and metaphors to convey their themes.

Emotion and Expression: Poetry is a powerful medium for expressing emotions and thoughts that may be difficult to communicate through conventional language.

Ambiguity: Poems often leave room for interpretation, allowing readers to engage with the text on multiple levels and derive personal meanings.

Sound Play: Besides rhyme, poets also use alliteration, assonance, consonance, and onomatopoeia to create musical and auditory effects.

Economy of Language: Poets carefully select words to convey a lot of meaning in a limited space, often with an emphasis on brevity and conciseness.

Poetry is an artistic expression, a form of creative expression that invites experimentation with language, form, and structure. Poetry can cover a wide range of topics, from love and nature to social issues and philosophical concepts. It captures the essence of human experience through the unique arrangement of words and the exploration of emotions and ideas. Different poets and cultures have produced countless styles and forms of poetry, making it a diverse and rich literary genre.

POEM

A poem is a literary work that uses language in a distinctive and artistic way to convey emotions, thoughts, ideas, or experiences. Poems often feature heightened language, carefully chosen words, and creative techniques to create a powerful impact on the reader or listener. They can be found in various forms and structures, each with its own unique characteristics.

Poems use language creatively and imaginatively, often employing figurative language, metaphors, similes, and other devices to convey meanings beyond literal interpretations
Poets use vivid descriptions and sensory language to create mental images that evoke emotions and engage the reader's senses.

Many poems have a rhythmic pattern created by stressed and unstressed syllables, known as meter. This rhythmic quality contributes to the musicality and flow of the poem.
The repetition of similar sounds at the end of lines or within lines, contributing to the poem's auditory appeal. Rhyming patterns vary among different poems.

Poems can take on a variety of forms, such as sonnets, haikus, ballads, free verse, and more. The structure and arrangement of lines and stanzas impact the visual appearance and pacing of the poem

Stanza: A group of lines in a poem, similar to a paragraph in prose. Different stanzas often mark shifts in theme, tone, or subject matter.
Theme: The central idea, message, or concept that the poem explores. Themes can be diverse and cover a wide range of topics.

Emotion and Tone: Poems often convey emotions, moods, and attitudes through carefully chosen words and their arrangement.

Conciseness: Poets strive to convey a lot of meaning in a limited space, often using economy of language to make every word count.

Artistic Expression: Poetry allows for creative expression and experimentation with language, rhythm, and form.

Interpretation: Poems may contain multiple layers of meaning, inviting readers to engage with the text and derive personal interpretations.

Sound Play: Beyond rhyme, poets use techniques like alliteration, assonance, consonance, and onomatopoeia to create auditory effects.

Ambiguity: Poems can intentionally leave certain aspects open to interpretation, encouraging readers to explore different meanings and perspectives.

Overall, a poem is a creative work of art that engages with language in a way that goes beyond straightforward communication. It encapsulates the complexities of human experience, thoughts, and emotions in a condensed and impactful form.

In simpler words "Poem" and "Poetry" are related terms in the realm of literature, but they refer to slightly different concepts.

Poem:

A poem is a specific work of literature that is characterized by its use of language, form, and structure to convey emotions, ideas, experiences, or imagery. It's a single, self-contained piece of writing that follows particular patterns of rhythm, rhyme, and/or line arrangement. A poem can take various forms, such as sonnets, haikus, ballads, or free verse. It is an individual creation that exists as a standalone artistic expression.

Poetry:

Poetry, on the other hand, is a broader and more encompassing term. It refers to the entire genre or category of literary works that use distinctive language and creative techniques to convey meaning and evoke emotions. Poetry includes not only individual poems but also the collective body of work that falls within the poetic tradition. It encompasses the various forms, styles, and themes that poets explore through their writing.

A poem is a specific instance of a single artistic creation within the broader category of poetry. Poetry includes the entire range of creative expression using poetic devices, structures, and techniques. While a poem is a single piece of literature, poetry is the genre or art form that encompasses all poems and the various approaches to using language creatively.

Objective Poetry and Subjective Poetry

Objective poetry and Subjective poetry refer to two different approaches or perspectives that poets can take when writing their poems. These terms relate to how the poet's personal emotions, thoughts, and experiences are presented within the poem.

Objective Poetry

Objective poetry, also known as impersonal or imagist poetry, focuses on presenting the external world and its details in a precise and vivid manner. In objective poetry, the poet attempts to convey sensory experiences, observations, and imagery without inserting their own emotions or opinions. The emphasis is on objective descriptions and capturing the essence of the subject matter without letting personal feelings interfere. This style often uses clear and concise language, striving to create a direct and unfiltered portrayal of the world.

Subjective Poetry

Subjective poetry, on the other hand, places a strong emphasis on the poet's personal emotions, thoughts, and experiences. In this style, the poet's feelings and perspectives are openly expressed, and the poem becomes a vehicle for sharing the poet's inner world with the reader. The poet's emotions and opinions play a significant role in shaping the poem's content and tone. This approach allows for a more introspective and emotionally charged exploration of themes, often leading to a deeper connection between the poet and the reader.

It's important to note that many poems contain elements of both objective and subjective perspectives. The distinction between these approaches is not always clear-cut, and poets often blend these elements to create unique and nuanced works. The choice between objective and subjective poetry depends on the poet's intention, the themes they want to explore, and the emotional impact they seek to convey to their audience.

OBJECTIVE POETRY

Objective Poetry, also known as imagist poetry or impersonal poetry, focuses on presenting the external world and its details in a clear, vivid, and precise manner. This style of poetry aims to provide objective descriptions and imagery without delving into the poet's personal emotions or opinions. Here are some types or characteristics of objective poetry:

Epic Poetry: Epic poetry is a genre of literature that tells a long narrative story about heroic deeds, often involving gods, legendary figures, and grand adventures. Epics are typically written in a formal and elevated style. While epic poetry can contain both objective and subjective elements, it is usually considered more objective because it often focuses on external events, actions, and the portrayal of grand themes. Examples of epic poetry include Homer's "The Iliad" and "The Odyssey."

Drama: Drama is a genre of literature intended for performance, typically on a stage. It includes plays, scripts, and theatrical works. Drama can incorporate both objective and subjective elements, as it involves the depiction of characters, their actions, and their internal thoughts and emotions. The balance between objective and subjective elements in drama can vary depending on the playwright's style and intentions. Famous playwrights like William Shakespeare have created a wide range of dramatic works.

Ballads: Ballads are a form of narrative poetry often characterized by their simple and repetitive structure. They typically tell a story in a concise and emotionally charged manner. Ballads can contain both objective and subjective elements, depending on the storyteller's approach. Some ballads may focus on external events and actions (objective), while others delve into the emotions and perspectives of the characters (subjective). Examples of ballads include "The Ballad of Bonnie and Clyde" and "The Rime of the Ancient Mariner."

Subjective Poetry focuses on expressing the poet's personal emotions, thoughts, and experiences. This style of poetry delves into the inner world of the poet, often conveying feelings, perspectives, and introspection.
Here are some types or characteristics of subjective poetry:

Lyric Poetry: Lyric poetry is one of the most common forms of subjective poetry. It expresses the poet's emotions, thoughts, and personal reflections in a highly personal and often musical way. Lyric poems can encompass a wide range of emotions, from love and joy to sorrow and melancholy. These poems typically have a musical quality and often use first-person perspective. Famous examples of lyric poetry include poems by Emily Dickinson and Walt Whitman.

Sonnet: A sonnet is a specific form of poetry that consists of 14 lines, typically written in iambic pentameter. Sonnets often express personal feelings, including themes of love, beauty, and the passage of time. The most famous type of sonnet is the Shakespearean or English sonnet, which consists of three quatrains followed by a final rhymed couplet. Sonnets are known for their concise and emotionally charged nature.

Ode: An ode is a type of lyric poem that is typically characterized by its formal structure and elevated, often celebratory tone. Odes can express the poet's personal emotions or observations but are often directed toward a specific subject, such as a person, event, or even an abstract concept like love or beauty. Odes often employ elaborate language and complex metaphors. Famous examples include John Keats's "Ode to a Nightingale" and Pablo Neruda's "Ode to the Tomato."

Elegy: An elegy is a poem that expresses deep sorrow or mourning, often in response to a death or loss. Elegies are highly subjective, as they convey the poet's grief, reflection, and personal connection to the deceased. They may also reflect on the transient nature of life. Elegies can vary in tone, from melancholic to celebratory, depending on the poet's approach. Notable elegies include Thomas Gray's "Elegy Written in a Country Churchyard" and Walt Whitman's "When Lilacs Last in the Dooryard Bloom'd."

EPIC POETRY

An epic is a long and narrative poem that tells the story of heroic deeds, legendary figures, and grand adventures. Epics often explore the origins of a culture, civilisation, or a nation, and they are known for their grand scale, elevated language, and the incorporation of myth, legend, and history. Epics are a form of narrative poetry that provides insight into the values, beliefs, and ideals of a society.

Characteristics of an epic poem include:

Heroic Protagonist: Epics typically feature a heroic main character who embarks on a journey or quest and faces challenges, often representing the virtues and values of their culture.

Vast Setting: Epics often take place in a broad and expansive setting, involving multiple locations, realms, and landscapes.

Supernatural Elements: Epics often include gods, goddesses, mythical creatures, and magical elements that influence the story.

Long and Complex Narrative: Epics are lengthy poems, often divided into books or cantos, with intricate plot lines and multiple subplots.

Invocation of the Muse: Many epics begin with an invocation to a muse or deity, seeking inspiration and guidance for the storyteller.

Elevated Language: Epics use formal and elevated language, including poetic devices, metaphors, and similes, to enhance the grandeur of the narrative.

Cultural Significance: Epics often reflect the values, ideals, and beliefs of the society from which they originate.

Character Development: Epics provide in-depth character development for the main characters and often explore their motivations, conflicts, and growth.

Oral Tradition: Historically, many epics were passed down through oral tradition before being written down, contributing to their distinctive rhythms and patterns.

Moral and Ethical Themes: Epics often address moral dilemmas, ethical choices, and the consequences of actions, reflecting societal norms and ideals.

Famous examples of epic poems include:

Homer's "Iliad" and "Odyssey": These ancient Greek epics narrate the events of the Trojan War and the adventures of Odysseus as he attempts to return home after the war.

Virgil's "Aeneid": This Roman epic tells the story of Aeneas, a Trojan hero, and his journey to establish the foundations of Rome.

Milton's "Paradise Lost": This epic explores the fall of man and the struggles between good and evil, based on the biblical story of Adam and Eve.

Beowulf: An Old English epic poem that follows the hero Beowulf as he battles monstrous creatures to protect his people.

Epic poetry serves as a window into the cultural heritage and values of different societies throughout history. It often combines myth, history, and legend to create a larger-than-life narrative that captures the imagination of readers and listeners.

Epic poetry is a genre of literature that tells a long and grand narrative, often centered around heroic deeds and legendary figures. Epics typically feature larger-than-life characters, epic quests, battles, and adventures.

There are two primary types of epic poetry:

1. Primary or traditional epics and
2. Literary or secondary epics

1. Primary or Traditional Epics:
These are ancient epics that have roots in oral tradition and often originate from early cultures and civilisations. They are considered the foundational epics of literature and have been passed down through generations.

Examples:

a. **The Epic of Gilgamesh:** One of the oldest known epics, "The Epic of Gilgamesh" is from ancient Mesopotamia and tells the story of Gilgamesh, a historical king, and his quest for immortality.

b. **The Iliad and The Odyssey (Homer):** Attributed to the Greek poet Homer, "The Iliad" and "The Odyssey" are two of the most famous primary epics. "The Iliad" recounts the Trojan War, while "The Odyssey" follows the adventures of Odysseus on his journey home from the war.

c. **The Mahabharata:** An ancient Indian epic, "The Mahabharata" is one of the longest epic poems in the world. It tells the story of the Kurukshetra War and includes philosophical and moral teachings.
The Ramayana: Ancient Indian Epic, the story of Shri Ram with the human moral teaching " The truth always wins over the Evil".

2. Literary or Secondary Epics:
These are epics written by individual authors who draw inspiration from the style and themes of primary epics. Literary epics often serve as deliberate imitations or reinterpretations of the ancient epic tradition.
Examples:

a. **"Paradise Lost" (John Milton):** "Paradise Lost" is an epic poem that retells the biblical story of the fall of mankind, focusing on the character of Satan and his rebellion against God. It is considered a literary epic due to its imitation of classical epic conventions.

b. **"The Aeneid"** (Virgil): Virgil's "The Aeneid" is an epic poem that tells the story of Aeneas, a Trojan hero who becomes the legendary ancestor of the Romans. It draws heavily on the style and themes of earlier epics, such as Homer's works.

c. **"The Divine Comedy"** (Dante Alighieri): Although often categorized as an allegorical epic, Dante's "The Divine Comedy" shares many characteristics with traditional epics. It follows Dante's journey through Hell, Purgatory, and Heaven and explores themes of salvation and divine justice.

d. **"Beowulf":** While "Beowulf" is often considered a primary epic due to its ancient origins, it is also recognized as a literary epic due to its written form. It tells the story of the hero Beowulf and his battles against monsters and dragons.

These are just a few examples of epic poetry, illustrating both the primary and literary subtypes. Epics are renowned for their epic heroes, epic quests, and exploration of universal themes, making them enduring and influential works of literature.

Some famous lines/ Quotes from various epic poems:

1. "The Iliad" by Homer:
"Sing, O goddess, the anger of Peleus' son Achilles."
"There is the heat of Love, the pulsing rush of Longing, the lover's whisper, irresistible—magic to make the sanest man go mad."

2. "The Odyssey" by Homer:

"Tell me, O Muse, of that ingenious hero who travelled far and wide."
"We are all fools in love."

3. "The Epic of Gilgamesh"

"I will make my name known to the oppressed, I will be their light."
"The life that you are seeking you will never find. When the gods created man they allotted to him death, but life they retained in their own keeping."

4. "The Aeneid" by Virgil:
"I sing of arms and the man, he who, exiled by fate, first came from the coast of Troy to Italy."
"Fate will find a way."

5. "Paradise Lost" by John Milton:
"Better to reign in Hell than serve in Heaven."
"The mind is its own place, and in itself can make a heaven of hell, a hell of heaven."

6. "The Divine Comedy" by Dante Alighieri:
"In His will is our peace."
"Abandon all hope, ye who enter here."

7. "Beowulf":
"Fate often saves an undoomed man when his courage is good."

"A man's heart must love, must live, must love life."

8. "The Mahabharata":
"One who stands up and confronts the fear created by the adversities of life becomes one whose mind remains undisturbed."
"The true teacher is he who does not seek to impress you with his own authority, but who seeks to impress upon your mind the authority of the truth."

9. "The Ramayana":
"Whatever happened, happened for the good. Whatever is happening, is happening for the good. Whatever will happen, will also happen for the good."
"A person can rise through the efforts of his own mind; he can also sink, in the same mind, because of his own mind."

These lines capture the essence of their respective epics and are often quoted and referenced in literature and popular culture due to their profound themes and insights.
drama

DRAMA

Drama is a genre of literature that involves the creation and performance of stories through dialogue, action, and conflict. It is primarily intended to be performed on stage by actors, bringing characters and their interactions to life in front of an audience. Drama encompasses a wide range of themes, styles, and formats, from tragedies to comedies and everything in between.

Elements and features of drama include:

Characters: Dramas feature characters who interact with each other and drive the plot forward through their actions and dialogue. Characters' personalities, motivations, and conflicts are central to the story.

Dialogue: The primary mode of communication in drama is through spoken dialogue between characters. Dialogue reveals their thoughts, emotions, and relationships.

Conflict: Conflict is a driving force in drama, creating tension and propelling the plot. Conflicts can be internal (within a character) or external (between characters or circumstances).

Plot: The plot of a drama involves a sequence of events that unfold in a specific order. It includes the exposition, rising action, climax, falling action, and resolution.

Setting: The setting provides the context in which the events of the drama take place. It includes the time, place, and social environment in which the characters interact.

Stage Directions: Stage directions are instructions provided by the playwright for the actors, directors, and crew. They describe actions, movements, expressions, and other elements of the performance.

Themes: Dramas explore a variety of themes, such as love, power, morality, social issues, identity, and more. Themes provide depth and meaning to the story.

Genres: Drama includes various genres, such as tragedy, comedy, tragicomedy, farce, melodrama, and more, each with its own tone and conventions.

Monologue and Soliloquy: These are extended speeches delivered by a character, often revealing their thoughts, emotions, or inner conflicts. A monologue is addressed to other characters, while a soliloquy is a private speech to oneself.

Ensemble Cast: Larger dramas may have an ensemble cast with multiple characters playing significant roles in the narrative.

Symbolism: Dramas can incorporate symbolism to represent deeper meanings and ideas through actions, props, or gestures.

Catharsis: In tragedies, drama can evoke catharsis—an emotional release or purging—by bringing audiences face-to-face with intense emotions and experiences.

Famous playwrights and their works include William Shakespeare ("Hamlet," "Romeo and Juliet"), Anton Chekhov ("The Seagull," "The Cherry Orchard"), Tennessee Williams ("A Streetcar Named Desire," "The Glass Menagerie"), and Arthur Miller ("Death of a Salesman," "The Crucible").

Drama is a versatile form of artistic expression that engages audiences by exploring human emotions, relationships, and the complexities of life through dynamic storytelling and performance.

A comprehensive overview of various types of drama, along with detailed explanations and examples for each:

1. Tragedy:

Tragedy is a dramatic genre that explores serious and often somber themes, typically involving the downfall or suffering of the main character, who is usually a noble or heroic figure. Tragic plays aim to evoke catharsis, an emotional release or purging of feelings in the audience.

Example: William Shakespeare's "Hamlet" is a classic tragedy that tells the story of Prince Hamlet's quest for revenge against his uncle, exploring themes of ambition, betrayal, and the consequences of inaction.

"Romeo and Juliet" by William Shakespeare: A tragic love story of two young lovers from feuding families, leading to their untimely deaths.

"Macbeth" by William Shakespeare: The tale of a Scottish nobleman's descent into tyranny and madness after he becomes consumed by his ambition for power.

"Oedipus Rex" by Sophocles: A Greek tragedy that follows King Oedipus as he seeks to uncover the truth behind a curse that has befallen his kingdom.

2. Comedy:

Comedy is a dramatic genre that aims to amuse and entertain the audience through humor and lighthearted situations. Comedies often revolve around misunderstandings, mistaken identities, and comedic conflicts that are resolved in a positive and joyful manner.

Example: William Shakespeare's "A Midsummer Night's Dream" is a comedic play that weaves together the stories of several couples and mischievous fairies in a magical forest, exploring themes of love and the absurdity of human behavior.

"The Importance of Being Earnest" by Oscar Wilde: A satirical comedy that pokes fun at the societal norms and expectations of Victorian England.

"Twelfth Night" by William Shakespeare: A comedy of mistaken identities and romantic entanglements, with a plot full of humor and misunderstandings.

3. Dramatic Monologue:

In a dramatic monologue, a single character delivers a lengthy speech that reveals their inner thoughts, emotions, and experiences to the audience. This form allows the audience to gain insight into the character's psyche.

Example: Robert Browning's "My Last Duchess" is a dramatic monologue in which the Duke of Ferrara describes the portrait of his late wife, revealing his jealousy and possessiveness.

4. Tragicomedy:

Tragicomedy is a dramatic genre that blends elements of tragedy and comedy, combining serious and often dark themes with moments of humor and levity. Tragicomedy explores the complexities of human existence by juxtaposing tragic and comedic elements.

Example: William Shakespeare's "The Winter's Tale" begins as a tragedy, featuring jealousy and betrayal, but transitions into a comedy in its latter part, focusing on reconciliation and forgiveness.

"The Tempest" by William Shakespeare: A play that combines elements of both tragedy and comedy, exploring themes of power, forgiveness, and transformation on a remote island.

"Waiting for Godot" by Samuel Beckett: A modern tragicomedy that follows two characters as they wait for a person named Godot, engaging in existential discussions while waiting.

5. Historical Drama:

Historical drama is set in a specific historical period and often explores the lives and events of historical figures. These plays provide insights into past cultures, politics, and societal norms. "Henry IV, Part 1" by William Shakespeare: A historical drama that follows the reign of King Henry IV and the political and personal challenges he faces.

6. Musical Drama:

Musical drama combines elements of drama and music, featuring songs and musical numbers as integral parts of the narrative. Musicals explore a wide range of themes and emotions. Example: Andrew Lloyd Webber's "The Phantom of the Opera" is a musical drama that tells the story of the masked Phantom who haunts the Paris Opera House.

"Les Misérables" by Victor Hugo (adapted into a musical): A novel and musical that explores the lives of various characters against the backdrop of 19th-century France, focusing on themes of justice, love, and redemption.

7. Absurdist Drama:

Absurdist drama defies conventional logic and embraces themes of existentialism, alienation, and the absurdity of human existence. These plays often challenge traditional narrative structures. Example: Samuel Beckett's "Waiting for Godot" is a classic absurdist play featuring two characters waiting for someone who never arrives, exploring themes of existentialism and the human condition.

8. Political Drama:

Political drama focuses on political themes, conflicts, and power struggles. These plays often explore social and political issues and their impact on individuals and society.

Example: Henrik Ibsen's "An Enemy of the People" revolves around the conflict between a town's economic prosperity and the moral principles of one man who seeks to expose a public health threat.

9. Domestic Drama:

Domestic drama revolves around family dynamics, relationships, and conflicts within the home. These plays often explore interpersonal relationships and the complexities of family life. Example: Henrik Ibsen's "A Doll's House" delves into the constraints of gender roles and societal expectations in a marriage, following the story of Nora Helmer seeking personal freedom.

10. Experimental Drama:

- Experimental drama challenges traditional narrative structures and may incorporate unconventional elements such as non-linear plots, multimedia, and audience interaction. Playwrights experiment with form and content.
Example: Samuel Beckett's "Krapp's Last Tape" is an experimental drama that explores memory and self-reflection as the character Krapp listens to recordings of himself at different stages of life.

11. Mystery and Thriller Drama:

- Mystery and thriller dramas are characterized by suspense, tension, and a focus on solving mysteries or uncovering secrets. These plays often engage the audience with suspenseful and mysterious elements.
- Example: Agatha Christie's "The Mousetrap" is a classic mystery play involving a group of strangers trapped in a guesthouse during a snowstorm, with a murder mystery unfolding among them.

12. Radio Drama:

Radio drama is a form of drama created specifically for radio broadcasting. These dramas rely on sound effects, voice acting, and dialogue to convey the story to the audience.

Example: Orson Welles' radio adaptation of H.G. Wells' "War of the Worlds" (1938) famously caused panic among listeners who believed the story of a Martian invasion was real.

13. Site-Specific Drama:

Site-specific drama is performed in a specific location that is integral to the story. The setting is chosen for its relevance to the plot and can include unconventional locations.
Example: "Sleep No More" by Punchdrunk is an immersive, site-specific theatrical experience that takes place in a multi-story, immersive environment, where audience members move through the space as they follow the narrative of Shakespeare's "Macbeth."

14. Naturalism:

Naturalism is a style of drama that seeks to depict life as realistically as possible, often focusing on the struggles and hardships of everyday people. It emphasizes the influence of environment and heredity on characters' lives and decisions.
Example: Henrik Ibsen's "Ghosts" is a naturalistic play that explores the consequences of societal taboos and the impact of heredity on the characters, portraying a stark portrayal of family and societal issues.

15. Epic Drama:

Epic drama often involves a grand narrative with a large cast of characters and explores monumental themes such as heroism, destiny, and societal change.
Example: Bertolt Brecht's "Mother Courage and Her Children" is an epic drama set during the Thirty Years' War and follows the story of a canteen-wagon-driving woman named Mother Courage.

16. Experimental Performance Art:

Experimental performance art pushes the boundaries of traditional theater and often incorporates avant-garde elements, multimedia, and audience participation.

Example: Marina Abramović's performance art pieces, such as "The Artist Is Present," involve intense and often physically demanding interactions with the audience, challenging the conventional boundaries of art and theater.

17. Epic Theatre:

Epic theatre, pioneered by playwright Bertolt Brecht, is characterized by its use of distancing techniques that prevent the audience from becoming emotionally absorbed in the story. It encourages critical thinking about social and political issues.
Example: Bertolt Brecht's "The Threepenny Opera" employs epic theatre techniques to critique capitalism and societal corruption.

18. Expressionist Drama:

Expressionist drama emphasizes the emotional and psychological experiences of characters, often depicting distorted or nightmarish realities. It seeks to convey the inner turmoil of individuals.
Example: Georg Kaiser's "From Morning to Midnight" is an expressionist play that explores the disillusionment and despair of its protagonist as he seeks meaning in an alienating urban environment.

19. Theatre of the Absurd:

Theatre of the Absurd is a post-World War II movement that explores the irrationality and meaninglessness of human existence. It often features surreal and absurd situations.
Example: Eugène Ionesco's "The Bald Soprano" is a classic Theatre of the Absurd play where ordinary conversation becomes increasingly absurd and devoid of meaning.

20. Puppetry and Puppet Theater:

Puppet theater involves the use of puppets to convey stories and themes. It encompasses various forms, including hand puppets, marionettes, and shadow puppetry.

Example: "Avenue Q" is a contemporary puppet musical that combines puppetry with adult-oriented humor and themes.

21. Mime and Physical Theatre:

Mime and physical theatre rely on body movements, gestures, and facial expressions to convey stories and emotions without spoken words.

Example: Marcel Marceau, a renowned mime artist, created silent performances that engaged audiences through the art of pantomime.

22. Environmental Theatre:

Environmental theatre immerses the audience in a unique physical environment or space, often blurring the boundaries between performers and spectators.

Example: "Sleep No More," mentioned previously, is a notable environmental theatre production that invites audience members to explore a multi-story, immersive setting while experiencing Shakespeare's "Macbeth."

23. Dance Theatre:

Dance theatre combines dance and movement with narrative storytelling, often using choreography as a primary means of expression.

Example: "Billy Elliot: The Musical" is a dance theatre production that tells the story of a young boy's journey into the world of ballet against the backdrop of a mining community in England.

Famous lines and quotes from various dramatic works:

From Shakespearean Plays:
"To be or not to be, that is the question." - Hamlet in "Hamlet"
"All the world's a stage, and all the men and women merely players." - Jaques in "As You Like It"
"What's in a name? That which we call a rose by any other name would smell as sweet." - Juliet in "Romeo and Juliet"
"The better part of Valour, is Discretion." - Falstaff in "Henry IV, Part 1"
"Though she be but little, she is fierce!" - Helena in "A Midsummer Night's Dream"

From Classic Plays:
"Tomorrow, and tomorrow, and tomorrow, creeps in this petty pace from day to day." - Macbeth in "Macbeth" by William Shakespeare
"All happy families are alike; each unhappy family is unhappy in its own way." - Leo Tolstoy, opening line of "Anna Karenina"
"We are all fools in love." - "The Country Wife" by William Wycherley
"The only way to get rid of temptation is to yield to it." - Lord Henry in "The Picture of Dorian Gray" by Oscar Wilde
"In the middle of difficulty lies opportunity." - Albert Einstein, referenced in various plays and adaptations
"I have nothing to declare except my genius." - Oscar Wilde, from the Customs Declaration Form upon arriving in the United States.
"All the variety, all the charm, all the beauty of life is made up of light and shadow." - Leo Tolstoy, from "Anna Karenina."
"To thine own self be true." - Polonius in "Hamlet" by William Shakespeare.
"Is this a dagger which I see before me?" - Macbeth in "Macbeth" by William Shakespeare.
"If music be the food of love, play on." - Duke Orsino in "Twelfth Night" by William Shakespeare.

From Modern Plays:
"Life is a moderately good play with a badly written third act." - Truman Capote
"The world is a stage, but the play is badly cast." - Oscar Wilde
"You can't handle the truth!" - Colonel Jessup in "A Few Good Men" by Aaron Sorkin
"Goodnight stars, goodnight air, goodnight noises everywhere." - Margaret Wise Brown, quoted in "Goodnight Moon" (a popular children's book)
"There are no small parts, only small actors." - Konstantin Stanislavski, influential Russian theatre practitioner
"I want to be alone." - Greta Garbo, often associated with her role in the film "Grand Hotel" and later referenced in various works.
"You had me at 'hello.'" - Dorothy Boyd in the movie "Jerry Maguire," written by Cameron Crowe.
"I'm mad as hell, and I'm not going to take this anymore!" - Howard Beale in the film "Network," written by Paddy Chayefsky.
"I am big! It's the pictures that got small." - Norma Desmond in the film "Sunset Boulevard," written by Charles Brackett, Billy Wilder, and D.M. Marshman Jr.
"Fasten your seatbelts, it's going to be a bumpy night." - Margo Channing in the film "All About Eve," written and directed by Joseph L. Mankiewicz.

From Musicals:
"The sun'll come out tomorrow." - Annie in "Annie" by Charles Strouse and Martin Charnin
"Seasons of love." - Cast in "Rent" by Jonathan Larson
"Do you hear the people sing?" - Enjolras in "Les Misérables" by Alain Boublil and Claude-Michel Schönberg
"I could have danced all night." - Eliza Doolittle in "My Fair Lady" by Alan Jay Lerner and Frederick Loewe
"Defying gravity." - Elphaba in "Wicked" by Stephen Schwartz

These famous lines and quotes capture the essence of the characters and themes in a wide range of dramatic works, from classic plays to contemporary musicals. They continue to resonate with audiences and are often quoted and referenced in various contexts.

BALLAD

A ballad is a type of narrative poem or song that tells a story, often with a strong focus on emotions, adventures, or legendary events. Ballads have been an important part of oral and written traditions in various cultures throughout history. They typically have a simple and rhythmic structure, making them easy to remember and pass down through generations.

The characteristics of ballads include:

Narrative Structure: Ballads convey a story with a clear beginning, middle, and end. They often present a single dramatic event or a series of connected events.

Rhythm and Meter: Ballads have a distinctive rhythm and meter that contribute to their musical quality. The most common meter for ballads is alternating lines of iambic tetrameter and trimeter.

Refrain: Some ballads include a refrain—a repeated line or stanza that recurs at regular intervals throughout the poem. The refrain often emphasizes a key theme or emotional element.

Strong Emotions: Ballads often evoke strong emotions, whether they are tragic, romantic, heroic, or supernatural. The emotional impact is a central aspect of their appeal.

Simplicity: Ballads use straightforward language and tend to avoid complex or elaborate descriptions. The language is often accessible and easy to understand.

Dialogue: Many ballads include direct speech or dialogue between characters, allowing the characters to express themselves and advance the plot.

Quatrain Stanzas: Ballads are often composed of quatrains (four-line stanzas) with an alternating rhyme scheme (ABCB), though variations exist.

Folk Traditions: Ballads have strong ties to folk traditions and were often passed down orally before being written down. They were often performed as songs and accompanied by musical instruments.

Examples of well-known ballads include:

"The Rime of the Ancient Mariner" by Samuel Taylor Coleridge: A narrative poem that tells the tale of a mariner's supernatural experiences at sea and his subsequent redemption.

"Bonnie George Campbell": A Scottish ballad that recounts the tragic death of a young nobleman in battle and the sorrow of his lover.

"Barbara Allen": A traditional English ballad that tells the story of a young woman's rejection of a dying man's love and her later regret.

"The Ballad of Tam Lin": A ballad of Scottish origin that features a supernatural element involving a young woman rescuing her lover from the grip of the Queen of Fairies.

"The Highwayman" by Alfred Noyes: A narrative ballad about a highwayman and his love, Bess, set against a backdrop of adventure and tragedy.

Ballads continue to be an important part of literary traditions, and their influence can be seen in various forms of storytelling, including poetry, song lyrics, and even modern ballads found in contemporary music.

Some famous lines from various ballads:

From "The Rime of the Ancient Mariner" by Samuel Taylor Coleridge:
> *"Water, water, everywhere, nor any drop to drink."*
> *"He holds him with his skinny hand."*

From "The Ballad of John Henry" (Traditional American Ballad):
> *"John Henry said to the Captain, 'A man ain't nothin' but a man.'"*

From "Barbara Allen" (Traditional Scottish Ballad):
> *"All in the merry month of May, when the green buds they were swellin'."*
> *"Love gave me a cruel wound, and love's the cause of my mournin'."*

From "Bonnie Barbara Allan" (Traditional Scottish Ballad):
> *"O dinna ye mind, young man," said she, "when ye was in the tavern?"*
> *"O dinna ye mind, young man," said she, "when ye was but a stranger?"*

From "The Unquiet Grave" (Traditional English Ballad):
> *"Cold blows the wind to my true love, and gently drops the rain."*
> *"The life of man is but a span; it's like a morning flower."*

From "The Highwayman" by Alfred Noyes:
> *"The moon was a ghostly galleon tossed upon cloudy seas."*

> *"And the highwayman came riding, riding, riding, the*
> *highwayman came riding up to the old inn-door."*

From "Annabel Lee" by Edgar Allan Poe:

> *"But we loved with a love that was more than love—*
> *I and my Annabel Lee—*
> *With a love that the wingèd seraphs of Heaven*
> *Coveted her and me."*

From "The Ballad of Lucy Jordan" by Shel Silverstein (popularised by Marianne Faithfull):

> *"At the age of thirty-seven she realized she'd never ride*
> *through Paris in a sports car with the warm wind in her*
> *hair."*

Types of Ballads

Traditional Ballad (or Folk Ballad):

Originated from the oral tradition; passed down verbally from one generation to the next.

Typically have a simple rhyme scheme and meter.

Often include repeated lines or refrains.

Characters and settings are often generic.

Common themes include love, death, the supernatural, and historical or mythical tales.

Literary Ballad:

Written by known poets in imitation of the style and form of the traditional ballads.

While they mimic the form of folk ballads, they might have more intricate language and themes.

Examples include "La Belle Dame sans Merci" by John Keats and "The Rime of the Ancient Mariner" by Samuel Taylor Coleridge.

Broadside Ballad (or Street Ballad):

Printed on one side of a sheet of paper and sold on the streets.

Often about current events, local legends, or tales of tragedy.

Became popular from the 16th to the 19th centuries.

Blues Ballad:

Rooted in the African American musical tradition.

Merges the narrative quality of ballads with the emotional expressiveness of the blues.

Themes often revolve around personal woes, societal problems, or lost love.

Pop Ballad:

Modern ballads often found in popular music.

Typically slower tempo songs that emphasize emotion and a narrative.

Subjects range from love and heartbreak to personal introspection.

Rock Ballads:

A subtype of pop ballad but with a rock musical backdrop.

Characterized by emotional storytelling and are often anthemic in nature.

They became especially popular in the 1970s and 1980s.

Epic Ballads:

Longer narrative poems that depict heroic deeds or significant events.

They might blend myth, history, and fiction.

Examples from ancient traditions include the "Epic of Gilgamesh" and "Beowulf," though these are often just categorized as epics.

Each type of ballad has its own distinct characteristics and serves a unique cultural or artistic purpose. Over time, the ballad has proven to be a versatile form, adapting to the changing tastes and sensibilities of different eras and audiences.

SUBJECTIVE POETRY

Subjective poetry often expresses the personal emotions, thoughts, and experiences of the poet, and one of the primary forms of subjective poetry is the lyric poem. Lyric poetry is highly introspective and emotional, and it often explores the poet's inner world, personal feelings, and observations.

LYRIC

Emotional Expression: Lyric poetry is characterized by its intense emotional expression. It allows poets to convey their deepest feelings, whether they are love, joy, sorrow, anger, or any other emotion.

First-Person Perspective: Lyric poems are typically written from the first-person perspective, making them highly personal and subjective. They often use pronouns like "I" and "me."

Short and Musical: Lyric poems are usually shorter in length compared to other forms of poetry. They often feature musical qualities, such as rhyme, rhythm, and meter, that make them pleasant to read aloud.

Themes: Lyric poetry explores a wide range of themes, including love, nature, beauty, mortality, and the passage of time. These themes are often presented through the lens of the poet's personal experiences and emotions.

Imagery and Symbolism: Lyric poems often employ vivid imagery and symbolism to evoke emotional responses in the reader. They use metaphors and similes to create striking comparisons and associations.

Subjective Language: The language in lyric poetry is subjective and highly descriptive, allowing the poet to communicate their innermost thoughts and feelings. It can be both straightforward and metaphorical, depending on the poet's style.

Historical Examples: Some famous examples of lyric poetry include William Wordsworth's "I Wandered Lonely as a Cloud" (often referred to as "Daffodils"), Emily Dickinson's "Because I could not stop for Death," and John Keats' "Ode to a Nightingale."

Contemporary Examples: In contemporary poetry, lyricism continues to be a prominent style. Poets like Mary Oliver, Billy Collins, and Rupi Kaur have gained popularity for their emotionally charged and introspective lyric poems.

Lyric poetry offers a direct and intimate connection between the poet and the reader, inviting readers to enter the poet's emotional world and share in their experiences and reflections. It remains a vital and enduring form of subjective poetry.

Examples of lyric poetry along with some famous lines:

1. Emily Dickinson:
Famous Line: *"Hope is the thing with feathers / That perches in the soul / And sings the tune without the words / And never stops at all."*
2. Langston Hughes:
Famous Line: *"Hold fast to dreams / For if dreams die / Life is a broken-winged bird / That cannot fly."*
3. Pablo Neruda:
Famous Line: *"I want to do with you what spring does with the cherry trees."*
4. Maya Angelou:
Famous Line: *"You may write me down*

Types Of Lyrics

"Lyrics" primarily refer to the words of a song. Over time, song lyrics have been categorized based on their themes, style, and the emotions they evoke. Here are some types of lyrics based on these categorizations:

Narrative Lyrics:

Tell a story or narrate an event or series of events. Examples include many country songs or ballads that unfold a tale from beginning to end.

Descriptive Lyrics:

Paint a picture of a place, person, or emotion. They immerse the listener in vivid imagery and detail.

Emotive or Expressive Lyrics:

Focus on expressing deep emotions or feelings. This can be about love, loss, joy, sorrow, anger, etc.

Philosophical or Reflective Lyrics:

Explore deep philosophical questions or personal reflections about life, existence, society, etc. Songs that ponder the meaning of life or the nature of existence fall into this category.

Inspirational Lyrics:

Meant to inspire, motivate, or uplift the listener. Often found in gospel, devotional songs, or anthems that stir feelings of hope and encouragement.

Humorous or Satirical Lyrics:

Intended to entertain by being funny or by satirizing certain aspects of society or human behavior.

Abstract or Experimental Lyrics:

Might not follow conventional songwriting structures. Can be open to multiple interpretations and may delve into experimental themes or wordplay.

Political or Protest Lyrics:

Address societal issues, injustices, or political sentiments. Songs from the 1960s and 1970s anti-war movement or those advocating for civil rights are examples.

Romantic Lyrics:

Center on themes of love, passion, heartbreak, and relationships.

Social Commentary Lyrics:

Comment on societal norms, trends, or behaviors.

Offer critique or insights into cultural aspects of society.

Personal or Confessional Lyrics:

Share personal experiences, thoughts, or confessions.

They are intimate, offering a glimpse into the songwriter's personal life or psyche.

Anthemic Lyrics:

Crafted to be catchy and are often repeated by large groups.

Songs that are meant for stadiums or large audiences,

where the chorus becomes an anthem for the crowd.

It's important to note that a song's lyrics can often fit into multiple of these categories simultaneously. For instance, a romantic song can also be deeply emotive, and a song with political lyrics can also serve as a form of social commentary. The categorizations are merely tools to understand the diverse themes and styles lyrics can encompass.

SONNET

A sonnet is a 14-line poem with a specific rhyme scheme, meter, and often, a thematic structure. Sonnets have been used by poets for centuries to explore themes of love, beauty, time, and mortality. There are several types of sonnets, each with its own unique characteristics.

1. Shakespearean Sonnet (or English Sonnet):

Structure: Consists of 14 lines divided into three quatrains (four-line stanzas) followed by a final rhymed couplet (two-line stanza).
Rhyme Scheme: ABAB CDCD EFEF GG.
Meter: Traditionally written in iambic pentameter (ten syllables per line with alternating stressed and unstressed syllables).
Example: William Shakespeare's Sonnet 18, often referred to as "Shall I compare thee to a summer's day?"
Famous Lines:
> *"Shall I compare thee to a summer's day?"*
> *"So long as men can breathe or eyes can see,*
> *"So long lives this, and this gives life to thee."*

2. Petrarchan Sonnet (or Italian Sonnet)

Structure: Comprises an octave (eight lines) and a sestet (six lines).
Rhyme Scheme: ABBAABBA CDCDCD or ABBAABBA CDECDE.
Meter: Often written in iambic pentameter.
Example: Francesco Petrarch's Sonnet 18 from his "Canzoniere," where he expresses his unrequited love for Laura.
Famous Lines:
> *"Blest be the day, and blest the month and year,*
> *"And blest the hour, the day, the month, the year,*
> *"The season and the time, and blest the place."*

3. Spenserian Sonnet:

Structure: Comprises three quatrains and a final couplet, similar to the Shakespearean sonnet.

Rhyme Scheme: ABAB BCBC CDCD EE.
Meter: Typically written in iambic pentameter.
Example: Edmund Spenser's Sonnet 1 from his sequence "Amoretti."
Famou*s Lines:*

> *"Happy ye leaves when as those lily hands,*
> *"Which hold my life in their dead-doing might*
> *"Shall handle you and hold in love's soft bands."*

4. Miltonic Sonnet (or Miltonic)

Structure: Follows the same structure as the Petrarchan sonnet but is often written in blank verse (unrhymed lines of iambic pentameter).
Example: John Milton's Sonnet 19, also known as "On His Blindness," where he reflects on his own blindness and God's purpose.
Famous Lines:

> *"When I consider how my light is spent*
> *"Ere half my days, in this dark world and wide,*
> *"And that one talent which is death to hide*
> *"Lodged with me useless, though my Soul more bent."*

These examples showcase the different types of sonnets, each with its own structure, rhyme scheme, and meter, but all used by poets to explore a wide range of themes and emotions.

5. Curtal Sonnet:

Structure: A curtal sonnet is a shorter form of the traditional sonnet, developed by Gerard Manley Hopkins. It consists of 11 lines, typically divided into one six-line stanza and one five-line stanza.
Rhyme Scheme: The rhyme scheme can vary, but a common one for the 11 lines is ABCABC DEDE.
Meter: Like other sonnets, it can be written in iambic pentameter or other meters.

Example: Gerard Manley Hopkins' "Pied Beauty" is a curtal sonnet known for its celebration of the beauty and diversity of nature.

6. American Sonnet:

Structure: The American sonnet is a free-verse form of the sonnet, which means it does not strictly adhere to the traditional rhyme scheme or meter. It allows for more flexibility in terms of structure.
Rhyme Scheme: Variable, as there is no fixed rhyme scheme.
Meter: Meter is not required, making it a more modern and flexible form.
Example: "Sonnet in Search of an Author" by David Lehman is an example of an American sonnet that combines humor and reflection in a contemporary style.

7. Modern Sonnet:

Structure: Modern sonnets are often experimental and may deviate from traditional structures, both in terms of rhyme and meter. They allow for greater freedom and innovation.
Rhyme Scheme: Variable, depending on the poet's choice.
Meter: May or may not follow a strict meter, allowing for more fluidity in verse.
Example: E.E. Cummings' "silently if, out of not knowable" is a modern sonnet that showcases the poet's unique style and disregard for traditional sonnet conventions.

These variations of the sonnet form demonstrate how poets have adapted and evolved this classic poetic form to suit their artistic intentions and to explore a wide range of themes and emotions in contemporary poetry.

Some famous lines from various sonnets:

From William Shakespeare's Sonnets:
"Shall I compare thee to a summer's day?" - Sonnet 18
"When in disgrace with fortune and men's eyes," - Sonnet 29
"Let me not to the marriage of true minds" - Sonnet 116
"When to the sessions of sweet silent thought" - Sonnet 30
"My mistress' eyes are nothing like the sun" - Sonnet 130

From Petrarch's Sonnets (translated from Italian):
"You who hear the sound, in scattered rhymes," - Sonnet 1
"To my own self I turned with a cold heart" - Sonnet 90
"Death, which can take from me what I hold dear" - Sonnet 181

From John Milton's Sonnets:
"When I consider how my light is spent" - Sonnet 19
"Methought I saw my late espoused Saint" - Sonnet 23

From Elizabeth Barrett Browning's Sonnets from the Portuguese:
"How do I love thee? Let me count the ways." - Sonnet 43
"I love thee to the depth and breadth and height" - Sonnet 29

From Pablo Neruda's 100 Love Sonnets (translated from Spanish):
"I want to do with you what spring does with the cherry trees." - Sonnet 12
"Love is so short, forgetting is so long." - Sonnet 20
From William Wordsworth's Sonnets:
"The world is too much with us; late and soon" - Sonnet 14
"A gentle answer did the saint return" - Sonnet 35

These lines capture the beauty, depth, and range of emotions found in sonnets, making them memorable and enduring in the world of poetry. Sonnets continue to be celebrated for their eloquence and ability to convey complex feelings and ideas within a compact form.

ODE

An ode is a form of lyrical poetry that is typically characterized by its elevated and often formal tone, as well as its focus on a specific subject, theme, or object of admiration. Odes are known for their elaborate and structured style, making them a suitable vehicle for expressing profound emotions, celebrating an individual or an event, or contemplating philosophical or aesthetic ideas.

Some key features of odes
Structure: Odes often follow a structured pattern in terms of stanzas and rhyme scheme. Classical odes, such as those by the ancient Greek poet Pindar and the Roman poet Horace, adhered to strict patterns. Commonly, odes have three parts: the strophe, antistrophe, and epode.

Stanza Form: Odes are typically composed of stanzas with a fixed number of lines, such as 10-line stanzas in the Pindaric ode and 13-line stanzas in the Horatian ode.

Rhyme Scheme: Odes often have a specific rhyme scheme within each stanza, contributing to their musical quality. The rhyme scheme varies depending on the specific type of ode.

Elevated Language: Odes employ elevated and formal language, which may include archaic words and phrases. This contributes to the dignified and reverential tone.

Addressing the Subject: Odes directly address and celebrate the subject of the poem, whether it's a person, an event, an abstract concept, or even an inanimate object. The subject is often praised or revered.

Emotional Intensity: Odes convey intense emotions, whether it's admiration, love, reverence, or deep reflection. The poet's emotional response to the subject is a central aspect of the ode.

Philosophical or Reflective Elements: Odes may also incorporate philosophical or reflective elements, exploring broader themes and ideas related to the subject.

There are two major types of odes:

1. **A Pindaric Ode** is a type of ode named after the ancient Greek poet Pindar (c. 518-438 BCE), who is credited with popularizing this form of lyric poetry. Pindaric odes are known for their elaborate and structured nature, typically consisting of three distinct parts: the strophe, the antistrophe, and the epode. These parts serve to create a balanced and rhythmic composition.

The characteristics and components of a Pindaric ode:

Tripartite Structure:
> Strophe: The strophe is the first part of the ode, and its lines are often performed while the chorus moves from right to left. It presents the main theme or subject of the ode and typically has a specific metrical pattern and rhyme scheme.
> Antistrophe: The antistrophe is the second part of the ode and mirrors the strophe in metrical and structural terms. It is usually performed while the chorus moves from left to right. The antistrophe often provides a contrasting perspective or idea related to the theme presented in the strophe.
> Epode: The epode is the final part of the ode and differs from the strophe and antistrophe in terms of its metrical structure. It often has a different rhyme scheme and may serve to summarize or conclude the ode's themes or arguments.

Elaborate Language and Imagery:
> Pindaric odes are characterized by their use of elevated and elaborate language, as well as vivid and complex imagery. The poet employs rich metaphors and symbolism to convey deeper meanings and emotions.

Celebratory Themes:
> Pindaric odes often celebrate significant events, achievements, or individuals. Pindar himself was renowned for composing odes in honor of victorious athletes in ancient Greece, but the form has been adapted to various celebratory contexts.

Musical and Rhythmic:
> The musical and rhythmic qualities of Pindaric odes are important. The strophe and antistrophe are meant to be sung or chanted with music, and the interplay between the two sections contributes to the ode's overall impact.

Varied Meter and Rhyme:
> Pindaric odes do not adhere to a fixed meter or rhyme scheme, but rather, they exhibit a flexibility in their metrical patterns and rhyme schemes, depending on the poet's choice and the specific ode.

Complex Themes and Ideas:
> Pindaric odes often explore complex themes, such as the relationship between humans and the divine, the nature of glory and fame, and the significance of individual achievement within a broader cultural or historical context.

Pindaric odes are known for their formal complexity and artistic craftsmanship. They require careful attention to meter, rhyme, and structure, and they aim to elevate the subject of the ode through poetic language and celebration. While Pindaric odes were popular in ancient Greece, they have influenced later poets and continue to be appreciated for their artistic qualities.

Few examples of Pindaric odes:

Olympian Odes by Pindar:
Pindar's own Olympian Odes are some of the most famous examples of the Pindaric ode form. They were written to celebrate the victories of athletes at the ancient Olympic Games. One of his well-known odes is "Olympian 1," which praises the boxer Theagenes of Thasos.

"Ode on the Death of the Duke of Wellington" by Alfred, Lord Tennyson:
This 19th-century ode by Tennyson pays tribute to the Duke of Wellington, a British military hero. It follows the Pindaric ode structure, with strophes, antistrophes, and an epode, and it celebrates the duke's achievements.

"Ode to a Nightingale" by John Keats:
While not a traditional Pindaric ode in terms of structure, Keats's "Ode to a Nightingale" exhibits Pindaric elements, including elevated language and intricate imagery. It reflects on the contrast between the ephemeral nature of human existence and the eternal song of the nightingale.

"The Progress of Poesy" by Thomas Gray:
Gray's ode, inspired by Pindaric odes, celebrates the power of poetry and the imagination. It is divided into three parts, each with its own metrical and rhyming patterns, reminiscent of the strophe, antistrophe, and epode.

"To Poesy" by Samuel Taylor Coleridge:
Coleridge's ode, "To Poesy," pays tribute to the muse of poetry. It features a structured and elaborate form with

sections that correspond to the strophe and antistrophe. The ode explores the role of poetry in inspiring creativity and transcending reality.

These examples showcase the influence of Pindaric odes on poets from different eras and cultures. While not all of them strictly adhere to the traditional Pindaric structure, they share the spirit of celebrating and honoring various subjects through elevated and lyrical poetry.

2. A Horatian Ode is a type of lyric poem that takes its name from the Roman poet Horace (Quintus Horatius Flaccus, 65-8 BCE), who popularized this form of poetry. Horatian odes are characterized by their simpler and more informal structure compared to the more elaborate Pindaric odes. They often have a personal and contemplative tone, making them suitable for a wide range of subjects and themes.

The characteristics of a Horatian ode include:
Stanzaic Structure: Horatian odes are typically divided into regular stanzas, often quatrains (four-line stanzas) or tercets (three-line stanzas). These stanzas maintain a consistent metrical and rhyme scheme.

Varied Themes: Horatian odes can address a wide variety of themes and subjects, including love, friendship, the joys of life, the passage of time, and philosophical musings. They are known for their versatility in exploring everyday human experiences.

Personal and Reflective Tone: Unlike the more formal and elevated tone of Pindaric odes, Horatian odes often have a personal and introspective quality. They may express the poet's thoughts, emotions, or observations in a conversational manner.

Accessible Language: Horatian odes typically use everyday language and avoid highly formal or archaic diction. This approachable language contributes to their relatability.

Musical Quality: While not as structured as Pindaric odes, Horatian odes still exhibit a musical quality in their language and rhythm. They are often meant to be sung or chanted, enhancing their lyrical appeal.

Focus on the Present and Simple Pleasures: Many Horatian odes celebrate the pleasures of the present moment, the enjoyment of life's simple delights, and the importance of seizing the day ("carpe diem").

Examples of Horatian odes include:
"Odes" by Horace: The original Horatian odes were written by Horace himself. They encompass a wide range of themes, often emphasizing the enjoyment of life, friendship, and the fleeting nature of time. Notable odes include "Ode 1.11," often quoted with its famous opening line, "Tu ne quaesieris" ("Do not ask").

"To Autumn" by John Keats: Keats's "To Autumn" is considered a Horatian ode. It celebrates the beauty and richness of the autumn season and reflects on the cyclical nature of life and death.

"Ode to a Nightingale" by John Keats: While this ode by Keats exhibits some Pindaric elements, it also contains characteristics of Horatian odes. It explores the contrast between the ephemeral nature of human existence and the enduring song of the nightingale.

Horatian odes offer poets a versatile and accessible form of lyrical expression, allowing them to engage with a wide range of themes and convey personal reflections in a relatable and conversational manner.

In addition to the Pindaric and Horatian odes, there are other variations and types of odes, each with its own unique characteristics and structures:

3. Irregular or Free Ode:

Structure: These odes do not adhere to a strict form or rhyme scheme. They are characterized by their freedom in terms of structure, length, and stanza patterns.

Content: Irregular odes allow poets to explore a wide range of themes and emotions without the constraints of traditional ode structures.

Example: William Wordsworth's "Ode: Intimations of Immortality from Early Childhood" is an irregular ode that reflects on the loss of childhood wonder and the persistence of its influence in adulthood.

4. Sapphic Ode:

Structure: The Sapphic ode is characterized by its adherence to the Sapphic stanza, a four-line stanza with a specific metrical pattern. This type of ode is often associated with the ancient Greek poet Sappho.

Meter: The Sapphic stanza typically consists of three lines of 11 syllables each followed by a fourth line of five syllables.

Example: Algernon Charles Swinburne's "Sapphics" is a well-known example of a Sapphic ode that follows Sappho's poetic tradition.

5. Elegiac Ode:

Structure: The elegiac ode is a subgenre of the ode that often combines elements of the ode and the elegy. It reflects on themes of loss, mourning, or sorrow while maintaining some characteristics of the ode.

Content: Elegiac odes may express admiration and reverence for a subject while also addressing themes of mortality and grief.

Example: Thomas Gray's "Elegy Written in a Country Churchyard" is considered an elegiac ode that reflects on the lives of common people buried in a churchyard.

These additional types of odes illustrate the versatility of this poetic form, allowing poets to adapt and experiment with structure and content while maintaining the ode's core qualities of elevated language, emotional intensity, and a reverential tone toward the subject.

Some examples of odes from various poets and time periods:
1. "Ode to a Nightingale" by John Keats:
This famous ode by John Keats reflects on the transcendence of art and the contrast between the ideal world of the nightingale's song and the real world of human suffering.
Famous Lines: *"Thou wast not born for death, immortal Bird!"*
2. "Ode to the West Wind" by Percy Bysshe Shelley:
Shelley's ode to the west wind explores themes of change, inspiration, and the power of nature. The wind is depicted as a force of renewal and transformation.
Famous Lines: *"Make me thy Lyre, even as the foreset is."*
3. "Ode on a Grecian Urn" by John Keats:
In this ode, Keats contemplates the timeless beauty of a Grecian urn and the frozen scenes depicted on it, contrasting the urn's permanence with human transience.
Famous Lines: *"Beauty is truth, truth beauty,—that is all / Ye know on earth, and all ye need to know."*
4. "Ode to Autumn" by John Keats:
Keats celebrates the beauty and abundance of autumn in this ode. He vividly describes the sights and sounds of the season, emphasizing its ripeness and maturity.
Famous Lines: *"Season of mists and mellow fruitfulness, / Close sister of the maturing sun."*
5. "Ode to a Skylark" by Percy Bysshe Shelley:
Shelley's ode to a skylark praises the bird's joyful and untroubled existence. The skylark becomes a symbol of the poet's idealized vision of art and nature.
Famous Lines: *"Hail to thee, blithe Spirit! / Bird thou never wert."*
6. "Ode on Melancholy" by John Keats:
In this ode, Keats explores the complex nature of melancholy and advises on how to embrace it as a source of beauty and inspiration.

Famous Lines: *"She dwells with Beauty—Beauty that must die."*
7. "Ode to a Tomato" by Pablo Neruda:
Neruda's ode celebrates the humble tomato, exalting its earthy qualities and sensual appeal. It is a playful and affectionate ode to a common fruit.
Famous Lines: *"The street filled with tomatoes, / midday, summer, / light is / halved like / a / tomato."*
8. "Ode to Joy" (from Beethoven's Ninth Symphony):
While not a written poem, Beethoven's "Ode to Joy" sets Friedrich Schiller's poem to music. It is a celebration of universal brotherhood and the joy of life.
Famous Lines: *"Freude, schöner Götterfunken"* (German for "Joy, beautiful divine spark").

9. "Ode to Psyche" by John Keats:
In this ode, Keats addresses the Greek goddess Psyche and explores the idea of the imagination as a gateway to the divine. It's a reflection on the power of art and the creative mind.
Famous Lines: *"Yes, I will be thy priest, and build a fane / In some untrodden region of my mind."*

10. "Ode to a Large Tuna in the Market" by Pablo Neruda:
- In this playful ode, Neruda celebrates the ordinary sight of a large tuna fish in a market, turning it into a poetic and humorous tribute.
Famous Lines: "Salt / advanced / a secret / tower, / it rose / slower / than / the / imagination."

11. "Ode on Indolence" by John Keats:
- In this introspective ode, Keats contemplates the temptation of idleness and the ephemeral nature of inspiration.
Famous Lines: "The melancholy fit shall fall / Sudden from heaven like a weeping cloud."

12. "Ode to a Butterfly" by Thomas Wentworth Higginson:
- Higginson's ode is a tribute to the butterfly, celebrating its fleeting beauty and grace as it flits through the natural world.
Famous Lines: "Thou hast no flowers, no herbs, no thorns to fear, / No lurking foe in leaf or grass to dread."

13. "Ode to My Socks" by Pablo Neruda:
- In this ode, Neruda humorously celebrates a pair of handmade socks gifted to him, emphasizing their warmth and the craftsmanship that went into making them.
Famous Lines: "Marriage of blue / socks / and yellow socks, / two freshly / dyed / socks."

14. "Ode to the Confederate Dead" by Allen Tate:
- Tate's modernist ode reflects on the cultural and historical significance of the Confederate soldiers' graves and contemplates the impact of the Civil War.
- Famous Lines: *"Carved stone to ivory / Is slick with power."*
These examples illustrate the diverse range of subjects, tones, and styles that odes can encompass, from the contemplative and philosophical to the playful and observational. Odes continue to be a versatile and enduring form of poetry.

ELEGY

An elegy is a poetic form that typically reflects on themes of loss, mourning, and remembrance. It is often written in response to the death of a person or the contemplation of something lost, such as love, beauty, or a way of life. Elegies are characterised by their somber and reflective tone, as well as their exploration of grief and sorrow.

Characteristics:

Reflective and Mourning Tone: Elegies convey a sense of sadness, lament, and reflection. They express grief and sorrow over the loss of someone or something dear.

Expression of Emotions: Elegies provide a platform for poets to express their emotions, whether it's the pain of loss, longing for what's gone, or a sense of nostalgia.

Diverse Subjects: Elegies can be written about a wide range of subjects, including deceased individuals, historical events, personal experiences, or even abstract concepts like lost innocence.

Formal Structure: While elegies may not adhere to a strict rhyme or meter, they often have a structured and organised form that helps convey the poet's thoughts and emotions.

Exploration of Transience: Elegies often explore the transient nature of life and the inevitability of death. They may ponder the fragility of human existence.

Famous Elegies:

"Elegy Written in a Country Churchyard" by Thomas Gray:

> This is one of the most famous elegies in English literature. It reflects on the lives of ordinary people buried in a rural churchyard and contemplates the universality of death. "The paths of glory lead but to the grave."

"In Memoriam A.H.H." by Alfred, Lord Tennyson:

> Tennyson's elegy is a lengthy and introspective work written in memory of his close friend Arthur Henry Hallam.

It explores the themes of grief, faith, and the passage of time.
"Be near me when my light is low, / When the blood creeps, and the nerves prick."

"Lycidas" by John Milton:
Written in response to the death of Milton's friend Edward King, "Lycidas" is a pastoral elegy that reflects on the loss of a talented young poet and laments the unpredictable nature of death.
"Fame is the spur that the clear spirit doth raise / (That last infirmity of noble mind)."

"Adonais" by Percy Bysshe Shelley:
Shelley's elegy is dedicated to the memory of John Keats. It mourns Keats's untimely death and praises his poetic genius while reflecting on the impermanence of human life.
"He is made one with Nature: there is heard / His voice in all her music, from the moan / Of thunder, to the song of night's sweet bird."

"When Lilacs Last in the Dooryard Bloom'd" by Walt Whitman:
Whitman's elegy is written in response to the assassination of President Abraham Lincoln. It is a deeply moving and somber reflection on loss, death, and the American Civil War.
"O starry-eyed, star-haired visionary! / With the sad voice of death chants he."

6. "To an Athlete Dying Young" by A.E. Housman:
This elegy mourns the premature death of a young athlete who was celebrated in his prime. It reflects on the fleeting nature of fame and glory.
"The time you won your town the race / We chaired you through the market-place."

7. "Dirge Without Music" by Edna St. Vincent Millay:
In this modern elegy, Millay reflects on the inevitability of death and the absence of solace or consolation in the face of loss.

> "Down, down, down into the darkness of the grave / Gently they go, the beautiful, the tender, the kind."

8. "Requiem" by Anna Akhmatova:
Akhmatova's elegy reflects on the suffering and loss experienced during the tumultuous period of the Russian Revolution and its aftermath. It mourns the deaths of loved ones and the destruction of a way of life.

> "I'll always keep the wonder in my eyes / And I won't let a single memory go."

9. "O Captain! My Captain!" by Walt Whitman:
While not a traditional elegy, this poem mourns the assassination of President Abraham Lincoln. It uses the metaphor of a ship and its captain to express grief and loss.

My Captain does not answer, his lips are pale and still,
My father does not feel my arm, he has no pulse nor will,

10. "Funeral Blues" by W. H. Auden:
Auden's poem, also known as "Stop all the clocks," is a contemporary elegy that expresses profound grief and the desire to stop time in response to the death of a loved one.

> "He was my North, my South, my East and West, / My working week and my Sunday rest."

11. "The Soldier" by Rupert Brooke:
This elegy is written in the form of a sonnet and reflects on the idea of an English soldier's death as a noble and heroic sacrifice for his country

> "In that rich earth a richer dust concealed;"

12. "Elegy for Jane" by Theodore Roethke:
Roethke's poem is a personal elegy written for a student who died tragically. It reflects on the impact of her death on the poet and the sense of loss.

> "All the tides of the world / Can christen you, / Though it never could."

These elegies come from various time periods and cultures, showcasing the universal theme of mourning and the human response to loss and mortality. They continue to resonate with readers for their poignant expressions of grief and reflection on the fleeting nature of life.

Elegy It is a mournful, melancholic, or plaintive poem that can address different themes and subjects, not just death. Over time, several types of elegies have been identified based on their content and the context in which they were written. Here are some types of elegies:

Personal Elegy:
> Laments the death of a particular person.
> The focus is on personal grief, sorrow, and remembrance.
> Examples include "In Memory of W. B. Yeats" by W. H. Auden and "Lycidas" by John Milton (though "Lycidas" also touches upon broader societal issues).

Pastoral Elegy:
> Uses pastoral elements, like shepherds or rural landscapes, as metaphors.
> Often includes a progression from grief to acceptance, sometimes concluding with a sense of solace or hope.
> Classic examples are "Adonais" by Percy Bysshe Shelley and "The Waste Land" by T.S. Eliot (though the latter can also be seen as a modernist elegy).

Mourning Elegy:

Expresses a sense of loss or sorrow for something that has passed, not necessarily death.

Can mourn the loss of youth, past times, or a way of life.

War Elegy:

Mourns the loss of life due to wars or battles.

These elegies often comment on the senselessness or brutality of war.

Examples include some war poems from World War I poets like Wilfred Owen and Siegfried Sassoon.

Romantic Elegy:

Combines elements of romantic poetry with the traditional themes of elegy.

Emphasizes personal emotion, nature, and individual experience.

"Elegy Written in a Country Churchyard" by Thomas Gray can be considered a precursor to this type.

Cultural or Political Elegy:

Laments societal changes, the loss of cultural values, or the passing of a particular way of life.

Can also mourn the death of a significant political or cultural figure.

Modernist Elegy:

Explores the themes of loss and mourning within the context of the modern world.

May challenge traditional forms or expressions of the elegy.

T.S. Eliot's "The Waste Land" can be seen as a modernist elegy mourning the decline of Western civilization after World War I.

Consolatory Elegy:

While starting with the expression of grief or sorrow, it eventually offers consolation or solace, either through the remembrance of the deceased, the hope of an afterlife, or acceptance of the inevitable cycle of life and death.

Elegies can often transcend these categories, blending elements from multiple types into a single work. The primary characteristic that binds them is their reflection on loss, whether that's of a person, an ideal, a cultural norm, or any other form of absence.

TYPES OF LITERARY TERMS / DEVICES

FIGURATIVE DEVICES

MUSICAL DEVICES

RHETORICAL DEVICES

ADVANCED LITERARY TERMS

FIGURATIVE DEVICES

SIMILE

A simile is a figure of speech that involves comparing two unlike things using the words "like" or "as" to highlight their similarities. Similes create vivid and imaginative comparisons, allowing readers to better understand or visualise the characteristics of one thing by comparing it to something familiar.
Few examples of similes:

"Her smile was as bright as the sun on a clear summer day."
"His voice was as smooth as velvet, soothing and comforting."
"The water in the lake sparkled like a field of diamonds."
"The wind howled through the trees like a pack of wolves in the night."
"His laughter echoed like the joyful chimes of a bell."

In each of these examples, the use of "as" or "like" establishes a comparison between two different elements, drawing a connection between their qualities or characteristics. Similes enhance descriptions, create imagery, and engage readers by helping them form mental associations between the known and the new.

Similes come in various forms and serve different purposes in language and literature.

Some types of similes that showcase their versatility and use:

Simple Simile: The most common type of simile, where two dissimilar things are directly compared using "like" or "as." For example: "Her laughter was like music."

Extended Simile: A simile that is elaborated over several lines or even an entire paragraph, providing detailed comparisons and often enhancing the imagery. An example can be found in Homer's "The Iliad," where extended similes are used to describe characters and events.

Homeric Simile: is a special type of simile found in the epic poems of Homer, particularly in "The Iliad" and "The Odyssey." These similes are known for their extended and elaborate nature, often spanning several lines or even an entire paragraph. Homeric similes are designed to provide vivid and imaginative comparisons, enhancing the epic narrative and offering readers a deeper understanding of the characters and events.

Here's an example of a Homeric simile from "The Iliad" by Homer:

Example from "The Iliad":

In Book 16 of "The Iliad," there is a Homeric simile that compares Patroclus's battle with the Trojan hero Hector to a pair of lions. It emphasizes the intensity of the battle and the fierce combat between the two warriors. The simile goes as follows:

"Like lions in the pride of their strength they sprang upon one another,
glaring dreadfully, and fought in fury of heart for the
sake of the victory and the slain. Thus did Achilles give
chase to Hector, and as a lion in the mountains flags not in
pace or spring till he has got back to his lair, even so did
Achilles not give over to pursue Hector son of Priam, that
he might slay him and strip him of his armour."

In this simile, the epic battle between Patroclus and Hector is likened to the fierce combat of two lions, emphasising their strength, intensity, and determination.

Homeric similes serve to enrich the storytelling in epic poetry, providing readers with vivid and memorable comparisons that enhance their engagement with the narrative. These extended similes are a hallmark of Homer's poetic style and contribute to the enduring impact of his epic works.

Implicit Simile: Also called an implied simile, this type of simile doesn't use "like" or "as" explicitly but still creates a comparison through context. For example: "His eyes were fire."

Appositive Simile: This type uses an appositive—a noun or noun phrase—to draw a comparison. For instance: "She walked with the grace of a dancer, light and elegant."

Hyperbolic Simile: These similes use exaggeration to emphasize the comparison, often pushing the boundaries of believability for dramatic effect. For example: "He was as hungry as a thousand wolves."

Compressed Simile: This is a brief simile that conveys a comparison in a concise manner. For example: "Her smile, like a sunrise."

Mixed Simile: A simile that combines elements from two or more different comparisons to create a unique or unexpected comparison. For example: "He was as strong as an ox and as swift as the wind."

Proverbial Simile: A simile that has become a common saying or idiom, often carrying a universal truth or advice. For example: "As busy as a bee."

Direct Simile: The traditional form of simile, where the comparison is stated directly using "like" or "as." For example:

"Her eyes were as bright as stars."

Indirect Simile: This type implies a comparison without using "like" or "as," relying on context and the use of vivid descriptions. For example: "Her words cut through the room like a knife."

Contrasting Simile: This type highlights the differences between two elements while still using "like" or "as." For example: "He was calm like the eye of a storm."

These different types of similes provide writers with a wide range of tools to create comparisons that are imaginative, expressive, and engaging for readers.

More examples of similes to help you further understand how they work and how they can be used in different contexts:

"She danced across the stage like a fluttering butterfly."
"His voice was as smooth as silk, soothing and gentle."
"The stars shone like diamonds in the velvet sky."
"Her hair was as golden as the rays of the morning sun."
"The old house creaked like an aging wooden ship."
"His courage in the face of danger was as unwavering as a mountain."
"Her laughter echoed through the room like the peal of bells."
"The water flowed gently, like a whispering stream."
"His smile lit up the room like a burst of sunlight."
"The storm raged outside, sounding like a ferocious beast."
"She was as quick-witted as a fox, always one step ahead."
"The toddler's energy was boundless, like a bouncing ball."
"His determination was as unyielding as a stone wall."
"The wind whispered through the trees like a secret message."
"Her cooking was a disaster; the kitchen looked like a war zone."
"The athlete's speed on the track was as swift as a cheetah."
"The evening sky was painted with hues as vibrant as a painter's palette."
"The tension in the room was thick, like the fog on a misty morning."
"His bravery on the battlefield was as fierce as a lion's roar."
"The ice cream melted in the sun as quickly as snowflakes on a warm day."
These examples showcase different ways similes can be used to create vivid imagery and comparisons in various contexts. Similes enhance the descriptive quality of language and contribute to the overall impact of a literary work.

METAPHOR

A metaphor is a figure of speech that involves comparing two unlike things by stating that one thing is another, implying a direct similarity or identification between them. Unlike a simile, which uses "like" or "as" to make a comparison, a metaphor makes the comparison more directly and often creates a deeper connection between the two elements. Metaphors are used to add depth, imagery, and layers of meaning to language and literature.

Here are a few examples of metaphors:

"Time is a thief that steals our youth."
"Her heart is a fragile glass, easily shattered."
"The world is a stage, and we are all actors."
"His voice was a velvet blanket, wrapping around me."
"Life is a journey with ups and downs, twists and turns."
"The city streets were a bustling river of people."
"Love is a beacon that guides us through the darkness."
"Her smile is a ray of sunshine on a cloudy day."
"The classroom was a zoo, filled with restless animals."
"His words were a sword, cutting through the silence."

In each of these examples, a metaphor creates a direct comparison between two different elements, suggesting a shared characteristic or quality. Metaphors can be both subtle and powerful, adding depth and resonance to language by connecting abstract concepts with concrete imagery.

Types of Metaphors

Metaphors come in various types, each serving a different purpose and creating different effects in language and literature. Here are some types of metaphors:

Conventional Metaphor: This is a common or widely recognized metaphor that has become part of everyday language. For example, "time is money" is a conventional metaphor that implies the value of time.
"Time is money."
"She's a shining star."
"Love is a battlefield."
"Life is a roller coaster."
"His words were music to my ears."

Dead Metaphor: A dead metaphor is a metaphor that has been used so often that its original vividness has faded, and it's now treated as a literal expression. For example, "the foot of the mountain" uses "foot" metaphorically, but it's so commonly used that people often don't think of it as a metaphor.
"Face the facts."
"The heart of the matter."
"The arms of a chair."
"The leg of the table."

Extended Metaphor: An extended metaphor is a metaphor that is developed over several lines or throughout an entire work. It elaborates on the comparison, providing more depth and detail. For example, in Shakespeare's "All the world's a stage" speech from "As You Like It," the world is compared to a stage, and various aspects of human life are compared to actors and roles.
In Martin Luther King Jr.'s "I Have a Dream" speech, he extended the metaphor of "the bank of justice" and "insufficient funds of freedom" to describe the challenges faced by African Americans.

Mixed Metaphor: A mixed metaphor occurs when two or more metaphors are used together in a way that creates confusion or an illogical comparison.
For example, "He's a diamond in the rough, and it's time to strike while the iron is hot."

"Let's grab the bull by the horns and think outside the box."
"We'll cross that bridge when the ball is in our court."

Implied Metaphor: An implied metaphor suggests a comparison without directly stating it. It relies on context and the reader's understanding to make the connection.
 For example, "She barked her orders" implies a comparison between the speaker and a dog without explicitly saying "like a dog."
"His words cut deeper than a knife."
"She danced through life with grace."
"His smile lit up the room."

Root Metaphor: A root metaphor is a fundamental or underlying metaphor that shapes a person's perception, beliefs, or culture. It's often deeply ingrained and influences how people view the world. For
example, the idea of "time as a journey" is a root metaphor that shapes how people think about time.

Submerged Metaphor: A submerged metaphor is a metaphor that is not immediately obvious, requiring the reader to think deeper to uncover the comparison. It adds a layer of complexity to the language. For example, "The seeds of rebellion were sown" uses a gardening metaphor to describe the beginning of a rebellion.

Absolute Metaphor: An absolute metaphor is a self-contained metaphor that doesn't need context to make sense. It's a direct comparison that stands on its own. For example, "His heart of gold" compares someone's heart to gold to convey their kindness and generosity.

Visual Metaphor: A visual metaphor uses visual elements to create a comparison, often using images or scenes to represent abstract concepts. For example, a broken mirror can visually symbolise shattered self-image or identity.

Catachresis: While not a traditional metaphor, a catachresis is an extreme or strained metaphor that pushes the boundaries of language. It uses words in new and unconventional ways to create unique comparisons. For example, "I will speak daggers to her" from Shakespeare's "Hamlet" combines the literal meaning of "speak" with the metaphor of "daggers" to express strong words. "I smell a rat" combines the literal sense of smelling with the metaphor of detecting deception.

These different types of metaphors showcase the versatility and creativity of language when it comes to making comparisons and expressing abstract ideas in tangible terms.

Metaphor and Simile are both figures of speech used to make comparisons between two unlike things, but they do so in slightly different ways.

 The key differences between metaphor and simile:
Metaphor:
Comparison Type: In a metaphor, a direct comparison is made between two unlike things by stating that one thing is another. The comparison is more straightforward and direct.

Use of "Like" or "As": Metaphors do not use "like" or "as" to create the comparison. Instead, they equate the two things without explicitly stating the comparison method.

Example: "His words were daggers," where the speaker is directly equating the words to daggers without using "like" or "as."

Effect: Metaphors often create a stronger and more direct connection between the two elements being compared. They can be more powerful and evocative.

Simile:
Comparison Type: In a simile, a comparison is made between two unlike things using "like" or "as." The comparison is more explicit and indicated by these words.
Use of "Like" or "As": Similes use "like" or "as" to signal that a comparison is being made. This makes the comparison more evident and provides a clear point of comparison.
Example: "Her smile was as bright as the sun," where the comparison between her smile and the sun is made using "as."
Effect: Similes often provide a softer and more indirect comparison. They allow for a more gradual or nuanced connection between the two elements being compared.

In summary, the primary difference between metaphor and simile lies in the way the comparison is presented. Metaphors directly equate one thing with another, while similes use "like" or "as" to create a comparison that is more explicit and stated. Both figures of speech serve to enhance language by creating imaginative connections and vivid imagery.

PERSONIFICATION

Personification is a literary device in which non-human objects, abstract concepts, or animals are given human-like qualities or attributes, ascribing human characteristics to them.
This technique allows writers to make their descriptions more vivid, relatable, and engaging, as well as to create deeper connections between the reader and the subject.
Personification adds depth and imagery to language by anthropomorphising elements that are not human.

Few examples of personification:
"The wind whispered through the trees."
"The stars danced in the night sky."
"The flowers nodded their heads in agreement."
"The sun smiled down upon the earth."
"The ocean waves embraced the shoreline."
"Fear gripped his heart tightly."
"Time flies by so quickly."
"The old house groaned as it settled."
"The leaves rustled in the breeze, telling secrets to each other."
"The river chattered as it flowed over the rocks."

In each of these examples, non-human elements (such as wind, stars, flowers, etc.) are endowed with human-like actions, emotions, or qualities. Personification adds a layer of imagery and emotional resonance to the language, helping readers to better understand and relate to the subject being described.

Personification comes in various forms, each serving different purposes in literature and language.

Types of personification:
Simple Personification: This is the most basic form of personification, where non-human objects or concepts are given human attributes. For example, "The sun smiled."

Extended Personification: In extended personification, the human-like qualities or actions are sustained over a longer passage or throughout a work, contributing to a more immersive experience. For example, "The old tree stood with arms outstretched, as if welcoming the dawn."

Pathetic Fallacy: This type of personification involves attributing human emotions to elements of nature, often to reflect the mood or emotions of characters or the narrative. For example, "The stormy sky mirrored her heartache."

Visual Personification: Visual personification assigns human facial or bodily features to non-human entities or objects. For example, "The moon stared down at the world with its one eye."

Psychological Personification: This type imbues non-human elements with human psychological traits, such as thoughts, intentions, or desires. For example, "The fire hungered for more wood to consume."

Narrative Personification: Here, non-human elements are given the ability to perform actions typically attributed to humans, contributing to the plot. For example, "Time raced against them as they worked to finish the task."

Symbolic Personification: In this form, non-human entities represent abstract concepts or ideas, often adding depth to allegorical or symbolic works. For example, "Justice held her scales with unwavering balance."

Emphatic Personification: Emphatic personification emphasizes certain qualities or attributes of an object or concept to create a more vivid or intense description. For example, "The wind howled with anger."

Ironical Personification: This type of personification uses human-like traits to convey irony or sarcasm. For example, "The clock mocks me with its relentless ticking."

Reverse Personification: In reverse personification, humans are attributed with non-human characteristics. This approach can create unexpected perspectives or evoke certain emotions. For example, "He was a stone, unmoved by her pleas."

Zoomorphism: While not a strict form of personification, zoomorphism attributes animal qualities to humans or non-human elements. For example, "The politician was a sly fox."

These different types of personification demonstrate the creative ways writers use this literary device to enhance language, create imagery, and establish deeper connections between readers and the subjects being described.

Here are more examples of personification in various forms:
Simple Personification:
"The wind whispered secrets through the trees."
"The flowers danced in the meadow."
"The stars winked in the night sky."
"The door creaked in protest as it opened."
"The rain tapped gently on the windowpane."

Extended Personification:
"The river, tired from its journey, sighed as it flowed lazily through the valley."
"The abandoned house stood alone on the hill, its windows staring vacantly into the distance."
"The mountain held its head high, unmoved by the passing storms."
"The city streets buzzed with life, as if they had stories to tell to those who would listen."

Pathetic Fallacy:
"The stormy sky mirrored their turbulent emotions."
"The sun smiled warmly upon the joyful scene."
"The thunder roared in anger as the conflict escalated."
"The calm sea reflected the tranquility of their hearts."

Visual Personification:
"The moon's face beamed down on the earth."
"The mountain's shoulders were covered in a blanket of snow."
"The river's winding path resembled a serpent slithering through the landscape."

Psychological Personification:
"The flames of curiosity burned brightly within her."
"The forest whispered secrets that only the trees could hear."
"The ocean waves sang a lullaby to the weary travelers."

Narrative Personification:
"Time raced against them, urging them to finish before it was too late."
"The door slammed shut, as if it wanted to keep them out."
"The storm raged, battling against the efforts to bring back calm."

Symbolic Personification:
"Freedom spread its wings and soared above the horizon."

"Love embraced them, wrapping them in its warm embrace."
"Hope held a lantern, guiding them through the darkness."

Emphatic Personification:
"The wind howled with rage, tearing through the trees."
"The ocean waves roared in defiance against the shore."
"The silence of the night was broken by the thunder's mighty voice."

Ironical Personification:
"The clock, with its infinite patience, continued ticking as if time were never-ending."
"The door protested loudly as it was forced open, as if it had a choice."

Reverse Personification:
"She carried the weight of the world on her shoulders, a burden she couldn't escape."
"His heart of stone showed no mercy to those in need."
"They were like moths, drawn to the flame of temptation."

Zoomorphism:
"He had the cunning of a fox when it came to negotiation."
"Her eyes had the curiosity of a cat, always exploring."

These examples highlight the various ways personification is used to enrich language, create imagery, and bring inanimate or abstract concepts to life through human-like qualities and actions.

HYPERBOLE

Hyperbole is a figure of speech that involves intentional exaggeration for emphasis or effect. It's used to create a strong impact, evoke emotions, or make a point, often by stretching the truth to an extreme degree.

Hyperbole is not meant to be taken literally; instead, it serves to emphasise a particular aspect of the subject being described.

Some examples of hyperbole:

"I'm so hungry, I could eat a horse."
"Her backpack weighs a ton."
"I've told you a million times not to do that."
"The line for the concert stretched for miles."
"I'm dying of embarrassment."
"His smile could light up the entire room."
"She's as tall as a skyscraper."
"I've been waiting for ages for you to call."
"The car was going at a million miles an hour."
"This suitcase weighs a ton; I can't even lift it."

In each of these examples, hyperbole is used to exaggerate the situation or characteristics being described. The purpose of hyperbole is to create emphasis, evoke strong emotions, or make a statement more memorable by presenting it in an extreme or exaggerated manner.

TYPES OF HYPERBOLES

Hyperbole comes in various types, each serving different purposes in language and literature. Here are some types of hyperbole:

General Hyperbole: This is the most common type of hyperbole, where exaggeration is used to emphasize a point or create an effect. For example, "I've been waiting forever."

Comic Hyperbole: In comic hyperbole, exaggeration is used for comedic effect, often to create humor through over-the-top statements. For example, "I'm so hungry I could eat a whole elephant."

Catastrophic Hyperbole: This type involves exaggeration to describe a disastrous or catastrophic situation. For example, "The party was a total disaster."

Gross Hyperbole: Gross hyperbole uses extreme exaggeration to describe something in a way that's vivid and attention-grabbing. For example, "It's a million degrees outside."

Understatement Hyperbole: This involves using exaggeration to understate something, creating a sense of irony. For example, "I'm just a little bit busy."

Antithetical Hyperbole: Antithetical hyperbole combines contrasting ideas with exaggeration for emphasis. For example, "The book is as light as a ton of bricks."

Hyperbolic Questions: Hyperbolic questions use exaggeration to pose questions that are meant to be rhetorical or humorous. For example, "Could you be any slower?"

Emphatic Hyperbole: This type uses hyperbole to emphasize a point with strong emotion. For example, "I'm so proud I could burst."

Flattery Hyperbole: Flattery hyperbole involves exaggerated praise to emphasise admiration or express positive feelings. For example, "You're the smartest person on the planet."

Sarcastic Hyperbole: In sarcastic hyperbole, the exaggeration is used to convey the opposite of what's being said, often for a satirical or critical effect. For example, "Oh, great! Another Monday morning."

These different types of hyperbole showcase the ways writers use exaggerated statements to create emphasis, evoke emotions, add humour, and make their language more engaging and memorable.

Few examples of poets and their works that include the use of hyperbole:
Poet: William Shakespeare
> Work: "Hamlet"
> Hyperbole: "I could be bounded in a nutshell and count myself a king of infinite space."

Poet: Emily Dickinson
> Work: Various poems
> Hyperbole: "I'm nobody! Who are you? / Are you nobody, too?"

Poet: Langston Hughes
> Work: "The Negro Speaks of Rivers"
> Hyperbole: "My soul has grown deep like the rivers."

Poet: Walt Whitman
> Work: "Song of Myself"

Hyperbole: "I sound my barbaric yawp over the roofs of the world."

Poet: Pablo Neruda
Work: Various poems
Hyperbole: "My feet will want to walk to where you are sleeping, but / I shall go on living."

Poet: Sylvia Plath
Work: "Lady Lazarus"
Hyperbole: "Dying / Is an art, like everything else."

Poet: Shel Silverstein
Work: Various poems (often in his children's poetry)
Hyperbole: "I'm as big as the sky, the trees, and the sun. / I'm as big as the world! Anyone."

Poet: Ogden Nash
Work: Various poems (known for humorous poetry)
Hyperbole: "Candy is dandy, but liquor is quicker."

Poet: William Wordsworth
Work: "I Wandered Lonely as a Cloud" (also known as "Daffodils")
Hyperbole: "Ten thousand I saw at a glance."

Poet: Edgar Allan Poe
Work: "The Raven"
Hyperbole: "Quoth the Raven 'Nevermore.'"

These examples demonstrate how hyperbole is used by various poets to enhance their poems, create impact, evoke emotions, and add unique qualities to their literary works.

William Shakespeare - "Hamlet":
Hyperbole: *"I could be bounded in a nutshell and count myself a king of infinite space."*
Explanation: In this line, Hamlet is using hyperbole to express his feelings of confinement and vastness. He's saying that even if he were as small as a nutshell, he could still consider himself a ruler of boundless space, emphasizing his sense of limitless imagination and grandeur.

Emily Dickinson - Various Poems:
Hyperbole: *"I'm nobody! Who are you? / Are you nobody, too?"*
Explanation: In these lines, Dickinson is using hyperbole to playfully downplay her own identity and question the reader's identity. By claiming to be "nobody," she exaggerates her anonymity, inviting readers to join her in a shared sense of humility or insignificance.

Langston Hughes - "The Negro Speaks of Rivers":
Hyperbole: *"My soul has grown deep like the rivers."*
Explanation: In this line, Hughes employs hyperbole to convey the profound connection between the speaker's soul and the ancient rivers. By saying his soul has grown as deep as the rivers, he exaggerates the depth of his experiences and emotions, emphasizing the lasting impact of history and heritage.

Walt Whitman - "Song of Myself":
Hyperbole: *"I sound my barbaric yawp over the roofs of the world."*
Explanation: Whitman uses hyperbole to emphasize the expansiveness of his voice and message. By describing his voice as a "barbaric yawp" that reaches over the world, he exaggerates the boldness and scope of his expression, symbolizing his desire for self-discovery and connection with humanity.

Pablo Neruda - Various Poems:
Hyperbole: *"My feet will want to walk to where you are sleeping, but / I shall go on living."*
Explanation: In these lines, Neruda uses hyperbole to express the intensity of his emotions. By saying his feet will want to walk to where someone is sleeping, he exaggerates his longing, emphasizing his struggle between desire and the reality of continuing to live his life.

Sylvia Plath - "Lady Lazarus":
Hyperbole: *"Dying / Is an art, like everything else."*
Explanation: Plath employs hyperbole to make a provocative statement. By calling dying an "art," she exaggerates the complexity and calculated nature of her struggles with mental health. This hyperbolic description captures the intensity of her emotions and the meticulous effort she feels goes into managing her pain.

Shel Silverstein - Various Poems:
Hyperbole: *"I'm as big as the sky, the trees, and the sun. / I'm as big as the world! Anyone."*
Explanation: In this excerpt from one of Silverstein's poems, the speaker uses hyperbole to express a childlike sense of empowerment and confidence. By claiming to be as big as the sky, trees, and sun, the speaker exaggerates their self-importance in a playful and imaginative way.

Ogden Nash - Various Poems:
Hyperbole: *"Candy is dandy, but liquor is quicker."*
Explanation: Nash employs hyperbole for humorous effect in this line. By saying that liquor is "quicker" than candy, he exaggerates the idea that alcohol provides faster satisfaction or relief. The hyperbolic contrast adds a lighthearted and witty twist to the comparison.

William Wordsworth - *"I Wandered Lonely as a Cloud"*:
Hyperbole: *"Ten thousand I saw at a glance."*
Explanation: In this line, Wordsworth uses hyperbole to emphasize the sheer abundance of daffodils he encountered. By exaggerating the number to "ten thousand," he vividly portrays the image of a vast field of flowers, enhancing the reader's sense of the scene's beauty and impact.

Edgar Allan Poe - "The Raven":
Hyperbole: *"Quoth the Raven 'Nevermore.'"*
Explanation: Poe employs hyperbole in the repetition of the word "Nevermore" by the raven. The raven's exaggerated refusal to provide any other answer intensifies the atmosphere of melancholy and despair in the poem, emphasizing the speaker's sense of hopelessness.

ANTITHESIS

Antithesis is a rhetorical device that involves placing contrasting or opposing ideas or elements within a sentence or parallel structure to create a striking juxtaposition.
This technique is used to highlight the differences between the two contrasting ideas, making them more noticeable and impactful. Antithesis adds depth and complexity to language, often leading to a deeper understanding of the concepts being presented.

"To be or not to be, that is the question."
"Love is an ideal thing, marriage a real thing."
"Man proposes, God disposes."
"It was the best of times, it was the worst of times."
"Patience is bitter, but it has a sweet fruit."
"Speech is silver, but silence is golden."
"Money is the root of all evil, but it's also the source of comfort."
"Give me liberty or give me death."
"You are easy on the eyes, but hard on the heart."
"Art is long, and Time is fleeting."

In each of these examples, antithesis is used to contrast two opposing ideas or qualities, creating a balanced and thought-provoking comparison. This technique adds depth and complexity to language by highlighting the inherent contradictions between the elements being juxtaposed.

Antithesis comes in various types, each offering a different way to present contrasting or opposing ideas for rhetorical effect. Here are some types of antithesis:

Single Antithesis: This is the basic form of antithesis, where a single sentence or phrase presents a direct contrast between two opposing elements. For example, *"To err is human, to forgive* *divine."*

Compound Antithesis: In compound antithesis, two or more parallel phrases or clauses are contrasted within the same sentence. For example, *"It was the age of wisdom, it was the age of foolishness, it was the epoch of belief, it was the epoch of incredulity..."*

Emphatic Antithesis: In this type, the contrasted elements are intentionally exaggerated for emphasis. For example, *"She's not just smart; she's a genius."*

Juxtapositional Antithesis: This form involves placing two contrasting ideas side by side in order to highlight their differences more effectively. For example, "You're easy on the eyes, but hard on the heart."

Antithesis of Words: Here, opposing words are used to create a clear and direct contrast. For example, "Darkness cannot drive out darkness; only light can do that."

Antithesis of Ideas: Instead of using contrasting words, this type contrasts opposing ideas or concepts to create a profound comparison. For example, "The greater our knowledge increases, the greater our ignorance unfolds."

Antithesis in Poetry: Antithesis is often used in poetry to create rhythm and impact. For example, in Robert Frost's poem "Fire and Ice," the lines "Some say the world will end in fire, / Some say in ice" present contrasting ideas in a poetic structure.

Balanced Antithesis: In this type, the contrasting elements are presented in a balanced and parallel structure, creating a sense of symmetry and rhythm. For example, "Not that I loved Caesar less, but that I loved Rome more."

Rhetorical Antithesis: This type involves the deliberate use of antithesis to persuade or influence the audience. For example, "Ask not what your country can do for you; ask what you can do for your country."

Sequential Antithesis: In sequential antithesis, a series of contrasting ideas is presented one after the other to build a complex contrast. For example, "We will not be satisfied until justice rolls down like waters and righteousness like a mighty stream."

These different types of antithesis showcase the versatility of this rhetorical device, allowing writers to create contrasts that enhance the impact of their ideas and statements.

Different types of antithesis, along with explanations for each:
Single Antithesis:
"To err is human, to forgive divine."
Explanation: In this single antithesis, the contrasting ideas of human fallibility and divine forgiveness are juxtaposed. The contrast highlights the difference between human nature and a higher moral quality attributed to the divine.

Compound Antithesis:
"It was the age of wisdom, it was the age of foolishness, it was the epoch of belief, it was the epoch of incredulity..."
Explanation: Charles Dickens employs compound antithesis in the opening lines of "A Tale of Two Cities." By contrasting different qualities of the two ages (wisdom/foolishness, belief/incredulity), Dickens sets the stage for the themes of duality and contrast in the novel.

Emphatic Antithesis:
"She's not just smart; she's a genius."
Explanation: In this example, the contrast is emphasized by using the word "just" to indicate that the first quality is not sufficient to describe the extent of the person's intelligence. The word "genius" is used to heighten the impact of the statement.

Juxtapositional Antithesis:
"You're easy on the eyes, but hard on the heart."
Explanation: This antithesis places two contrasting qualities side by side, creating a sharp comparison between the external appearance ("easy on the eyes") and the emotional impact ("hard on the heart") of a person.

Antithesis of Words:
"Darkness cannot drive out darkness; only light can do that."
Explanation: Here, the contrast between "darkness" and "light" is used to convey a profound idea. The antithesis emphasizes that negative qualities cannot be eliminated by more of the same negativity, but only through positive qualities.

Antithesis of Ideas:
"The greater our knowledge increases, the greater our ignorance unfolds."
Explanation: This antithesis contrasts the expansion of knowledge with the revelation of ignorance. The more knowledge we acquire, the more we become aware of the vast amount we still do not know.

Balanced Antithesis:
"Not that I loved Caesar less, but that I loved Rome more."
Explanation: In this balanced antithesis, the speaker clarifies that their love for Rome was the stronger motivation, although their love for Caesar was not diminished. The balanced structure creates a sense of symmetry and rhythm.

Rhetorical Antithesis:
"Ask not what your country can do for you; ask what you can do for your country."
Explanation: In this famous line from John F. Kennedy's inaugural address, the contrasting ideas of personal responsibility and national service are presented. The antithesis serves as a call to action, urging citizens to prioritise contributing to their country.

Sequential Antithesis:
"We will not be satisfied until justice rolls down like waters and righteousness like a mighty stream."
Explanation: In this sequential antithesis, Dr. Martin Luther King Jr. contrasts the imagery of justice flowing like water with the image of righteousness as a mighty stream. The repetition of "like" emphasizes the continuous and forceful nature of change.

Antithesis in Poetry:
"Fire and Ice" by Robert Frost
"Some say the world will end in fire,
Some say in ice."
Explanation: In these lines, Frost presents two contrasting elements, fire and ice, to explore different ways the world might come to an end. The antithesis adds rhythm and impact to the poem's theme of destruction.
These examples illustrate how antithesis can be used in different ways to create contrasts, emphasize ideas, and enhance the rhetorical impact of language and literature.

OXYMORON

An oxymoron is a rhetorical device that involves the combination of two contradictory or opposing words to create a meaningful expression.
Despite the apparent contradiction, oxymorons are used to convey complex ideas, provoke thought, or create a unique and memorable effect. Oxymorons often highlight the tension between the conflicting words and encourage the reader or listener to consider their underlying meaning.

Here are some examples of oxymorons:
Jumbo shrimp: The contradiction between "jumbo" (large) and "shrimp" (small) creates a playful and memorable expression.

Bittersweet: The combination of "bitter" (unpleasant) and "sweet" (pleasant) captures the mix of emotions or experiences.

Deafening silence: The contrast between "deafening" (extremely loud) and "silence" (absence of sound) emphasizes the absence of expected noise.

Living dead: This oxymoron combines "living" (alive) and "dead" (not alive) to describe something or someone that appears alive but lacks vitality.

Awfully good: The pairing of "awful" (negative) and "good" (positive) creates a sense of irony or surprise.

Pretty ugly: The juxtaposition of "pretty" (attractive) and "ugly" (unattractive) creates a contradiction that catches the reader's attention.

Open secret: The contrast between "open" (accessible) and "secret" (hidden) plays with the idea of something known to many but not openly discussed.

Act naturally: This phrase combines "act" (pretend) and "naturally" (genuinely) to create a humorous instruction.

Same difference: The oxymoron highlights a subtle distinction while acknowledging similarities.

Original copy: The combination of "original" (unique) and "copy" (duplicate) raises questions about authenticity.

Oxymorons serve to engage readers or listeners by presenting them with unexpected word combinations that invite deeper thought and reflection on the meanings behind the contradictory terms.

Jumbo shrimp:
Explanation: This oxymoron combines "jumbo" (meaning large or huge) with "shrimp" (a type of small seafood), creating a playful contradiction. It highlights the unexpected pairing of two words that are typically associated with different sizes.

Bittersweet:
Explanation: "Bittersweet" combines "bitter" (referring to something unpleasant or sharp) with "sweet" (referring to something pleasant or sugary). This oxymoron conveys a complex emotional experience where happiness is tinged with sadness, much like the mingling of contradictory flavors.

Deafening silence:
Explanation: In this oxymoron, "deafening" (meaning overwhelmingly loud) is combined with "silence" (absence of sound). The contrast between the two words emphasises the powerful and impactful absence of noise.

Living dead:
Explanation: "Living dead" combines "living" (alive) with "dead" (not alive). This oxymoron is often used to describe creatures like zombies or to convey a sense of lifelessness despite physical presence.

Awfully good:
Explanation: "Awfully good" juxtaposes "awful" (meaning extremely bad or unpleasant) with "good" (meaning positive or desirable). The combination creates irony, suggesting that something is surprisingly enjoyable despite its potential negative aspects.

Pretty ugly:
Explanation: This oxymoron pairs "pretty" (meaning attractive) with "ugly" (meaning unattractive). The contradiction catches attention by presenting two opposing descriptions within one expression.

Open secret:
Explanation: "Open secret" combines "open" (meaning accessible or not hidden) with "secret" (meaning concealed or unknown to many). The phrase suggests that the information is widely known yet not openly acknowledged.

Act naturally:
Explanation: In this phrase, "act" (meaning pretend or perform) is combined with "naturally" (meaning genuinely or as one would naturally behave). The oxymoron humorously instructs someone to behave in a way that appears spontaneous and unscripted.

Same difference:
Explanation: "Same difference" is a playful contradiction that emphasizes a subtle distinction between two things while acknowledging their similarities. It points out that although there

may be differences, they are ultimately inconsequential.

Original copy:
Explanation: "Original copy" combines "original" (meaning authentic or unique) with "copy" (meaning a duplicate or reproduction). This oxymoron raises questions about the authenticity of something presented as an original.

These examples illustrate how oxymorons creatively combine opposing words to create memorable and thought-provoking expressions that often evoke deeper contemplation or convey layered meanings.

Act naturally: This phrase instructs someone to behave in a genuine and unforced manner, using the contradictory pairing of "act" and "naturally."

Freezer burn: This oxymoron describes the damage that occurs when frozen food is exposed to air, combining "freezer" (where things are preserved) with "burn" (a destructive process).

Found missing: The oxymoron "found missing" creates a paradoxical situation where something is located but also absent or lost.

Minor crisis: Combining "minor" (small in importance) with "crisis" (a significant event or problem) creates a contrast that highlights a situation that may be serious but is not of utmost importance.

Original reproduction: "Original reproduction" juxtaposes "original" (unique and first) with "reproduction" (a copy or duplicate) to suggest a form of copying that is considered authentic.

Pretty terrible: This oxymoron combines "pretty" (attractive or pleasant) with "terrible" (unpleasant or bad), resulting in a description that contrasts positive and negative qualities.

Serious fun: The combination of "serious" (grave or significant) and "fun" (enjoyable and lighthearted) creates a contrast that suggests an enjoyable experience with a certain level of importance.

Virtual reality: This oxymoron pairs "virtual" (something that exists in a simulated or digital environment) with "reality" (the actual world), emphasizing the contradiction between the two concepts.

Clearly confused: The contradictory pairing of "clearly" (obviously or distinctly) and "confused" (lacking clarity or understanding) creates a paradox that describes a state of perplexity.

Dark light: "Dark light" combines "dark" (lacking light or visibility) with "light" (illumination), creating a paradoxical expression that challenges the usual associations between the two words.

These additional examples demonstrate the versatility of oxymorons in conveying complex ideas, creating contrasts, and adding depth to language through the pairing of contradictory terms.

IRONY

It seems like there might be a typo or misunderstanding in your question. The term "irony" doesn't seem to correspond to a recognised literary or rhetorical device. It's possible that you intended to ask about irony.

Irony is a rhetorical device in which there's a discrepancy between what's expected to happen and what actually occurs, creating an unexpected twist or contrast between appearance and reality. There are several types of irony, each serving a different purpose in literature and communication:

Verbal Irony: This occurs when someone says something but means the opposite. It often involves sarcasm or a play on words. For example, if someone remarks, "Oh, great! Another rainy day," on a sunny day, that's verbal irony.

Situational Irony: This type of irony involves a situation in which the outcome is significantly different from what was expected. For example, a fire station burning down would be a case of situational irony.

Dramatic Irony: Dramatic irony occurs when the audience or readers know something that the characters in a story do not. This creates tension and anticipation. For instance, in a horror movie, the audience might see the killer lurking behind a character while the character remains unaware.

Tragic Irony: Tragic irony is a subtype of dramatic irony, specifically in tragic situations where a character's actions lead to their own downfall or a negative outcome, often because of their own ignorance or misunderstanding.

Cosmic Irony: This refers to a situation in which fate or the universe seems to be playing a cruel joke on characters. It suggests that events are orchestrated against the characters' desires or efforts.

Socratic Irony: Named after the philosopher Socrates, this type of irony involves pretending ignorance to expose the flaws in someone else's argument or to provoke deeper thought.

Situational Cosmic Irony: This occurs when situational irony aligns with cosmic irony, creating a sense that fate itself is orchestrating the unexpected outcome.

These various types of irony serve different purposes in literature, adding layers of meaning, complexity, and often a sense of surprise or revelation for the audience or readers. If you intended to ask about "irony," feel free to ask for more information or examples!

Types of Irony along with explanations for each:

Verbal Irony:
Situation: On a freezing cold day, someone says, "What a lovely weather we're having."
Explanation: The speaker's statement is ironic because the actual weather is unpleasant, but they express the opposite sentiment.
Situation: Someone receives a terrible gift and exclaims, "Oh, this is just what I've always wanted!"
Explanation: The person uses verbal irony to sarcastically express dissatisfaction with the gift while pretending to be enthusiastic.

Situational Irony:
 Situation: A fire station burns down while the firefighters are responding to a fire in another part of the town.

Explanation: This situation is ironic because fire stations are expected to prevent fires, yet the fire station itself becomes a victim of fire.

Situation: A health-conscious person who never smoked a day in their life dies of lung cancer.

Explanation: This situation is situational irony because the expected outcome (healthy habits lead to health) contrasts with the actual outcome (lung cancer).

Dramatic Irony:

Situation: In a play, the audience knows that a character is planning a surprise party for another character, but the character being surprised remains unaware.

Explanation: The audience's knowledge creates dramatic irony, as they have information that the character on stage does not.

Situation: In a horror movie, the audience sees the killer hiding behind a door, but the character about to enter the room is unaware of the danger.

Explanation: The audience's awareness of the killer's presence creates dramatic irony, intensifying suspense and tension.

Tragic Irony:

Situation: In Shakespeare's play "Romeo and Juliet," Romeo believes Juliet is dead and drinks poison to join her, unaware that she is actually alive.

Explanation: Romeo's tragic fate is a result of his misunderstanding, creating tragic irony where the audience knows more than the character.

Cosmic Irony:

Situation: A lifeguard who has spent years training to save lives drowns in a shallow pool.

Explanation: The lifeguard's ironic fate suggests that despite their expertise, they were unable to save themselves, giving a sense that fate is playing a cruel joke

Socratic Irony
Situation: During a debate, a speaker pretends not to understand a complex argument and asks questions that reveal flaws in the opponent's reasoning.
Explanation: The speaker uses Socratic irony to expose weaknesses in the opponent's argument by feigning ignorance.

Situational Cosmic Irony:
Situation: A self-proclaimed climate change denier's home is destroyed by a natural disaster linked to climate change.
Explanation: This situation combines situational irony (the unexpected destruction) with cosmic irony (the person's beliefs leading to their own misfortune).

These examples illustrate how different types of irony create contrasts between expectations and outcomes, adding layers of meaning, complexity, and often a sense of surprise or commentary on human nature and fate.

IMAGERY

Imagery is a literary device that appeals to the senses, creating vivid mental pictures or sensory experiences in the reader's mind. Writers use imagery to enhance their writing by providing readers with a sensory-rich and immersive experience, allowing them to visualise and feel the scenes, characters, and emotions being described.
Imagery engages the reader's imagination and helps create a deeper understanding and emotional connection to the text.

There are several types of imagery, each appealing to a different sense:
Visual Imagery: Appeals to the sense of sight. It describes scenes, colors, shapes, and visual details in a way that allows readers to visualize the setting or characters. For example, "The sky was painted with hues of orange and pink as the sun dipped below the horizon."

Auditory Imagery: Appeals to the sense of hearing. It describes sounds and auditory experiences to create an auditory atmosphere. For example, "The distant howl of a wolf echoed through the silent forest."

Olfactory Imagery: Appeals to the sense of smell. It describes scents and odors to evoke a sensory experience related to the sense of smell. For example, "The aroma of freshly baked bread wafted through the air."

Gustatory Imagery: Appeals to the sense of taste. It describes flavors and tastes to engage the reader's sense of taste. For example, "The soup was a rich blend of savory spices that danced on the palate."

Tactile Imagery: Appeals to the sense of touch. It describes textures, temperatures, and tactile sensations to create a tangible and physical experience. For example, "Her skin was as smooth as silk to the touch."

Kinaesthetic Imagery: Appeals to the sense of movement and physical sensations. It describes bodily movements and actions to make the reader feel the motion. For example, "He danced with such grace that his movements seemed to defy gravity."

Organic Imagery: Appeals to internal sensations, emotions, and physiological experiences. It describes feelings in a way that helps readers connect emotionally with the text. For example, "His heart raced with excitement as he approached the finish line."

Thermal Imagery: Appeals to the sense of temperature. It describes sensations of heat or cold to evoke a sense of temperature. For example, "The icy wind cut through her jacket, sending shivers down her spine."

Imagery enriches writing by creating a sensory experience that brings words to life and allows readers to immerse themselves in the world of the text. Writers use imagery to paint a vivid and memorable picture in the reader's mind, making their writing more engaging, relatable, and evocative.

An example of imagery along with an explanation:
Example: "The sun dipped below the horizon, casting a warm golden glow over the tranquil ocean. The waves gently lapped against the shore, their rhythmic whispers creating a soothing melody. Seagulls soared overhead, their wings slicing through the sky as they called out to each other. The air carried a salty breeze that tousled the hair of those lucky enough to witness the serene spectacle."

Explanation: In this example, visual imagery is used to describe a scene of the sun setting over the ocean. The writer appeals to the sense of sight by vividly portraying the warm golden glow of the sun, the tranquil ocean, and the seagulls in flight. The reader can visualise the colours, shapes, and movements of the elements in the scene.

Additionally, auditory imagery is employed when the writer describes the waves "gently lapping" against the shore and creating a "soothing melody." This appeals to the sense of hearing, allowing the reader to imagine the sound of the waves and their calming effect.

Furthermore, tactile imagery is incorporated when the salty breeze is mentioned as "tousling the hair" of those present. This engages the sense of touch by describing how the breeze interacts with the environment.

Overall, this passage uses imagery to create a multi-sensory experience for the reader. By appealing to multiple senses, the writer paints a detailed and immersive picture of the setting, allowing the reader to feel as if they are right there, witnessing the scene themselves.

Many poets have used irony in their work to add depth, complexity, and thought-provoking elements to their poetry. Here are a few poets who are known for their use of irony in their literary creations:

William Shakespeare: Shakespeare's plays and sonnets often feature various forms of irony, including dramatic, verbal, and situational irony. His characters' speeches and interactions are rich with layers of irony that contribute to the complexity of their emotions and relationships.

Alexander Pope: Pope, an 18th-century poet, was known for his satirical and ironic style. His famous poem "The Rape of the Lock" employs irony to mock the triviality and vanity of society while also highlighting its absurdities.

John Donne: Donne's metaphysical poetry often features intricate and paradoxical language that carries elements of irony. His exploration of themes like love, death, and spirituality is characterized by his use of wit and intellectual irony.

T.S. Eliot: Eliot's modernist poetry frequently employs irony to reflect the disillusionment and fragmentation of the post-World War I era. His poem "The Love Song of J. Alfred Prufrock" is a notable example of his use of ironic self-reflection.

Dorothy Parker: Parker was known for her sharp wit and satirical style. Her poems often contain ironic commentary on societal norms, relationships, and the human condition. Her poem "Résumé" is a prime example of her use of irony.

Sylvia Plath: Plath's poetry delves into the complexities of mental health, identity, and femininity. Her use of dark and poignant irony serves to explore personal struggles and societal expectations in a powerful way.

Langston Hughes: Hughes employed irony to address issues of race, identity, and social inequality in his poems. His poem "Theme for English B" is a skillful example of how he used irony to examine the complexity of racial identity.

W.H. Auden: Auden's poems often contain layers of irony, exploring themes of love, politics, and the human experience. His poem "September 1, 1939" uses irony to reflect on the onset of World War II and its impact on humanity.

Robert Frost: Frost's poems often feature subtle irony, inviting readers to contemplate the contrasts between appearances and underlying realities. His poem "The Road Not Taken" is a famous example that challenges conventional interpretations.

Oscar Wilde: Wilde, known for his wit and satire, used irony extensively in his poetry. His poem "The Ballad of Reading Gaol" is a powerful work that employs irony to critique the cruelty of the penal system.

These poets used irony in diverse ways, whether to critique society, explore inner thoughts and emotions, or challenge established norms. Their use of irony has contributed to the depth and lasting impact of their poetic works.

Examples of poets known for their use of irony in their work, along with explanations for each:
William Shakespeare:
Example: In Shakespeare's play "Julius Caesar," Mark Antony's funeral oration is a classic example of verbal irony. He repeatedly refers to Brutus and the other conspirators as "honourable men,"

while subtly undermining their integrity by recounting Caesar's virtues.

Explanation: The verbal irony lies in Antony's tone and the contrast between his words and his true intention. While he appears to be praising the conspirators, his actual purpose is to criticise and incite the crowd against them.

Alexander Pope:

Example: In "The Rape of the Lock," Pope employs situational irony to highlight the extravagant importance placed on a trivial event—the cutting of a lock of hair. The epic treatment of a seemingly minor incident satirises the superficiality of high society.

Explanation: The irony arises from the mismatch between the gravity of the situation, a lock of hair, and the grandiose and mock-heroic language used to describe it.

John Donne:

Example: In Donne's poem "The Flea," the speaker uses verbal irony to persuade his beloved to engage in physical intimacy by downplaying the significance of their actions, comparing them to the seemingly harmless act of a flea biting both of them.

Explanation: The irony lies in the way the speaker uses the flea as a metaphor to suggest that their physical union would be insignificant, while he actually desires a deeper connection.

T.S. Eliot:

Example: In "The Love Song of J. Alfred Prufrock," Eliot employs dramatic irony as the speaker engages in self-reflective monologue. The gap between Prufrock's perceptions of himself and the readers' observations creates a sense of irony and introspection.

Explanation: The dramatic irony is created by the contrast between Prufrock's internal thoughts and his external actions, revealing his insecurity and hesitations.

Dorothy Parker:

Example: Parker's poem "Résumé" is a prime example of situational irony. The speaker casually lists various failed suicide attempts, suggesting that life's disappointments have become so common that they are just part of her "résumé."
Explanation: The irony lies in the juxtaposition of the grim subject matter with the lighthearted and almost dismissive tone, revealing a bleak view of life.

Sylvia Plath:
Example: In Plath's poem "Daddy," the speaker's complicated relationship with her father is explored through intense and sometimes sarcastic imagery. The poem's use of irony underlines the speaker's conflicting emotions and struggles.
Explanation: The poem employs dark imagery and the speaker's mocking tone to convey the complexity of her feelings toward her father, juxtaposing both admiration and resentment.

Langston Hughes:
Example: In "Theme for English B," Hughes uses situational irony to examine the complexities of racial identity. The speaker's assignment to write about themselves becomes a larger exploration of their place within a racially divided society.
Explanation: The situational irony arises from the contrast between the simplicity of the assignment and the deeper societal implications that the speaker uncovers.

W.H. Auden:
Example: In "September 1, 1939," Auden uses verbal irony to reflect on the onset of World War II. He describes the day as a time of "low dishonesty," highlighting the irony of the destructive events unfolding.
Explanation: The irony is present in Auden's use of understatement to convey the gravity of the situation, revealing his disillusionment with the state of the world.

Robert Frost:
Example: In "The Road Not Taken," Frost employs situational irony to challenge the conventional interpretation of the poem. The speaker's description of two diverging paths suggests that they took the less traveled one, yet the paths were actually worn about the same.
Explanation: The situational irony arises from the revelation that the paths were equally worn, complicating the poem's message about individual choices.

Oscar Wilde:
Example: In "The Ballad of Reading Gaol," Wilde uses situational irony to critique the harsh penal system. The speaker observes the prisoners and reflects on the cruelty they face, contrasting their reality with the poem's opening lines that describe the prison as "silent, save for the night."
Explanation: The irony emerges from the contrast between the supposed silence and the harsh reality of life in the prison, highlighting the dissonance between appearance and truth.
These examples illustrate how these poets used various forms of irony to add complexity, commentary, and depth to their poetry, engaging readers and inviting them to consider multiple layers of meaning.

SYMBOL

A symbol is a literary device in which a word, character, object, or concept is used to represent something beyond its literal meaning. Symbols are often used to convey complex ideas, emotions, or themes in a more compact and meaningful way.
They add depth and layers of interpretation to a work of literature by allowing readers to connect the symbolic element with broader concepts or ideas. Symbols can be both tangible and abstract, and their meanings can evolve based on the context of the story or poem.

Examples of symbols and their meanings:
Dove: A dove is often used as a symbol of peace and purity. In literature, it can represent harmony, freedom, and hope. For example, in various cultures, a dove carrying an olive branch is a common symbol of peace after a conflict.

Red Rose: A red rose is a symbol of love and passion. In many poems and stories, it is used to convey deep emotions and romantic feelings. The red color of the rose is associated with intensity and desire.

Cross: The cross is a powerful symbol in Christianity, representing sacrifice, redemption, and the teachings of Jesus Christ. It can evoke religious themes and convey messages of faith and salvation.

Green Light: In F. Scott Fitzgerald's novel "The Great Gatsby," the green light at the end of Daisy Buchanan's dock symbolizes Gatsby's unattainable dreams and desires. It represents the unreachable ideal and his longing for the past.

Mockingbird: In Harper Lee's novel "To Kill a Mockingbird," the mockingbird symbolises innocence and goodness. Atticus Finch's advice to his children to never harm a mockingbird becomes a metaphor for not causing harm to those who are vulnerable and kind.

Hourglass: An hourglass is often used as a symbol of time's passage and the inevitability of mortality. It can also represent the fleeting nature of life and the need to make the most of the time we have.

The Colour Black: In literature, the colour black can symbolise darkness, evil, mystery, or death. It is often used to convey negative emotions or foreboding situations.

Phoenix: In mythology, the phoenix is a bird that is reborn from its own ashes, symbolising renewal, resurrection, and the cycle of life. It can also represent overcoming adversity and starting anew.

River: A river can symbolise the passage of time, change, and the flow of life. It's often used to represent the journey of characters as they undergo personal growth and transformation.

White Flag: A white flag is universally recognised as a symbol of surrender and truce. It signifies a desire for peace and the cessation of conflict.
Symbols can vary in their meanings based on cultural, historical, and contextual factors. Writers use symbols to add layers of depth and meaning to their works, inviting readers to explore and interpret the text on different levels.

Symbolism is a literary technique in which symbols are used to represent ideas, emotions, concepts, or themes in a work of literature. These symbols can be objects, characters, actions, or even words that carry a deeper meaning beyond their literal significance.

Symbolism adds depth, complexity, and layers of interpretation to a story, allowing readers to engage with the text on multiple levels and uncover hidden messages or themes. Here's a more in-depth look at how symbolism works:

Function of Symbolism
Enhancing Themes: Symbols are often chosen by authors to amplify and emphasize the central themes of a story. They provide a visual or tangible representation of abstract ideas, making the themes more accessible and relatable.

Conveying Emotions: Symbols can convey emotions and feelings that might be difficult to express directly through words. By associating an emotion with a symbol, authors can evoke a certain mood or atmosphere.

Adding Depth: Symbolism adds depth to characters and their development. A symbol associated with a character can reveal their inner thoughts, conflicts, and growth throughout the story.

Engaging the Reader: Symbols invite readers to actively engage with the text by deciphering the hidden meanings and connecting the dots between the symbol and the story's larger message.

Universality: Some symbols have universal meanings that transcend cultural boundaries. This allows readers from different backgrounds to interpret the symbolism and relate to the themes.

Examples of Symbolism:
The Scarlet Letter (Letter "A"): In Nathaniel Hawthorne's novel "The Scarlet Letter," the red letter "A" worn by Hester Prynne is a symbol of her adultery. However, over the course of the story, the symbol transforms to represent not only her sin but also her strength and resilience in the face of societal judgment.

The Mockingbird ("To Kill a Mockingbird"): In Harper Lee's novel, the mockingbird symbolises innocence and purity. Atticus Finch's advice to "remember it's a sin to kill a mockingbird" emphasises the idea of not harming those who do good and bring no harm.

The Green Light ("The Great Gatsby"): In F. Scott Fitzgerald's novel, the green light at the end of Daisy's dock symbolises Gatsby's unattainable dreams and his aspiration for a better future. It represents his pursuit of the American Dream.

The Conch Shell ("Lord of the Flies"): In William Golding's novel, the conch shell represents order and civilisation. As the story progresses and the boys' society deteriorates, the conch shell loses its power as a symbol of authority.

The Road ("The Road"): In Cormac McCarthy's novel, the road symbolises the journey of survival in a post-apocalyptic world. It represents the challenges, uncertainties, and the human instinct to keep moving forward despite adversity.

Snow ("The Snows of Kilimanjaro"): In Ernest Hemingway's short story, the snow on Mount Kilimanjaro symbolizes purity and the unfulfilled ambitions of the protagonist, Harry. The melting snow reflects his fading dreams.

Symbolism enriches literature by allowing authors to convey complex ideas and emotions through visual and sensory elements. It encourages readers to analyze and interpret the text on a deeper level, uncovering hidden meanings and connecting with the story's themes on a more personal and profound level.

W.B. Yeats, a prominent Irish poet and playwright, often used symbolism in his works to explore themes of Irish mythology, mysticism, politics, and the human experience. His poetry is known for its rich imagery and layered symbolism that invite readers to delve into deeper meanings and interpretations.

Few examples of how Yeats used symbolism in his poetry:

The Tower: Yeats's collection of poems titled "The Tower" (1928) is filled with symbolic references. The tower itself is a recurring symbol representing both personal and collective spiritual journey and enlightenment. It signifies the process of transcending earthly concerns and connecting with higher truths.

The Gyres: Yeats developed a theory of history based on the concept of gyres—spiral-like cycles of history that reflect the rise and fall of civilizations. The gyres are symbolized by intersecting cones, and they represent the eternal struggle between opposing forces such as chaos and order, spiritual and material, and the changing ages.

The Swan: The swan is a symbol that appears in several of Yeats's poems, often representing different aspects of transformation, purity, and transcendence. In poems like "The Wild Swans at Coole," the swans evoke a sense of permanence and renewal amidst the passing of time.

The Mask: Yeats often explored the idea of masks and persona in his work. The mask symbolizes the different roles individuals play in society and how they conceal or reveal aspects of themselves. This theme is evident in poems like "The Mask" and "The Mask Before the King."

Leda and the Swan: In the poem "Leda and the Swan," Yeats uses the mythological story of Leda's encounter with Zeus in the form of a swan to explore themes of power, violence, and the impact of historical events on the present. The poem's imagery and symbolism create a complex narrative about fate and transformation.

The Rose: The rose is a recurring symbol in Yeats's work, often representing ideals such as love, beauty, and spiritual transformation. The dual nature of the rose, with its thorns and petals, reflects the coexistence of pain and beauty.

Innisfree: The poem "The Lake Isle of Innisfree" uses the symbol of Innisfree, a peaceful island, to represent a yearning for a simpler, idealized life in harmony with nature. The symbol of Innisfree embodies Yeats's desire to escape urban life and find solace in nature.

Cuchulainn: Yeats's interest in Irish mythology led him to write poems about figures from Irish folklore, such as the warrior Cuchulainn. These poems use the symbolism of heroic figures to explore themes of heroism, destiny, and the complexities of Irish identity.

Overall, W.B. Yeats's use of symbolism adds layers of meaning and depth to his poetry. His symbols are often multifaceted, inviting readers to explore themes of spirituality, history, identity, and the human condition through intricate imagery and metaphor.

SOLILOQUY

A soliloquy is a dramatic device used in literature, particularly in plays, where a character speaks their thoughts, feelings, or innermost reflections aloud, often when they are alone on stage. Soliloquies provide insight into a character's inner conflicts, motivations, and emotional state. They are a powerful tool for revealing a character's depth and complexity to the audience.

Characteristics:
Solo Speech: A soliloquy is a speech delivered by a character who is alone on stage or believes they are alone, allowing them to express their inner thoughts without addressing other characters.

Revealing Inner Conflict: Soliloquies often reveal a character's inner turmoil, doubts, desires, or moral dilemmas. They provide insight into the character's psychology.

Audience Address: While the character is not speaking to other characters on stage, they are addressing the audience directly, sharing their inner world.

Reflective and Emotional: Soliloquies tend to be introspective and emotionally charged, offering a window into the character's emotional state.

Types of Soliloquies:
Reflective Soliloquy: In this type of soliloquy, a character reflects on past events, decisions, or experiences. It often serves to provide backstory or reveal a character's motivations. An example is Hamlet's "To be or not to be" soliloquy.

Contemplative Soliloquy: Contemplative soliloquies involve a character pondering a moral dilemma, decision, or a choice they must make. They weigh the pros and cons and often express uncertainty. For instance, Macbeth's soliloquy before Duncan's murder.

Emotional Soliloquy: Emotional soliloquies are characterized by the character's intense emotional state, such as anger, grief, or love. Juliet's balcony soliloquy in Shakespeare's "Romeo and Juliet" is an example.

Descriptive Soliloquy: In these soliloquies, a character describes a scene, setting, or situation in detail, offering vivid imagery and sensory descriptions. It can serve to create atmosphere or foreshadow events. An example is Prospero's soliloquy in "The Tempest."

Examples:

"To be or not to be" - Hamlet: In this famous soliloquy, Hamlet reflects on the nature of existence and the consequences of life and death. It reveals his inner conflict and contemplation of suicide.

"Tomorrow, and tomorrow, and tomorrow" - Macbeth: This soliloquy occurs after Macbeth hears of his wife's death. He reflects on the futility of life and the inevitability of death, expressing his despair.

"But, soft! What light through yonder window breaks?" - Romeo and Juliet: Juliet's soliloquy on her balcony expresses her love for Romeo and her longing for their union, despite the obstacles they face.

"All the world's a stage" - As You Like It: In this soliloquy, spoken by Jaques, the character philosophizes about the stages of human life, from infancy to old age, using the metaphor of a play.

Soliloquies are a powerful literary and theatrical device that offer insight into characters' inner lives and contribute to the development of themes and dramatic tension in plays and literature.

ASIDE

An aside is a dramatic device used in plays and sometimes in literature, where a character briefly speaks their thoughts or lines directly to the audience or to themselves.
 Unlike a soliloquy, an aside is typically very brief and is not meant to be heard by other characters on the stage. It is a way for a character to share private thoughts, feelings, or commentary with the audience while the action of the play continues.

Characteristics:
Audience Address: An aside involves a character speaking directly to the audience or whispering lines to themselves, as if breaking the fourth wall and momentarily stepping outside the action of the play.

Privacy: The lines spoken in an aside are meant to be private, and the other characters on stage are usually unaware of what is being said.

Briefness: Asides are typically short and concise, often consisting of just a few lines or sentences.

Revealing Inner Thoughts: Like soliloquies, asides provide insight into a character's inner thoughts, motivations, or reactions to the events taking place in the play.

Purpose:
The primary purpose of an aside is to allow the audience to gain deeper insight into a character's perspective or emotions without other characters in the play being aware of it. Asides are a way for characters to express their true feelings, share secrets, or provide commentary on the unfolding events. They can be used for dramatic irony, where the audience knows something that the other characters do not.

Example:

In William Shakespeare's play "Julius Caesar," during the assassination scene, Brutus delivers an aside when he explains to the audience his reasons for participating in the conspiracy against Caesar. He says:

"Since Cassius first did whet me against Caesar,
I have not slept.
Between the acting of a dreadful thing
And the first motion, all the interim is
Like a phantasma or a hideous dream."

In this aside, Brutus reveals his inner turmoil and his struggle with the decision to betray Caesar, providing insight into his character and motivations.

Asides are a valuable tool in drama for adding depth to characters and enhancing the audience's understanding of the play's events and characters' inner lives.

Examples of asides from various literary works along with explanations of their significance:

"Hamlet" by William Shakespeare (Act 1, Scene 5):

HAMLET:

There are more things in heaven and earth, Horatio, Than are dreamt of in your philosophy.

> Explanation: Hamlet's aside reflects his contemplative nature and skepticism about the limits of human knowledge. It sets the tone for the play's exploration of uncertainty and the supernatural.

"Romeo and Juliet" by William Shakespeare (Act 2, Scene 2):

ROMEO:

But, soft! what light through yonder window breaks? / It is the east, and Juliet is the sun.

> Explanation: Romeo's aside expresses his profound love and admiration for Juliet's beauty. It emphasizes the intensity of his emotions.

"Julius Caesar" by William Shakespeare (Act 3, Scene 2):
MARK ANTONY:
O, pardon me, thou bleeding piece of earth, / That I am meek and gentle with these butchers.

> Explanation: Mark Antony's aside reveals his true intentions to seek revenge against Caesar's assassins. It foreshadows his cunning manipulation of the Roman populace.

"Macbeth" by William Shakespeare (Act 1, Scene 5)
LADY MACBETH:
Art thou afeard / To be the same in thine own act and valour / As thou art in desire?

> Explanation: Lady Macbeth's aside highlights her manipulation of Macbeth and his inner conflict between ambition and morality. It sets the stage for the murder of King Duncan.

"Richard III" by William Shakespeare (Act 1, Scene 1):
RICHARD:
Now is the winter of our discontent / Made glorious summer by this son of York.

> Explanation: Richard's aside introduces his character as a cunning and ambitious schemer who seeks power. It sets the tone for his villainous actions.

"Macbeth" by William Shakespeare (Act 5, Scene 5):
LADY MACBETH:
Out, damned spot! out, I say!

> Explanation: Lady Macbeth's aside reveals her guilt and descent into madness as she attempts to cleanse herself of her involvement in the murders.

"A Midsummer Night's Dream" by William Shakespeare (Act 3, Scene 2):
PUCK:
If we shadows have offended, / Think but this, and all is mended.
> Explanation: Puck's aside at the end of the play addresses the audience directly, acknowledging the play's fantastical nature and inviting them to accept any errors as mere dreams.

"Othello" by William Shakespeare (Act 5, Scene 2):
OTHELLO:
Yet she must die, else she'll betray more men.
> Explanation: Othello's aside reveals his inner turmoil as he contemplates killing Desdemona, torn between love and jealousy.

"The Tragedy of Julius Caesar" by William Shakespeare (Act 4, Scene 2):
BRUTUS:
O, that a man might know / The end of this day's business ere it come!
> Explanation: Brutus's aside expresses his desire to foresee the outcome of the impending battle, emphasizing his inner conflict and uncertainty.

"Macbeth" by William Shakespeare (Act 1, Scene 7):
MACBETH:
If it were done when 'tis done, then 'twere well / It were done quickly.
> Explanation: Macbeth's aside reflects his internal struggle with the decision to murder King Duncan and his desire for a swift resolution to his ambition.

Soliloquy and Aside are both dramatic devices used in plays and literature, but they have distinct differences in terms of their purpose, audience, and how they are delivered:

Soliloquy:

Audience: In a soliloquy, a character speaks their inner thoughts, feelings, and reflections aloud while alone on stage or when they believe themselves to be alone. The character is addressing the audience directly.

Privacy: Soliloquies are not meant to be heard by other characters on the stage. They provide a window into the character's inner world, allowing the audience to understand their motivations, doubts, and conflicts.

Duration: Soliloquies are often longer speeches, sometimes spanning several lines or even an entire scene. They provide a deeper exploration of the character's psyche.

Purpose: Soliloquies serve to reveal a character's innermost thoughts, dilemmas, and emotions. They offer insight into the character's development and contribute to the play's themes and dramatic tension.

Aside:

Audience: In an aside, a character briefly speaks their thoughts, comments, or lines directly to the audience or in an undertone to themselves while other characters are present on stage.

Privacy: Unlike soliloquies, asides are meant to be private, and the other characters on stage are typically unaware of what is being said. The dialogue is not meant for their ears.

Duration: Asides are usually very brief, often consisting of just a sentence or a few lines. They are concise and to the point.

Purpose: Asides allow characters to share private thoughts, reactions, or commentary with the audience. They can serve to create dramatic irony, as the audience gains insight that the other characters lack. Asides provide a layer of dramatic tension and humor.

Key Differences:
Soliloquies are longer, introspective speeches that reveal a character's inner thoughts and emotions, while asides are brief, private remarks meant for the audience's benefit.

In a soliloquy, the character is alone on stage or believes themselves to be alone. In an aside, other characters are present on stage.

Soliloquies offer a deeper exploration of a character's psyche and motivations, while asides provide immediate, often humorous, or dramatic commentary on the ongoing action.

Soliloquies are extended monologues where characters express their innermost thoughts directly to the audience, while asides are brief, private remarks meant to convey specific information or reactions to the audience while keeping other characters in the dark. Both devices serve to enhance the audience's understanding of the play and its characters.

ALLEGORY

An allegory is a literary device or narrative technique in which characters, events, and settings are used to symbolise a deeper, often abstract, moral, political, or philosophical concept. In allegorical stories, the surface narrative has a secondary or symbolic meaning. Allegories are often used to convey complex ideas or moral lessons in a more accessible and engaging way. Here are a few key points about allegory:

Symbolism: In allegories, characters, objects, and events are deliberately chosen and crafted to represent something else beyond their literal meaning. These symbols are used to convey a hidden message or theme.

Hidden Meanings: The true meaning of an allegory is not explicitly stated but must be inferred by the reader or audience. It requires critical thinking and interpretation to uncover the deeper message.

Moral and Philosophical Themes: Allegories are frequently employed to explore moral, philosophical, or political ideas. They can provide commentary on human behavior, societal issues, or ethical dilemmas.

Examples: Famous examples of allegory include George Orwell's "Animal Farm," which uses animals on a farm to symbolize political ideologies and events; John Bunyan's "The Pilgrim's Progress," where the journey of the protagonist represents the Christian life; and Plato's "Allegory of the Cave," a philosophical allegory about enlightenment and ignorance.

Universality: Allegories often have universal themes that can apply to various contexts and time periods. This universality contributes to their enduring appeal.
Art and Literature: Allegory is not limited to literature alone. It can

also be found in art, where visual symbols are used to represent abstract concepts, such as justice or love.

Educational and Didactic: Allegorical stories are often used for didactic or educational purposes, as they allow readers to explore complex ideas in a more engaging and relatable manner.

Multilayered Interpretation: Allegories can be multilayered, allowing for different interpretations and depths of meaning. They encourage readers to delve deeper into the narrative to uncover hidden truths.

Overall, allegory is a powerful literary device that adds depth and complexity to storytelling. It challenges readers to think critically and engage with the text on multiple levels, making it a valuable tool for writers and a rewarding experience for readers.

Some examples of allegory in literature along with explanations of their allegorical meanings:

"Animal Farm" by George Orwell:

> Allegorical Meaning: "Animal Farm" is an allegory for the events leading up to the Russian Revolution of 1917 and the early years of the Soviet Union. The farm animals represent different social classes and political figures. For example, the pig Napoleon symbolizes Joseph Stalin, and the horse Boxer represents the working class. The farm itself represents the Soviet state.

"The Pilgrim's Progress" by John Bunyan:

> Allegorical Meaning: This allegorical novel tells the story of a character named Christian, who embarks on a journey from the City of Destruction to the Celestial City. The journey symbolizes the Christian life and the challenges and temptations a believer faces on the path to salvation.

"The Lion, the Witch and the Wardrobe" by C.S. Lewis (from "The Chronicles of Narnia" series):

Allegorical Meaning: Aslan, the lion, is a Christ-like figure in the story, symbolizing sacrifice, redemption, and the battle between good and evil. The White Witch represents evil and temptation, and the children's adventures in Narnia mirror themes of faith and salvation.

"Lord of the Flies" by William Golding:

Allegorical Meaning: This novel uses a group of boys stranded on a deserted island to explore the darker aspects of human nature. The island and its transformation into chaos symbolize society and the inherent capacity for savagery within human beings.

"The Allegory of the Cave" by Plato:

Allegorical Meaning: In this philosophical allegory, prisoners in a cave are chained and can only see shadows on the wall, believing them to be reality. When one prisoner is freed and sees the outside world, it symbolises the journey from ignorance to enlightenment, with the cave representing the world of appearances and the outside world representing the world of reality and knowledge.

"The Divine Comedy" by Dante Alighieri:

Allegorical Meaning: Dante's epic poem follows his journey through Hell, Purgatory, and Heaven. It is an allegory of the soul's journey toward God, with various characters and settings representing different aspects of morality, sin, and salvation.

"The Chronicles of Narnia" series by C.S. Lewis (overall series allegory):

Allegorical Meaning: The entire series serves as an allegory for Christian theology and morality. The characters and events in Narnia mirror biblical themes, such as the creation, fall, redemption, and the ultimate battle between good and evil.

"The Wizard of Oz" by L. Frank Baum:

> Allegorical Meaning: While "The Wizard of Oz" is often interpreted as a simple children's story, it can also be seen as an allegory for political and economic issues in the late 19th century. The Yellow Brick Road represents the gold standard, the Scarecrow symbolizes farmers, the Tin Man stands for industrial workers, and the Cowardly Lion represents politicians. Dorothy's journey represents the struggles of everyday people during this period.

"The Crucible" by Arthur Miller:

> Allegorical Meaning: "The Crucible" is an allegory for the McCarthy era in American history when there was a witch hunt for suspected communists. The Salem witch trials depicted in the play symbolise the irrationality and hysteria of the McCarthy hearings, where innocent people were accused of being communist sympathisers.

"The Giver" by Lois Lowry:

> Allegorical Meaning: In this dystopian novel, the society is an allegory for a conformist and controlled world where individuality and emotions are suppressed. The story explores themes of free will, memory, and the consequences of eliminating pain and suffering from human existence.

"Fahrenheit 451" by Ray Bradbury:

> Allegorical Meaning: "Fahrenheit 451" serves as an allegory for censorship and the suppression of free thought in society. The burning of books in the novel symbolizes the control of information and ideas, and the protagonist's journey represents his awakening to the importance of literature and individual thought.

"The Chronicles of Prydain" series by Lloyd Alexander (overall series allegory):

> Allegorical Meaning: This fantasy series draws inspiration from Welsh mythology and serves as an allegory for the hero's journey and the battle between good and evil. The protagonist, Taran, undergoes personal growth and moral development throughout his adventures.

Allegories can be both short narratives or extended pieces that contain intricate symbolisms. Depending on their scope, function, and medium, there are several types of allegories:

Historical and Political Allegory:

> Reflects on specific historical or political events, or critiques a political system or structure.
> George Orwell's "Animal Farm" is an allegory for the Russian Revolution and the rise of the Soviet Union.

Moral or Religious Allegory:

> Aims to impart moral lessons or religious teachings.
> John Bunyan's "The Pilgrim's Progress" is an allegory of the Christian journey towards salvation.

Personal or Psychological Allegory:

> Represents internal psychological struggles or personal journeys.
> Franz Kafka's "Metamorphosis" can be interpreted as an allegory for alienation and the human condition.

Cultural or Social Allegory:

> Reflects on societal norms, behaviors, or cultural shifts.
> Aldous Huxley's "Brave New World" is an allegory about the dangers of unchecked technological advancement and its impact on society.

Classical Allegory:

> Originates from ancient or classical literature.
> Plato's "Allegory of the Cave" from "The Republic" is a philosophical allegory about enlightenment and understanding.

Symbolic Allegory:

> While all allegories are symbolic, this type of allegory often uses more abstract symbolism to convey its message, without a clear one-to-one correspondence between symbols and their meanings.
> Some interpretations of William Golding's "Lord of the Flies" view it as an allegory of the inherent evil in human nature.

Fable:

> A short story that typically uses animals as characters to impart moral lessons.
> Aesop's fables, such as "The Tortoise and the Hare," are allegorical tales with moral teachings.

Parable:

> A short, simple story designed to teach a moral or religious lesson.
> Many of Jesus' teachings in the Bible, like the Parable of the Good Samaritan, are allegories meant to convey spiritual truths.

Myth and Legend:

> Often contain allegorical elements, though they primarily function to explain natural phenomena, the cosmos, or historical events in a symbolic manner.

Extended or Continuous Allegory:

Maintains its allegorical nature throughout the entire narrative, with almost every element serving a symbolic purpose.
Dante's "Divine Comedy" is an allegory of the soul's journey towards God.
It's worth noting that a single work can fit multiple types of allegories, and not every reader or critic will agree on the exact allegorical interpretation of a particular work. The nature of allegory allows for layered readings, where multiple meanings can be derived from a single narrative.

ALLUSION

An allusion is a literary device that involves making a brief and indirect reference to a person, place, thing, event, or idea of historical, cultural, literary, or political significance. It is a way for authors to enrich their writing by drawing on the reader's prior knowledge or associations with the referenced subject. Allusions can be explicit or subtle and serve various purposes in literature. Here are some key points about allusions:

Reference to Known Works: Allusions often refer to famous literary works, such as the Bible, Shakespearean plays, or classical Greek and Roman mythology. However, they can also draw from historical events, popular culture, or other forms of art.

Conciseness: Allusions allow writers to convey complex ideas or themes in a concise manner. Instead of providing detailed explanations, they assume that readers will recognize the reference and its implications.

Layered Meaning: Allusions add depth and layers of meaning to a text. They can evoke emotions, create connections between different texts or ideas, and provide insight into character development.

Cultural Significance: Allusions can be culturally specific, relying on the reader's knowledge of the culture from which they originate. This can pose challenges for readers from different cultural backgrounds.

Symbolism: Allusions often carry symbolic weight. For example, an allusion to the Garden of Eden can symbolize innocence and temptation, while referencing Achilles' heel can symbolize vulnerability.

Subtle vs. Overt: Allusions can be subtle, requiring readers to make connections, or overt, clearly stating the reference. The choice depends on the author's intent and the context of the text.

Emphasis and Comparison: Authors use allusions to emphasize certain aspects of a story or to draw comparisons between characters, events, or situations.

Reader Engagement: Allusions engage readers who are familiar with the referenced material, inviting them to participate actively in the interpretation of the text.

Examples of allusions in literature include phrases like "sour grapes" (an allusion to Aesop's fable "The Fox and the Grapes") and "Pandora's box" (a reference to Greek mythology). Writers often use allusions to enrich their narratives, create atmosphere, or add depth to characters and themes.

Some examples of allusions in literature along with explanations of their meanings:
"He was a real Romeo with the ladies."

> Explanation: This is an allusion to Shakespeare's character Romeo from "Romeo and Juliet." Calling someone a "Romeo" implies that they are a passionate and romantic lover.

"She had the wisdom of Solomon."

> Explanation: This allusion refers to King Solomon, known for his legendary wisdom in the Bible (1 Kings 3:12). Saying someone has "the wisdom of Solomon" means they are exceptionally wise.

"Don't be such a Scrooge."

> Explanation: This allusion comes from Charles Dickens' "A Christmas Carol," where Ebenezer Scrooge is a miserly character who hoards his wealth. Calling someone a "Scrooge" suggests they are miserly or stingy.

"I was caught between a rock and a hard place."

> Explanation: This allusion to being caught between a "rock and a hard place" suggests being in a difficult or unwinnable situation. It may originate from the challenges of navigating rocky terrain.

"The garden was a veritable Eden."

> Explanation: Referring to a garden as an "Eden" alludes to the biblical Garden of Eden, a paradise described in Genesis. It implies that the garden is idyllic and perfect.

"His Achilles' heel proved to be his overconfidence."

> Explanation: This allusion to Achilles' heel comes from Greek mythology, where Achilles had one vulnerable spot —his heel. Describing someone's "Achilles' heel" means pointing out their weakness or vulnerability.

"She had a Midas touch in business."

> Explanation: This alludes to King Midas from Greek mythology, who could turn everything he touched into gold. Saying someone has a "Midas touch" suggests that they have a knack for success or making things profitable.

"It was a Titanic disaster."

> Explanation: This allusion to the RMS Titanic, a famous shipwreck, describes a massive and catastrophic failure or disaster.

"His voice was like a siren's call."

> Explanation: This alludes to the sirens in Greek mythology, whose enchanting songs lured sailors to their doom. Describing someone's voice as a "siren's call" means it is irresistibly alluring.

"She had a Mona Lisa smile."

> Explanation: This alludes to Leonardo da Vinci's famous painting "Mona Lisa," known for the enigmatic smile of the subject. Describing someone's smile as a "Mona Lisa smile" implies that it is mysterious or intriguing.

These examples demonstrate how allusions draw on well-known literary, historical, or mythological references to add depth, symbolism, and cultural resonance to language and literature. They allow authors to convey complex ideas or emotions succinctly and engage readers' prior knowledge and associations.

Here are a few more examples of allusions in literature:
"The journey felt like a modern-day Odyssey."

> Explanation: This alludes to Homer's epic poem "The Odyssey," in which the hero Odysseus embarks on a long and arduous journey home. Describing a journey as a "modern-day Odyssey" implies that it is an epic and challenging adventure.

"She was a real Cinderella story."

> Explanation: This allusion references the fairy tale of Cinderella, in which a kind-hearted girl is transformed from rags to riches. Calling someone's story a "Cinderella story" suggests a dramatic improvement in circumstances or success against the odds.

"The situation had become a Catch-22."

> Explanation: This allusion comes from Joseph Heller's novel "Catch-22," in which a paradoxical rule makes it impossible for soldiers to escape dangerous missions. Describing a situation as a "Catch-22" means it is a no-win or paradoxical scenario.

"Her beauty could rival that of Helen of Troy."

> Explanation: This alludes to Helen of Troy, a character in Greek mythology whose beauty was said to have caused the Trojan War. Comparing someone's beauty to that of Helen of Troy suggests exceptional attractiveness.

"He had the charisma of a Pied Piper."

> Explanation: This alludes to the legend of the Pied Piper of Hamelin, who played his flute to lead away rats and children from a town. Describing someone's charisma as

that of a "Pied Piper" implies the ability to attract and lead others.

"The situation was a real David and Goliath battle."

> Explanation: This alludes to the biblical story of David, a young shepherd who defeated the giant Goliath with a sling and a stone. Describing a situation as a "David and Goliath battle" means it involves a smaller, weaker entity facing a much larger and stronger opponent.

"She was the Hermione Granger of our class."

> Explanation: This allusion comes from J.K. Rowling's "Harry Potter" series, where Hermione Granger is a highly intelligent and studious character. Comparing someone to Hermione Granger suggests they are exceptionally smart and diligent.

"His decision was a real Hobson's choice."

> Explanation: This allusion refers to Thomas Hobson, a livery stable owner known for offering customers only one choice—the horse nearest the stable door. Describing a decision as a "Hobson's choice" means it's a situation in which there is no real choice or an apparent choice that is no choice at all.

The reader or audience is expected to grasp the implications of the allusion immediately, based on their prior knowledge or understanding. Allusions can be categorized based on what they reference or their source. Here are several types of allusions:

Literary Allusion:

> Refers to another work of literature, be it a novel, poem, play, etc.
>
> Example: The title of Aldous Huxley's "Brave New World" is an allusion to a line in Shakespeare's "The Tempest."

Historical Allusion:

> Refers to a historical event or period.

Example: If someone is described as having a "Napoleon complex," it alludes to Napoleon Bonaparte and the perception that his ambition was due to his short stature.

Mythological Allusion:

Refers to myths—often from Greek, Roman, Norse, or other world mythologies.

Example: Referring to someone's "Achilles' heel" is an allusion to the Greek hero Achilles and his one vulnerability.

Biblical Allusion:

Refers to events, figures, or stories from the Bible.

Example: The phrase "Adam's apple" is an allusion to the biblical story of Adam and Eve.

Cultural Allusion:

Refers to a contemporary cultural event or trend, often specific to a certain group or region.

Example: Referring to something as "the gold standard" alludes to a time when currency was backed by physical gold.

Artistic or Art Allusion:

Refers to a well-known piece of art, music, or film.

Example: Referring to a confusing scenario as "a Picasso" alludes to Picasso's abstract and unique style of painting.

Geographical Allusion:

Refers to a specific location or place known for a particular quality or historical event.

Example: Calling a lush, bountiful place "a Garden of Eden" alludes to the biblical paradise.

Pop Culture Allusion:

Refers to contemporary popular culture, such as movies, songs, celebrities, or current events.

Example: Calling someone "a real Sherlock" alludes to the fictional detective Sherlock Holmes, known for his brilliant deductive skills.

Scientific Allusion:

Refers to a scientific concept, discovery, or renowned scientist.

Example: Describing a transformative moment as "an Einstein moment" alludes to the genius of Albert Einstein.

Allusions serve to let readers or listeners make connections without the need to explain in detail. However, they are most effective when the audience is familiar with what's being alluded to; otherwise, the significance may be lost.

CLIMAX

In literature, the term "climax" refers to the highest point of tension or emotional intensity in a narrative or dramatic work. It is a critical moment within the plot when the conflict or central problem reaches its peak, and the outcome becomes uncertain. The climax is a pivotal juncture that often occurs toward the end of a story and leads to the resolution of the conflict.

Some key points about the climax in literature

Tension and Emotion: The climax is characterised by heightened tension and emotion. It is the moment that readers or viewers have been anticipating, and it typically evokes strong feelings, such as suspense, excitement, or anxiety.

Turning Point: The climax represents a turning point in the story. Up until this moment, the narrative has been building toward this critical juncture, and the actions of the characters and the events of the plot have led to this climax.

Conflict Resolution: The climax is where the central conflict or problem is confronted head-on, and the resolution begins to take shape. Depending on the type of story, the outcome can be positive or negative for the protagonist.

Character Growth: Often, the climax also serves as a moment of character growth or realization for the main characters. They are forced to make important decisions or confront their flaws.

Narrative Arc: The climax is an integral part of the narrative arc, which typically consists of exposition (introduction), rising action (build-up of tension), climax (highest point of tension), falling action (resolving the conflict), and denouement (conclusion or tying up loose ends).

Genres: The structure and nature of the climax can vary depending on the genre of the work. In a mystery novel, the climax might involve solving the mystery, while in an adventure story, it could be a life-or-death situation.

Importance of Timing: The timing of the climax is crucial to maintaining the reader's interest. If it occurs too early, it may result in an anticlimactic ending, while if it occurs too late, it can lead to frustration.

Examples: In William Shakespeare's play "Romeo and Juliet," the climax occurs when Romeo and Juliet die by suicide. In J.K. Rowling's "Harry Potter and the Deathly Hallows," the climax takes place during the final battle between Harry Potter and Lord Voldemort.

The climax is a critical element of storytelling because it captures the reader's or audience's attention and holds it until the story's resolution. It is the moment when the story's central questions or conflicts are answered, and it often leaves a lasting impact on the reader or viewer.

Some examples of climaxes in literature along with explanations of their significance:

"Romeo and Juliet" by William Shakespeare:
>Climax: The climax occurs in Act 5, Scene 3, when Romeo and Juliet both die by suicide.
>Explanation: This is the most intense and critical moment in the play. It marks the resolution of the feud between the Montagues and Capulets but at a heartbreaking cost. Romeo and Juliet's deaths result from a tragic

misunderstanding, and their love is proven to be powerful enough to overcome even death.

"To Kill a Mockingbird" by Harper Lee:

Climax: The climax takes place during the trial of Tom Robinson in Chapter 21, when Atticus Finch delivers his closing argument.

Explanation: This is the emotional high point of the novel. Atticus's powerful speech is the culmination of the racial tension and injustice that permeate the story. It represents a moral climax where Atticus, as a symbol of justice and decency, fights for what is right despite the odds.

"The Great Gatsby" by F. Scott Fitzgerald:

Climax: The climax occurs in Chapter 7 when Tom Buchanan confronts Gatsby about his relationship with Daisy, leading to a heated confrontation.

Explanation: This moment is pivotal because it brings to a head the conflict between Gatsby, Tom, and Daisy. The tension and rivalry that have been building throughout the novel reach their zenith, and the consequences of their actions become unavoidable.

"Lord of the Flies" by William Golding:

Climax: The climax occurs in Chapter 11 when the boys, driven by their primal instincts, hunt and kill Simon, mistaking him for the "beast."

Explanation: This is a harrowing and symbolic climax that represents the boys' descent into savagery. It marks a point of no return, as the group spirals further into chaos and violence.

"1984" by George Orwell:

Climax: The climax occurs in Part 3, Chapter 4, when Winston is tortured in the Ministry of Love and betrays Julia.

Explanation: This is the climactic moment of psychological and political oppression in the novel. Winston's betrayal of

Julia symbolizes the complete loss of his individuality and the crushing power of the totalitarian regime.

"The Catcher in the Rye" by J.D. Salinger:

Climax: The climax takes place when Holden Caulfield visits his little sister Phoebe's school and gives her his red hunting hat.

Explanation: This moment represents Holden's emotional climax and personal growth. He has been struggling with feelings of alienation and isolation throughout the novel, but this scene with Phoebe marks a turning point where he seeks connection and begins to accept responsibility for his actions.

These examples illustrate how climaxes in literature are pivotal moments that drive the narrative forward, reveal key truths or conflicts, and often lead to the resolution or denouement of the story. They are moments of emotional intensity and narrative significance that stay with readers long after they have finished the book.

ANTICLIMAX

An anticlimax is a literary device that involves an unexpected shift from a situation of heightened tension or expectation to one of lesser significance, often resulting in a disappointing or humorous outcome.
 Unlike the climax, which is the high point of a narrative, the anticlimax is characterized by a letdown, a sudden drop in tension, or an underwhelming resolution. Anticlimaxes are often used for comedic effect or to subvert the audience's expectations.

Key characteristics of an anticlimax:
Sudden Transition: An anticlimax typically occurs suddenly after the audience or reader has been led to expect a more significant or dramatic resolution.

Humor or Disappointment: Depending on the context, an anticlimax can evoke humor or disappointment. In humorous anticlimaxes, the abrupt shift to a less important outcome can be amusing, while in more serious works, it may create a sense of unfulfillment or frustration.

Subversion of Expectations: Anticlimaxes are often used to subvert the audience's or reader's expectations. They defy traditional narrative structures by intentionally avoiding a satisfying or predictable resolution.

Examples of anticlimaxes:
"Monty Python and the Holy Grail" (film): In this comedy, King Arthur and his knights embark on a quest to find the Holy Grail. The anticlimax occurs when they are stopped by police officers and arrested for the murder of a historian. The quest for the Holy Grail, which had been built up throughout the film, is abruptly halted in a humorous and unexpected way.

"The Adventures of Huckleberry Finn" by Mark Twain: In the novel's climax, Tom Sawyer devises an elaborate plan to rescue Jim, the runaway slave. However, the anticlimax occurs when Tom's plan is needlessly complicated and ultimately unnecessary, as Jim could have been freed much earlier in a simpler way.
"The Stranger" by Albert Camus: In this existential novel, the protagonist, Meursault, is put on trial for murder. The climax occurs during the trial, but the anticlimax comes when the trial devolves into a surreal and absurd spectacle, leading to Meursault's conviction and death sentence.

"A Modest Proposal" by Jonathan Swift: This satirical essay suggests that impoverished Irish people could solve their economic problems by selling their children as food to the wealthy. The entire essay builds up to a shocking proposal, which is presented as a serious solution. The anticlimax is the revelation that Swift's proposal is a satirical exaggeration meant to criticize the British treatment of the Irish.

Some more examples of anticlimaxes in literature and their explanations:
"The Tragedy of Macbeth" by William Shakespeare:
> Anticlimax: In the climax of the play, Macbeth confronts Macduff in a dramatic duel. However, the anticlimax occurs when Macbeth reveals that he cannot be killed by any man born of a woman, and Macduff informs him that he was born through a Caesarean section. Macbeth's realization of his impending doom and surrender is the anticlimax.
> Explanation: Shakespeare uses this anticlimax to subvert the audience's expectations and add a layer of dramatic irony. Macbeth's boastful confidence and subsequent despair serve to highlight the tragic consequences of his ambition and tyranny.

"The Importance of Being Earnest" by Oscar Wilde:
Anticlimax: In this comedy, the characters engage in a series of elaborate deceptions and misunderstandings, culminating in the climax when the truth is revealed. The anticlimax occurs when the characters quickly forgive each other, and all conflicts are resolved without any significant consequences.
Explanation: Wilde employs the anticlimax to emphasize the absurdity of societal conventions and the triviality of the characters' concerns. The resolution's lack of seriousness underscores the play's satirical commentary on the superficiality of the upper class.

"The Hitchhiker's Guide to the Galaxy" by Douglas Adams:
Anticlimax: In this science fiction comedy, the characters embark on a quest to discover the answer to the ultimate question of life, the universe, and everything. After a long journey, they learn that the answer is simply the number 42, and they must now find the question itself.
Explanation: The anticlimax in this story is both humorous and philosophical. It pokes fun at the idea of seeking a profound answer and highlights the absurdity of expecting a single answer to life's complex questions.

"Alice's Adventures in Wonderland" by Lewis Carroll:

Anticlimax: Throughout her adventures in Wonderland, Alice seeks to find her way home and encounters various peculiar characters and challenges. The anticlimax occurs when she wakes up from her dream, and the fantastical world of Wonderland is revealed to be a dream.
Explanation: Carroll uses this anticlimax to challenge the boundaries between reality and imagination. It invites readers to question the nature of reality and the role of imagination in shaping our perceptions.

"The Metamorphosis" by Franz Kafka:

    Anticlimax: The novella tells the story of Gregor Samsa, who wakes up one day transformed into a giant insect. The climax comes when his family, horrified by his appearance, locks him in a room. The anticlimax occurs when Gregor dies quietly in his room, and his family's reactions are surprisingly indifferent.

    Explanation: Kafka's use of an anticlimax serves to highlight the absurdity and isolation of the protagonist's existence. The family's lack of emotional response underscores the alienation and disconnect between Gregor and his family.

Anticlimaxes are versatile literary devices that can serve different purposes, from humor and satire to commentary on human nature and societal norms. They challenge conventional storytelling structures and often leave readers or viewers with unexpected and thought-provoking outcomes.

EPIGRAM

An epigram is a concise and witty statement, often in the form of a brief poem or verse, that conveys a single thought or observation, typically with a clever or humorous twist.
Epigrams are known for their brevity and their ability to pack a punch with a few well-chosen words. They are often used to satirise, criticise, or comment on various aspects of human nature, society, or the world. Key characteristics of epigrams include:
Brevity: Epigrams are short and to the point, often consisting of just a few lines or a couplet (a two-line verse).

Cleverness: They are characterised by clever wordplay, irony, or a surprising twist that catches the reader's attention.
Satire: Many epigrams employ satire, using humour or sarcasm to criticise or mock something, whether it's a social custom, a political figure, or a common human foible.
Insight: Despite their brevity, epigrams often contain profound insights into human behaviour, morality, or the human condition.
Memorability: A well-crafted epigram is memorable and leaves a lasting impression on the reader.
Variety of Themes: Epigrams can address a wide range of themes, from love and friendship to politics and ethics.

Examples of epigrams:
"Man is the only animal that blushes. Or needs to."
> Explanation: This epigram by Mark Twain humorously points out the unique self-awareness and social consciousness of humans.

"Familiarity breeds contempt."
> Explanation: This well-known epigram suggests that people often become critical or dismissive of things they are very familiar with, such as relationships or routines.

"In three words I can sum up everything I've learned about life: it goes on." - Robert Frost

Explanation: Frost's epigram reflects on the inevitability of life's continuous forward motion despite its challenges and complexities.

"I can resist everything except temptation." - Oscar Wilde

Explanation: Wilde's epigram uses humor to acknowledge the human tendency to succumb to temptation despite one's best intentions.

"The only way to get rid of temptation is to yield to it." - Oscar Wilde

Explanation: Here, Wilde employs irony by suggesting that yielding to temptation is the only way to eliminate its power over us.

"Little strokes fell great oaks."

Explanation: This epigram underscores the idea that consistent, small efforts can eventually achieve significant results.

"To err is human; to forgive, divine." - Alexander Pope

Explanation: Pope's epigram emphasizes the common human trait of making mistakes and contrasts it with the noble act of forgiveness.

"Age is a high price to pay for maturity." - Tom Stoppard

Explanation: Stoppard's epigram humorously suggests that growing older doesn't necessarily guarantee wisdom or maturity.

Epigrams are a versatile literary form, often found in various types of writing, including poetry, prose, and even speeches. They are valued for their ability to succinctly capture complex ideas or observations and present them in a memorable and thought-provoking manner.

"Better to reign in Hell than serve in Heaven." - John Milton, "Paradise Lost"

Explanation: This epigram, spoken by Satan in "Paradise Lost," reflects the character's defiant and prideful nature. It encapsulates the idea that some individuals would rather have power and freedom in a less desirable situation than submit to authority.

"Happiness is not an ideal of reason but of imagination." - Immanuel Kant

> Explanation: Kant's epigram distinguishes between rationality and imagination when it comes to the pursuit of happiness. It suggests that happiness often relies on our imagination's desires and fantasies rather than pure reason.

"The only thing we have to fear is fear itself." - Franklin D. Roosevelt

> Explanation: This famous epigram was part of Roosevelt's inaugural address during the Great Depression. It emphasizes the idea that fear can be a self-fulfilling prophecy and that overcoming fear is a key to overcoming challenges.

"Art for art's sake."

> Explanation: This succinct epigram encapsulates the idea of creating art purely for its intrinsic value and beauty, without ulterior motives or moral lessons.

"All animals are equal, but some animals are more equal than others." - George Orwell, "Animal Farm"

> Explanation: Orwell's epigram from "Animal Farm" satirically highlights the hypocrisy and corruption of those in power who claim equality but practice discrimination and inequality.

"To be yourself in a world that is constantly trying to make you something else is the greatest accomplishment." - Ralph Waldo Emerson

> Explanation: Emerson's epigram celebrates the value of individuality and authenticity in a world that often pressures people to conform to societal norms.

"In the midst of winter, I found there was, within me, an invincible summer." - Albert Camus

> Explanation: Camus' epigram reflects the resilience of the human spirit in the face of adversity. It suggests that even

in the darkest times, there is a spark of hope and strength within.

"The more I know, the less I understand." - Don Henley, "The Heart of the Matter"

Explanation: This epigram expresses the paradox of knowledge, where the acquisition of knowledge often reveals the complexity and depth of what is not known or understood.

"A little learning is a dangerous thing." - Alexander Pope

Explanation: Pope's epigram warns against the overconfidence that can arise from having a superficial or limited understanding of a subject. It suggests that incomplete knowledge can lead to misguided actions.

"The greatest trick the Devil ever pulled was convincing the world he didn't exist." - Verbal Kint in "The Usual Suspects" (film)

Explanation: This epigram, delivered by a character in the film, speaks to the idea that deception and manipulation can be most effective when they go unnoticed or unchallenged.

Epigrams, with their concise and clever expressions, offer insight, humor, and commentary on a wide range of topics. They have the power to encapsulate complex ideas in just a few words, making them memorable and impactful.

EPITHET

An epithet is a descriptive word or phrase that is used to characterize a person, place, thing, or quality. Epithets are often used in literature to provide additional information about the subject and to create vivid and memorable descriptions. They can be both positive and negative in nature and are employed to enhance the reader's understanding or emotional response to the subject.

Some key characteristics and examples of epithets:
Descriptive: Epithets are adjectives or adjective phrases that describe a specific quality or characteristic of the subject. They serve to provide additional details and imagery.

Figurative Language: Epithets often involve figurative language, such as metaphors or similes, to create vivid and imaginative descriptions. They can also include personification or alliteration for added effect.

Memorable: Epithets are chosen to be memorable and evocative, leaving a lasting impression on the reader or audience.

Characterization: Epithets are used to characterize individuals, objects, or places in literature. They can reveal personality traits, physical attributes, or emotional states.

Literary Devices: Epithets can function as literary devices when they are used for rhetorical effect, such as in epic poetry or formal speeches.

Examples of epithets:
"The Bard of Avon" for William Shakespeare
      This epithet combines "bard," a term for a poet or
      storyteller, with "Avon," the river that runs through

Shakespeare's birthplace, Stratford-upon-Avon. It characterizes him as a renowned poet from that region.

"The Man of Steel" for Superman

This epithet highlights Superman's invincible and superhuman qualities by comparing him to steel, a strong and durable material.

"The City of Lights" for Paris

This epithet emphasizes the city's reputation for its vibrant nightlife, cultural richness, and illuminated landmarks.

"The Dark Knight" for Batman

This epithet evokes the mysterious and vigilant nature of Batman's character as a crime-fighter in Gotham City.

"The Emerald Isle" for Ireland

This epithet describes Ireland's lush and green landscapes, evoking images of its natural beauty.

"The Great Emancipator" for Abraham Lincoln

This epithet characterizes Lincoln as a leader who played a pivotal role in the emancipation of enslaved individuals during the American Civil War.

"The Eternal City" for Rome

This epithet suggests Rome's enduring significance and historical longevity.

"The City that Never Sleeps" for New York City

This epithet reflects the bustling and vibrant nature of New York, known for its round-the-clock activity.

"The Mistress of the Seas" for the United Kingdom

This epithet highlights the historical dominance of the British Empire's navy and maritime influence.

"The Prince of Darkness" for Satan (in literature and mythology)

This epithet characterizes Satan as a malevolent and dark figure in religious and literary contexts.

Homer frequently uses epithets to refer to characters in The Iliad and The Odyssey, such as "swift-footed Achilles" and "the man of twists and turns."

Epithets are a literary tool used to create vivid and evocative descriptions that enhance the reader's understanding and engagement with the subject. They can contribute to the imagery, characterization, and atmosphere of a literary work.

IDIOM

An idiom is a phrase or expression that has a figurative, non-literal meaning. Idioms are typically deeply ingrained in a language and culture and may not be easily understood by looking at the individual words within the phrase. Instead, their meanings are often cultural or historical in nature, and they can be quite different from the literal meanings of the words used.
Idioms are widely used in everyday language to add color, humor, or depth to communication.

Some key characteristics and examples of idioms:
Figurative Meaning: Idioms do not mean exactly what the individual words suggest. Their meaning is figurative and often symbolic.

Cultural Context: Idioms are shaped by the culture and language in which they are used. Understanding idioms may require familiarity with the cultural references or historical events that gave rise to them.

Fixed Phrases: Idioms are typically fixed phrases that cannot be easily altered or substituted with other words.

Common Usage: Many idioms are used frequently in everyday language, making them an important part of informal communication.

Examples of idioms:
"Break a leg!"
> Meaning: This idiom is used to wish someone good luck, especially before a performance. It's an example of how idioms can have meanings that are unrelated to the literal words.

"Kick the bucket."

Meaning: This idiom means to die. It has a figurative, often humorous, and less direct way of expressing the concept of death.

"Bite the bullet."

Meaning: This idiom means to face a difficult or unpleasant situation with courage and determination. It doesn't involve actually biting a bullet but conveys the idea of enduring hardship.

"Piece of cake."

Meaning: This idiom means something is very easy to do. It doesn't refer to actual cake but suggests that a task is simple.

"The ball is in your court."

Meaning: This idiom means it's someone else's turn to take action or make a decision. It uses a sports metaphor to convey this idea.

"Cost an arm and a leg."

Meaning: This idiom means something is very expensive. It uses exaggerated body parts to emphasize the high cost.

"Let the cat out of the bag."

Meaning: This idiom means to reveal a secret or disclose information that was meant to be kept hidden. It uses a playful image of a cat escaping from a bag.

"Hit the nail on the head."

Meaning: This idiom means to describe something exactly as it is or to be completely accurate in one's assessment or statement. It uses a construction metaphor.

"Cry over spilled milk."

Meaning: This idiom advises against dwelling on past mistakes or regrets. It suggests that there's no use in being upset about something that has already happened, like spilled milk.

"The apple of my eye."

Meaning: This idiom is used to describe someone who is cherished or loved deeply. It uses the image of the pupil in the eye to convey affection.

Idioms add richness and depth to language, but their meanings may not always be immediately obvious to those who are learning a new language or encountering a different culture. Understanding and using idioms effectively often requires familiarity with the nuances and cultural context of the language in which they are used.

"The early bird catches the worm."

Meaning: This idiom encourages people to act promptly or get a head start because those who take action early are more likely to succeed.

"Actions speak louder than words."

Meaning: This idiom emphasizes that what people do is more important and revealing than what they say. It underscores the importance of behavior and deeds.

"Don't put all your eggs in one basket."

Meaning: This idiom advises against risking everything on a single plan or venture. Diversifying or having multiple options is considered a safer approach.

"The straw that broke the camel's back."

Meaning: This idiom refers to the final, seemingly insignificant event or issue that causes a person or situation to become overwhelmed or reach a breaking point.

"Under the weather."

Meaning: This idiom means that someone is not feeling well or is slightly sick. It doesn't involve actual weather but uses a metaphor to describe health.

"Don't count your chickens before they hatch."

Meaning: This idiom warns against assuming success or making plans based on something that has not yet occurred. It's a reminder that unexpected things can happen.

"In the same boat."

Meaning: This idiom means that people are facing the same situation or problem. It suggests that they are in it together.

"Burning the midnight oil."

Meaning: This idiom describes someone working late into the night or putting in extra hours to complete a task or project.

"A penny for your thoughts."

Meaning: This idiom is a way of asking someone what they are thinking or feeling, often when they appear lost in thought.

"Jumping on the bandwagon."

Meaning: This idiom refers to the act of joining a popular trend or following a crowd, often without careful consideration.

"To steal someone's thunder."

Meaning: This idiom means to take attention or credit away from someone, typically by doing something that eclipses their achievement or announcement.

"Read between the lines."

Meaning: This idiom suggests looking for hidden meanings or understanding a situation beyond its surface level. It encourages careful interpretation.

"Take it with a grain of salt."

Meaning: This idiom advises skepticism or caution when hearing information or advice. It implies not fully trusting or believing something without question.

"Walking on eggshells."

Meaning: This idiom describes a situation where people are being extremely cautious or sensitive, often because they want to avoid conflict or tension.

MONOLOGUE

A monologue is a speech or lengthy utterance by a single character in a work of literature, drama, or performance. Unlike a dialogue, where two or more characters engage in a conversation, a monologue involves one character speaking their thoughts, feelings, or ideas to themselves or to an audience. Monologues serve various purposes in literature and drama, such as providing insight into a character's inner thoughts, advancing the plot, or conveying thematic messages.

Some key characteristics and examples of monologues:
Single Speaker: A monologue features a single character speaking without interruptions from other characters.

Lengthy: Monologues can range from a few sentences to several pages or even longer, depending on their purpose and context.

Revealing: Monologues often reveal a character's innermost thoughts, emotions, motivations, and conflicts, offering insight into their psychology.

Addressing an Audience: In some cases, a character in a play may deliver a monologue directly to the audience, breaking the fourth wall and creating a sense of intimacy or connection.

Advancing the Plot: Monologues can be used to convey important plot information, backstory, or character development.

Reflective: Some monologues are introspective and allow characters to reflect on their experiences, dilemmas, or moral quandaries.

Examples of monologues:

Hamlet's "To be or not to be" soliloquy from William Shakespeare's "Hamlet":

> In this famous monologue, Hamlet contemplates the nature of existence and the moral dilemma of whether it is better to endure life's hardships or end them through death.

Juliet's balcony monologue from Shakespeare's "Romeo and Juliet":

> Juliet expresses her love for Romeo and her longing for their union, unaware that Romeo is listening below. This monologue is a classic expression of young love.

Iago's "I am not what I am" monologue from Shakespeare's "Othello":

> Iago speaks to the audience, revealing his deceptive and manipulative nature while plotting against Othello and other characters.

Macbeth's "Tomorrow, and tomorrow, and tomorrow" monologue from Shakespeare's "Macbeth":

> Macbeth reflects on the futility and meaninglessness of life as he grapples with the consequences of his actions and the inevitability of his own death.

Elie Wiesel's Nobel Prize acceptance speech:

> In his acceptance speech, Wiesel delivers a poignant monologue reflecting on the Holocaust, memory, and the importance of bearing witness to history.

Atticus Finch's closing argument in Harper Lee's "To Kill a Mockingbird":

> Atticus delivers a powerful monologue in the courtroom, defending Tom Robinson and addressing the jury's prejudice and moral responsibility.

Hedda Gabler's final monologue in Henrik Ibsen's "Hedda Gabler":

> In this tragic monologue, Hedda grapples with despair and fate as her actions lead to a devastating conclusion.

Monologues are a versatile literary and dramatic device that allows authors and playwrights to explore the inner lives of characters, convey complex ideas, and engage the audience in deep emotional and intellectual experiences. They are often memorable and impactful moments in literature and theater.

DIALOGUE

Dialogue is a written or spoken conversational exchange between two or more people in a literary work, play, film, or real-life communication. It is a fundamental component of storytelling and serves several essential functions, including character development, plot advancement, conveying information, and creating engagement with the audience or readers. Dialogues can be used in various forms of literature, from novels and short stories to plays and screenplays.

Some key characteristics and examples of dialogue:
Conversation: Dialogue involves characters engaging in a conversation, whether it's a casual chat, a heated argument, an exchange of information, or an emotional discussion.

Quotation Marks: In written form, dialogues are typically enclosed within quotation marks to distinguish spoken words from narrative or descriptive text.

Attributions: Dialogues often include attributions, which indicate who is speaking. These attributions can take the form of "he said," "she exclaimed," "they whispered," and so on.

Punctuation: Proper punctuation, such as commas, periods, question marks, and exclamation points, is used to clarify the tone, flow, and structure of the dialogue.

Revealing Character: Dialogues can reveal character traits, personalities, motivations, and relationships between characters. What characters say, how they say it, and what they don't say can all provide insights into their inner worlds.

Conflict and Tension: Conflict often arises in dialogues, driving the plot forward and creating dramatic tension. Characters may disagree, confront obstacles, or reveal hidden agendas through their conversations.

Realism: Dialogues aim to capture the natural flow of speech while remaining concise and purposeful. They should sound authentic to the characters and settings.

Examples of dialogue:

From "Romeo and Juliet" by William Shakespeare:
> Juliet: "Good night, good night! Parting is such sweet sorrow, That I shall say good night till it be morrow."
> Romeo: "Sleep dwell upon thine eyes, peace in thy breast! Would I were sleep and peace, so sweet to rest!"

From "To Kill a Mockingbird" by Harper Lee:
> Atticus Finch: "You never really understand a person until you consider things from his point of view... until you climb into his skin and walk around in it."
> Scout: "Atticus, he was real nice."
> Atticus Finch: "Most people are, Scout, when you finally see them."

From "Harry Potter and the Sorcerer's Stone" by J.K. Rowling:
> Hermione Granger: "Now, if you two don't mind, I'm going to bed before either of you come up with another clever idea to get us killed. Or worse, expelled."
> Ron Weasley: "She needs to sort out her priorities."

From "The Great Gatsby" by F. Scott Fitzgerald:
> Nick Carraway: "You can't repeat the past."
> Jay Gatsby: "Can't repeat the past? Why, of course, you can!"

From "The Lord of the Rings" by J.R.R. Tolkien:
> Frodo Baggins: "I wish the Ring had never come to me. I wish none of this had happened."

Gandalf: "So do all who live to see such times, but that is not for them to decide. All we have to decide is what to do with the time that is given us."

Dialogue is a fundamental element of storytelling that allows authors, playwrights, and filmmakers to bring characters to life, convey ideas, and engage audiences or readers in the narrative. Well-crafted dialogue can reveal character relationships, motivations, and conflicts, making it an essential tool for effective storytelling.

CONNOTATION AND DENOTATION

Connotation and denotation are two important aspects of word meaning in language and literature. They both contribute to the overall interpretation and impact of words and phrases, but they do so in different ways:

Denotation:
Denotation refers to the literal or dictionary definition of a word, i.e., its specific and objective meaning. It represents the basic and primary meaning that a word has, free from any emotional or cultural associations.
Denotative meanings are standardised and commonly understood by speakers of a language. They provide clarity and precision in communication.
For example, the denotation of the word "snake" is a long, legless reptile.

Connotation:
Connotation refers to the additional or secondary meanings and associations that words carry beyond their denotative meanings. These associations can be emotional, cultural, or subjective.
Connotations can vary among individuals and cultures, as they are influenced by personal experiences, emotions, and societal factors. Words with positive connotations evoke favourable emotions or ideas, while words with negative connotations evoke unfavourable emotions or ideas.
For example, the word "home" has a denotative meaning of a place where one lives, but it can have positive connotations of warmth, security, and comfort.

Examples of connotation and denotation:
Word: "House"
        Denotation: A building used as a residence.

Connotations: "House" may have connotations of shelter, family, and stability. It can also evoke feelings of belonging and comfort.

Word: "Cunning"

Denotation: Skilful or clever, especially in a deceitful or tricky way.

Connotations: While "cunning" denotes cleverness, its connotations may include slyness or deceitfulness, depending on the context.

Word: "Childish"

Denotation: Behaving in a manner typical of a child.

Connotations: "Childish" may have negative connotations, implying immaturity or irresponsibility.

Word: "Freedom"

Denotation: The state of being free from restraint or oppression.

Connotations: "Freedom" generally has positive connotations, evoking ideas of liberty, independence, and autonomy.

Word: "Slender"

Denotation: Thin or narrow in form.

Connotations: "Slender" typically conveys a sense of elegance or delicacy, with positive connotations.

Understanding the connotations and denotations of words is crucial for effective communication and literary analysis. Authors often use the connotations of words to create specific emotional or thematic effects in their writing. Additionally, awareness of connotations helps readers interpret the nuances and intentions behind the words they encounter in literature and everyday communication.

More examples of words with their denotations and connotations:

Word: "Economical"

Denotation: Using resources efficiently and sparingly.

Connotations: "Economical" can have positive connotations, suggesting frugality and responsible financial management.

Word: "Shack"

Denotation: A small, simple, and often poorly constructed dwelling.

Connotations: "Shack" typically carries negative connotations of poverty and lack of comfort.

Word: "Adventurous"

Denotation: Willing to take risks or seek new experiences.

Connotations: "Adventurous" generally has positive connotations, implying excitement, courage, and a spirit of exploration.

Word: "Dove"

Denotation: A type of bird belonging to the pigeon family.

Connotations: "Dove" often has connotations of peace, love, and innocence, as it is a symbol in many cultures.

Word: "Discipline"

Denotation: Training or control aimed at producing a specific behavior or outcome.

Connotations: "Discipline" can have both positive connotations, such as self-control and mastery, and negative connotations, such as punishment or strictness, depending on context.

Word: "Old"

Denotation: Having lived for a long time; not young.

Connotations: While "old" is a neutral descriptor, its connotations may include wisdom, experience, or deterioration, depending on how it is used.

Word: "Passionate"

Denotation: Expressing strong emotions, desires, or enthusiasm.

Connotations: "Passionate" generally has positive connotations, suggesting intensity, dedication, and fervor.

Word: "Nag"

Denotation: To annoy or criticize persistently.

Connotations: "Nag" typically carries negative connotations, implying irritation or constant complaining.

Word: "Mansion"

Denotation: A large, impressive, and often luxurious house.

Connotations: "Mansion" has connotations of opulence, wealth, and grandeur.

Word: "Sly"

Denotation: Cunning or deceitful in a secretive or sneaky way.

Connotations: "Sly" has negative connotations, suggesting dishonesty or trickery.

Word: "Innocent"

Denotation: Free from guilt or wrongdoing.

Connotations: "Innocent" generally has positive connotations, evoking notions of purity and blamelessness.

Word: "Fragile"

Denotation: Easily broken or delicate.

Connotations: "Fragile" carries connotations of vulnerability and the need for care.

Understanding the connotations of words is essential for effective communication, as it allows speakers and writers to convey not only the literal meanings but also the emotional nuances and associations associated with those words. Connotations can influence how a message is received and interpreted by others.

CLICHÉ

A cliché is an expression, idea, phrase, or element that has been overused to the point of losing its originality, impact, or effectiveness. Clichés are often considered trite or predictable because they have become so familiar that they no longer offer fresh or insightful meaning. Writers and speakers are encouraged to avoid clichés in their work, as they can weaken the impact of their writing or communication.

Some examples of clichés:

"A penny for your thoughts."

This cliché is often used to ask someone what they are thinking. It has become a common and unoriginal way to inquire about someone's thoughts or feelings.

"All's fair in love and war."

This cliché suggests that in matters of love and conflict, anything goes. It has been used so frequently that it lacks originality and depth.

"Don't judge a book by its cover."

This cliché advises against making judgments based on appearances. While it conveys a valuable lesson, its frequent use has made it a cliché.

"Better late than never."

This cliché implies that it's preferable for someone or something to arrive late than not at all. It is often used in situations involving tardiness or delays.

"Read between the lines."

This cliché suggests looking for hidden meanings or understanding a situation beyond its surface level. It encourages careful interpretation.

"Time heals all wounds."

This cliché conveys the idea that with time, emotional pain or trauma will gradually fade away. It is commonly used in discussions of grief or loss.

"Actions speak louder than words."

> This cliché emphasizes that what people do is more important and revealing than what they say. It underscores the importance of behavior and deeds.

"Every cloud has a silver lining."

> This cliché suggests that even in difficult or negative situations, there is a positive aspect or opportunity to be found.

"It's a piece of cake."

> This cliché means that something is very easy to accomplish. It is often used to describe simple tasks or activities.

"The calm before the storm."

> This cliché refers to a period of peace or tranquility that precedes a period of trouble or turmoil.

Clichés can be problematic in writing and communication because they can make the message sound unoriginal or uninspired. Writers and speakers are encouraged to seek fresh and unique ways to express their ideas to engage their audience more effectively. While some clichés may still hold value in certain contexts, relying on them too heavily can detract from the impact of one's communication.

Overusing clichés can indeed diminish the charm and impact of language and communication. Clichés, by their very nature, are phrases or expressions that have become overly familiar due to frequent use. When used excessively, they can make writing or speech sound predictable, unoriginal, and uninspired. Here are a few reasons why too much use of clichés can be detrimental:

Lack of Originality: Clichés often lack originality and fail to offer fresh or unique perspectives. They rely on well-worn phrases that may not capture the depth or complexity of a topic.

Diminished Impact: Clichés lose their power to engage and persuade an audience because they are so common. They may not evoke the intended emotional response or convey a sense of authenticity.

Reader or Listener Fatigue: Repeated encounters with clichés can lead to reader or listener fatigue. Audiences may become disengaged or lose interest if they encounter the same tired expressions.

Missed Opportunities: Overusing clichés can also prevent writers and speakers from exploring new ways to convey their ideas. There may be more creative and effective ways to communicate, but clichés can act as a shortcut that limits linguistic exploration.

Stifled Creativity: Clichés can stifle creativity and original thought. When writers or speakers rely on clichés, they may miss the opportunity to express themselves in a unique and authentic manner.

Loss of Individual Voice: Frequent use of clichés can make a writer or speaker's voice indistinguishable from others. It may mask their individuality and unique perspective.

While clichés can serve a purpose in communication by offering familiar shorthand for common ideas, it's important to use them judiciously. Mixing them with fresh, original language and ideas can help strike a balance and maintain the charm and impact of language. Effective communication often involves finding new ways to express thoughts and emotions, which can lead to more engaging and memorable interactions.

METONYMY

Metonymy is a figure of speech in which one word or phrase is substituted with another with which it is closely associated. Unlike a metaphor, where there is a direct comparison between two unlike things, metonymy involves the use of one term to stand in for something else that it is related to in some way. This relationship can be based on various factors, including proximity, cause-and-effect, or common associations. Metonymy is often used to create vivid and concise imagery or to emphasize a particular aspect of the subject.

Some common examples of metonymy:
The White House issued a statement.
> In this example, "The White House" is used as a metonym for the President of the United States or the presidential administration.

The crown will make an announcement.
> Here, "the crown" is used metonymically to refer to the monarchy or the royal authority.

Hollywood produces a lot of movies.
> "Hollywood" is often used as a metonym for the American film industry.

The pen is mightier than the sword.
> In this famous phrase, "the pen" represents writing or diplomacy, while "the sword" represents military force or violence.

The classroom was attentive during the lecture.
> In this case, "the classroom" is used to represent the students within it.

The track star broke a new record.
> "Track star" is a metonym for an athlete who participates in track and field events.

The press was at the scene of the accident.

"The press" is used metonymically to refer to journalists or news reporters.

The suits in the boardroom made the decision.

"The suits" refers to the business executives or decision-makers who typically wear suits.

The pen is red.

Here, "the pen" is used metonymically to refer to the writing that is done with the pen, emphasizing its color.

The stage lights stole the show.

In this case, "the stage lights" represents the overall visual and atmospheric elements of a performance.

Metonymy is a powerful literary device that can add depth and richness to language by allowing for subtle and evocative associations between words. It is commonly used in literature, rhetoric, and everyday language to convey ideas and create vivid imagery.

Some more examples of metonymy:

The press was buzzing with excitement.

In this example, "the press" represents the news media or journalists who are generating excitement and activity.

The pen is my livelihood.

"The pen" is used metonymically to refer to the act of writing, which is the writer's source of income.

The dish was delicious, and the kitchen deserves credit.

"The kitchen" here stands in for the chefs or cooks who prepared the dish.

The brass is playing a lively tune.

"The brass" is a metonym for the brass instruments being played in a musical performance.

He has a good heart.

In this case, "heart" is used metonymically to represent a person's kindness or compassionate nature.

The hospital is short-staffed.

"The hospital" is used to represent the medical staff working within it.

The team had strong bats this season.

"Bats" is used metonymically to refer to the players who use them in a sports context, such as baseball.

The classroom was focused on the lesson.

"The classroom" is used metonymically to represent the students' attention and engagement.

The boardroom made a decision.

"The boardroom" is used to represent the executives or decision-makers who meet there.

The paper is full of headlines.

"The paper" refers to a newspaper, and "headlines" represents the news stories featured prominently on its pages.

Metonymy can be a subtle yet effective way to convey complex ideas and create vivid mental images by using closely related terms. It allows writers and speakers to provide context and emphasize specific aspects of the subject they are discussing.

SYNECDOCHE

Synecdoche is a figure of speech in which a specific part of something is used to represent the whole, or vice versa. It involves substituting a part for the whole or the whole for a part. Synecdoche is a form of figurative language that can create vivid and concise imagery, emphasising a particular aspect of the subject.

Some common examples of synecdoche:

"All hands on deck."

> In this phrase, "hands" represents the whole crew or all the people on a ship. It uses a part (hands) to stand in for the whole (the crew).

"The United States won three gold medals in swimming."

> Here, "the United States" represents the athletes from the country who won the medals. The whole (the country) is used to refer to a part (the athletes).

"She has a new set of wheels."

> In this example, "wheels" refers to a car. The part (wheels) stands in for the whole (the car).

"The school sent a letter to all parents."

> "Parents" here represents the whole families of the students. The part (parents) is used to refer to the whole (families).

"The rancher had 500 head of cattle."

> In this case, "head" stands in for the whole animals, so it means the rancher had 500 cattle.

"Give me a hand with this."

> "Hand" is used to mean assistance or help. It represents the whole person providing help.

"The city mourned the loss of a brave firefighter."

> "Firefighter" represents the whole profession or the entire firefighting community.

"The White House issued a statement."

> In this instance, "The White House" is used to refer to the U.S. government or the administration as a whole.

Synecdoche is a versatile literary device that allows writers and speakers to emphasise specific aspects or details of a subject, making their language more evocative and precise. It can create vivid mental images and add depth to descriptions or narratives.

Metonymy and Synecdoche are closely related figures of speech that both involve substituting one term for another based on some form of association or relationship. While they share similarities, they have distinct characteristics and applications

Metonymy:

In metonymy, one word or phrase is substituted with another word or phrase based on a broader, more general association.

The substitution relies on a broader contextual or cultural relationship between the two terms.

Metonymy often involves substituting a term with something that is closely related or frequently associated with it, but not necessarily a part of it.

It can be used to create vivid and evocative imagery by emphasizing a broader concept or idea.

Example: Using "The White House" to refer to the U.S. government is a metonymic use because the White House is culturally associated with the government.

Synecdoche:

In synecdoche, a specific part of something is used to represent the whole, or vice versa.

The substitution involves a part-whole relationship, where a part is used to stand in for the whole, or the whole is used to represent a part.

Synecdoche often involves a more direct and literal connection between the part and the whole.

It can create concise and focused imagery by emphasizing a particular aspect or detail of the subject.

Example: Using "all hands on deck" to mean that everyone (the whole) should help with a task is a synecdoche because it uses a part (hands) to represent the whole (the crew).

In summary, while both metonymy and synecdoche involve substitutions based on associations, metonymy relies on broader cultural or contextual connections and often involves the substitution of something closely related but not necessarily a part. Synecdoche, on the other hand, emphasises the part-whole relationship and typically involves the substitution of an actual part for the whole or vice versa. These subtle distinctions make each figure of speech suitable for different expressive purposes in writing and speech.

PICTURESQUE

The term "picturesque" is a literary and artistic term used to describe a scene, landscape, or setting that is visually striking or picturesque, like a picture or painting. It conveys the idea that the scene is so visually appealing that it resembles a work of art. The picturesque often involves natural beauty, charming rural landscapes, or scenes with a sense of aesthetic harmony.

In literature, the term "picturesque" can be used to describe vivid and descriptive writing that paints a detailed and visually appealing picture in the reader's mind. Writers use picturesque descriptions to evoke a strong sense of place and to immerse readers in the world of the story.

The concept of the picturesque was influential in the Romantic movement in literature and art during the 18th and 19th centuries. Romantic writers and artists sought to capture and celebrate the beauty of the natural world, often emphasising the wild and untamed aspects of landscapes.

One famous work that incorporates the picturesque is William Wordsworth's poetry, particularly his poems celebrating the beauty of the Lake District in England. His descriptions of the landscape are often considered picturesque because they vividly depict the natural world and its aesthetic qualities.

Overall, the term "picturesque" is used to highlight the visual appeal and aesthetic qualities of scenes, settings, or descriptions in literature and art. It invites readers and viewers to appreciate the beauty and artistry in the world around them.

An example of a picturesque description from William Wordsworth's poem "Lines Composed a Few Miles Above Tintern Abbey," where he vividly depicts the natural beauty of the landscape:

"These beauteous forms,
Through a long absence, have not been to me
As is a landscape to a blind man's eye:
But oft, in lonely rooms, and 'mid the din
Of towns and cities, I have owed to them,
In hours of weariness, sensations sweet,
Felt in the blood, and felt along the heart;
And passing even into my purer mind
With tranquil restoration:—feelings too
Of unremembered pleasure: such, perhaps,
As have no slight or trivial influence
On that best portion of a good man's life,
His little, nameless, unremembered acts
Of kindness and of love."
In this passage, Wordsworth describes the landscape as "beauteous forms" and conveys how his memories of it have provided solace and inspiration throughout his life. His words paint a picturesque image of the natural world and its profound impact on his emotions and thoughts.

More examples of picturesque descriptions from literature:

From Jane Austen's "Pride and Prejudice":
"It is a truth universally acknowledged, that a single man in possession of a good fortune, must be in want of a wife."
This famous opening line of the novel humorously captures the social expectations and marriage prospects in the story's picturesque countryside setting.

From John Keats' "Ode to Autumn":
"Season of mists and mellow fruitfulness,
Close bosom-friend of the maturing sun;
Conspiring with him how to load and bless
With fruit the vines that round the thatch-eves run."
Keats beautifully describes the picturesque qualities of autumn,

painting a vivid image of the season's natural beauty.

From F. Scott Fitzgerald's "The Great Gatsby":
"In his blue gardens men and girls came and went like moths among the whisperings and the champagne and the stars."
This description of Gatsby's extravagant parties evokes a picturesque scene of opulence and decadence.

From Harper Lee's "To Kill a Mockingbird":
"Maycomb was an old town, but it was a tired old town when I first knew it."
The word "tired" in this description adds a picturesque quality to the town of Maycomb, suggesting a sense of weariness and stagnation.

From Charles Dickens' "Great Expectations":
"I was made awkward by his unexpected coming, and in a few moments began to feel that I had got myself into a picturesque scrape."
The term "picturesque scrape" humorously characterizes the protagonist's predicament, emphasizing its unusual and visually interesting nature.

These examples showcase how picturesque descriptions in literature can evoke striking and memorable images, immersing readers in the scenes and settings of the story.

SATIRE

Satire is a literary and rhetorical device that uses humor, irony, sarcasm, or ridicule to criticise and expose the flaws, vices, or follies of individuals, institutions, or society as a whole. It is often employed as a form of social or political commentary, aiming to bring about change or provoke thought by highlighting absurdities, hypocrisies, or injustices. Satire can take various forms, including written works, performances, visual art, and more.

Characteristics and examples of satire:
1. Exaggeration: Satire often employs exaggeration to emphasize and mock the flaws or weaknesses of its target. This can take the form of hyperbolic language, caricatures, or absurd situations.
Example: Jonathan Swift's "A Modest Proposal" suggests solving Ireland's economic problems by selling babies as a source of income. This extreme proposal exaggerates the callousness of British policies toward the Irish.

2. Irony: Satire frequently uses irony to convey a discrepancy between appearance and reality, or between what is said and what is meant. It can involve situational irony, verbal irony, or dramatic irony.
Example: In George Orwell's "Animal Farm," the animals revolt against their human oppressors, only to become oppressed by their fellow animals in a new regime. The ironic twist reveals the hypocrisy of the revolution's leaders.

3. Mockery: Satire often employs mockery or ridicule to lampoon its targets. This can include making fun of their behavior, beliefs, or characteristics.

Example: Mark Twain's "The Adventures of Huckleberry Finn" satirizes the racism and hypocrisy of the antebellum South through the character of the "King" and the "Duke," two con artists who exploit others' prejudices.

4. Social Commentary: Satire serves as a vehicle for social commentary, highlighting issues and problems in society. It may prompt readers or viewers to reflect on these issues critically.
Example: "Saturday Night Live" often satirizes contemporary political events and figures, using humor to comment on the state of politics and culture.

5. Parody: Satire may involve parody, where it imitates or mimics the style or conventions of a particular work, genre, or person, often for humorous effect.
Example: The satirical newspaper "The Onion" often publishes parodic articles that mimic the style of real news stories but exaggerate them to absurdity for comedic commentary.

6. Subversive Intent: Satire typically has a subversive intent, seeking to challenge the status quo, question authority, or provoke change. It can be a form of cultural critique.
Example: In "Brave New World" by Aldous Huxley, the novel satirises a dystopian future where the government controls every aspect of citizens' lives, questioning the consequences of a society obsessed with pleasure and conformity.

Satire can be a powerful tool for writers, comedians, and artists to engage with complex social and political issues while entertaining and challenging their audiences. It often relies on wit and cleverness to make its point, using humour as a means to deliver its critique.

Some examples of satire in literature, film, and other forms of media, along with explanations of their satirical elements:

"Animal Farm" by George Orwell:

Explanation: Orwell's "Animal Farm" is a satirical allegory that uses a group of farm animals who rebel against their human farmer as a metaphor for the Russian Revolution and the rise of Stalinism. The story exposes the corruption and hypocrisy of those in power, showing how the animals' idealistic vision of equality and freedom is corrupted by the ruling class.

"Gulliver's Travels" by Jonathan Swift:

Explanation: In this novel, Lemuel Gulliver's travels take him to various fantastical lands, each of which satirizes different aspects of 18th-century English society. For example, the land of Lilliput explores the absurdities of political and social hierarchies through its miniature inhabitants.

"The Daily Show" (TV Show) with Jon Stewart and Trevor Noah:

Explanation: "The Daily Show" is a satirical news program that uses humor, parody, and irony to critique political events, media coverage, and public figures. Through its humorous take on real-world issues, the show satirizes political and media absurdities.

"Dr. Strangelove or: How I Learned to Stop Worrying and Love the Bomb" (Film) by Stanley Kubrick:

Explanation: This satirical film explores the absurdity of nuclear warfare during the Cold War era. It uses dark humor and exaggerated characters to lampoon the military and political establishments, highlighting the dangers of a nuclear arms race.

"A Modest Proposal" by Jonathan Swift:

Explanation: In this satirical essay, Swift suggests that the impoverished Irish population should sell their infants as a source of income. Swift uses extreme exaggeration and irony to criticize British economic exploitation and the dehumanizing treatment of the Irish.

"The Onion" (Satirical News Website):

Explanation: "The Onion" is a satirical news outlet that publishes fictional news stories and headlines that mimic the style of real news reporting. Through humor and parody, it critiques various aspects of contemporary society, politics, and culture.

"1984" by George Orwell:

Explanation: "1984" is a dystopian novel that satirizes totalitarianism and government control. It portrays a bleak future in which the government exercises complete surveillance and propaganda, illustrating the dangers of a society stripped of individual freedoms.

"South Park" (TV Show) created by Trey Parker and Matt Stone:

Explanation: "South Park" is an animated series known for its irreverent and often controversial satire. It tackles a wide range of topics, from politics and religion to pop culture, using humor and parody to critique societal norms and taboos.

These examples demonstrate how satire uses humor, irony, exaggeration, and parody to criticize and comment on various aspects of society, politics, and human behavior. Satire often challenges the status quo and encourages critical thinking while entertaining its audience.

Types of Satire:
Horatian Satire:

Description: Horatian satire is characterized by its light-hearted and humorous tone. It seeks to gently mock and correct human folly and shortcomings.

Example: In Jane Austen's "Pride and Prejudice," the novel humorously satirizes the manners and social conventions of the British upper class during the early 19th century. The character of Mrs. Bennet, with her obsession with marrying off her daughters, is a source of light-hearted satire.

Juvenalian Satire:

Description: Juvenalian satire is often harsh, bitter, and angry. It aims to expose and condemn corruption, hypocrisy, and societal injustices.

Example: George Orwell's "Animal Farm" is a classic example of Juvenalian satire. The novel uses a farm allegory to critique the brutality and hypocrisy of totalitarian regimes, particularly the Soviet Union under Stalin.

Menippean Satire:

Description: Menippean satire features a diverse and complex structure, often including elements of parody, fantasy, and absurdity. It may critique multiple aspects of society and culture.

Example: Lewis Carroll's "Alice's Adventures in Wonderland" employs Menippean satire by creating a whimsical and absurd world where logic and reason are constantly undermined. It satirizes Victorian society and its rigid conventions.

Political Satire:

Description: Political satire targets political figures, institutions, and events. It uses humor, parody, and sarcasm to comment on political issues and often aims to expose the flaws and absurdities of the political world.

Example: "Saturday Night Live" (SNL) is known for its political satire through sketches and impersonations of political figures. One memorable example is Alec Baldwin's portrayal of Donald Trump, which provides a humorous commentary on his presidency.

Social Satire:

Description: Social satire addresses broader societal issues and norms. It critiques cultural practices, behaviors, and beliefs with the goal of highlighting their shortcomings or absurdities.

Example: Oscar Wilde's "The Importance of Being Earnest" satirizes the superficiality and hypocrisy of upper-class Victorian society. The characters' obsession with appearances and trivial matters is a source of social satire.

Religious Satire:

Description: Religious satire focuses on religious beliefs, practices, and institutions. It uses humor and irony to comment on religious matters, sometimes challenging religious dogma or hypocrisy.

Example: Mark Twain's "The Mysterious Stranger" satirizes religious beliefs and doctrines. It presents a skeptical view of organized religion through the character of Satan, who challenges conventional religious notions.

These examples demonstrate how different types of satire use humor, irony, parody, and wit to critique and comment on various aspects of society, culture, politics, and human behavior. Each type of satire has its own style and tone, ranging from light-hearted and humorous to harsh and critical, but all share the common goal of engaging and entertaining while providing social or political commentary.

More types of satire with examples:

Satirical Novels:

Description: Satirical novels are fictional works that use satire as a central theme or approach. They may employ satire to criticize society, politics, or human nature within a narrative framework.

Example: Joseph Heller's "Catch-22" is a satirical novel that explores the absurdities and contradictions of war and bureaucracy. The novel's title has even become synonymous with a paradoxical situation with no escape.

Satirical Cartoons and Comics:

Description: Satirical cartoons and comics use visual humor and satire to critique various subjects, including politics, culture, and current events. They often rely on caricatures and exaggerated visuals.

Example: "The Far Side" by Gary Larson is a comic strip known for its offbeat humor and satirical commentary on various subjects, including science, society, and the human condition.

Satirical News and Media:

Description: Satirical news outlets and shows, such as "The Onion" or "The Daily Show," use satire to parody real news and events. They employ humor and irony to comment on current affairs and societal issues.

Example: "The Onion" is a satirical news website that publishes fictional news stories and headlines. For instance, a headline like "Nation's Dogs Vow to Keep Barking at Nothing" humorously satirizes the idea of dogs' incessant barking.

Parody:

Description: Parody is a form of satire that imitates or mocks a specific work, genre, or individual, often for comedic effect. Parodies exaggerate or distort the original, highlighting its absurdities.

Example: The film "Spaceballs," directed by Mel Brooks, is a parody of the science fiction genre, particularly the "Star Wars" franchise. It uses humor and exaggeration to poke fun at the conventions of space opera and epic adventures.

Satirical Poetry:

Description: Satirical poems use verse and poetic techniques to criticize or ridicule their subjects. Poets employ satire to comment on a wide range of topics, from politics to human behavior.

Example: Alexander Pope's "The Rape of the Lock" is a mock-heroic poem that satirizes the triviality of a social incident involving a lock of hair. It elevates the event to epic proportions to highlight the absurdity of vanity.

Satirical Essays and Letters:

Description: Satirical essays and letters are written works that use satire to address various topics, often with humor and irony. They may take the form of open letters or editorials.

These additional examples showcase the versatility of satire as a literary and rhetorical device, as it can be applied to various forms of media and genres to provide commentary and entertainment while highlighting societal absurdities and flaws.

PARODY

Parody is a form of humor and satire that involves imitating or mimicking a particular work, style, artist, genre, or subject with the intention of creating a humorous or mocking effect. It often involves exaggerating or distorting elements of the original source to create a humorous or satirical commentary. Parodies can be found in literature, music, film, art, and various forms of media, and they are a way of both celebrating and critiquing the source material.

Some key aspects of parody:
Imitation: Parodies closely mimic the style, tone, and characteristics of the source material they are parodying. This includes elements such as language, visual aesthetics, music, and themes.

Exaggeration: Parodies often exaggerate or emphasize certain features of the original work to humorous effect. This exaggeration can take the form of caricature or hyperbole.

Satire: While parody is primarily comedic, it also serves as a form of satire. Parodies frequently comment on, critique, or lampoon aspects of the original work, as well as broader cultural or social phenomena.

Recognition: Effective parodies rely on the audience's recognition of the source material. Viewers or readers are expected to be familiar with the original work to fully appreciate the parody.

Playful Commentary: Parodies can provide a playful commentary on various aspects of popular culture, including literature, movies, television, music, and political figures.

Subversion: Parodies may subvert the expectations created by the original work. They can challenge conventions or reveal absurdities within the source material.

Examples of Parodies:
"Spaceballs" (1987): This comedy film directed by Mel Brooks is a parody of the science fiction genre, particularly the "Star Wars" franchise. It humorously imitates the characters, settings, and tropes of the original while adding comedic elements.

"Weird Al" Yankovic's Song Parodies: The musician "Weird Al" Yankovic is known for creating parodies of popular songs. For example, his parody of Michael Jackson's "Beat It" is titled "Eat It" and humorously addresses food-related themes.

"Scary Movie" Series: This film franchise parodies horror and thriller movies, including films like "Scream" and "The Sixth Sense." It exaggerates and mocks common horror movie tropes.

"Shrek" (2001): "Shrek" is an animated film that parodies traditional fairy tales, with characters like Shrek and Donkey providing humorous and satirical takes on classic fairy tale archetypes.

"The Onion" Satirical News Articles: "The Onion" is a satirical news publication that frequently parodies real news stories and journalistic conventions. Its headlines and articles often use humor to comment on current events and social issues.

"Austin Powers" Series: These films, starring Mike Myers as the titular character, parody the spy film genre, particularly the James Bond franchise. They exaggerate the conventions of spy films for comedic effect.

Parody is a form of creative expression that allows artists to both celebrate and critique the works and genres they parody. It relies on the audience's familiarity with the source material, making it a form of cultural commentary that can entertain and provoke thought simultaneously.

BURLESQUE

Burlesque is a form of entertainment that combines humor, parody, satire, and elements of theatrical performance, often characterized by exaggerated and risqué humor. It has a long history, dating back to the 17th century, and has evolved over time, incorporating various styles and themes. Burlesque performances typically involve comedy, music, dance, and elaborate costumes.

Some key aspects of burlesque:
Exaggeration: Burlesque often relies on exaggeration and caricature, with performers portraying characters or situations in an over-the-top and comedic manner. This can include exaggerated facial expressions, gestures, and physical movements.

Parody and Satire: Burlesque frequently parodies or satirizes established works, genres, or societal norms. It may mock serious or highbrow subjects with humor and irreverence.

Comedy: Humor is a central element of burlesque. Performers use wit, wordplay, and physical comedy to entertain the audience. Puns, double entendres, and slapstick humor are common.

Costumes and Glamour: Burlesque is known for its elaborate and often glamorous costumes. Performers may wear corsets, feathered headdresses, sequined outfits, and other extravagant attire.

Tease and Striptease: While not all burlesque acts involve striptease, it has been a prominent aspect of the genre's history. In classic burlesque, performers would tease the audience by gradually removing clothing, but they would not necessarily reveal everything.

Vaudeville Influence: Burlesque shares similarities with vaudeville, another form of variety entertainment. Both forms include a mix of acts, such as comedians, singers, dancers, and novelty acts.

Social Commentary: Some burlesque acts incorporate social commentary or political satire, using humor to address contemporary issues and challenges.

Music and Dance: Live music and dance routines are common in burlesque performances. Music can range from traditional jazz and blues to contemporary pop, depending on the style of the show.

Embracing Diversity: Modern burlesque has evolved to be more inclusive and diverse, with performers of various backgrounds, body types, and gender identities participating in the art form.

Examples of Burlesque:
Mae West: The actress and comedian Mae West is known for her provocative and humorous performances, both on stage and in films. Her witty one-liners and glamorous persona were emblematic of burlesque comedy.

Dita Von Teese: Dita Von Teese is a contemporary burlesque performer known for her elaborate, vintage-inspired acts, which often include striptease and luxurious costumes.

"The Rocky Horror Picture Show" (1975): This cult classic film incorporates elements of burlesque, parodying science fiction and horror genres while celebrating individuality and sexuality.

Burlesque Festivals: Various burlesque festivals and events are held worldwide, showcasing a diverse range of performers and styles, from classic to neo-burlesque.

Classic Burlesque: Performers like Gypsy Rose Lee and Sally Rand were iconic figures in classic burlesque, known for their humor, glamour, and innovative acts.

Burlesque continues to be a dynamic and evolving form of entertainment, with contemporary performers adding new twists and styles to the tradition while celebrating its history. It remains a space for creative expression, satire, and humor, captivating audiences with its unique blend of sensuality and comedy.

An example of a burlesque performance along with an explanation: Example: Imagine a burlesque performance set in the 1920s during the Prohibition era. The performer takes on the character of a flapper, complete with a short, fringed dress, feathered headband, and long strands of pearls. She starts with a sultry dance routine to a jazz tune, swaying her hips and moving with exaggerated grace.

As the performance continues, the humor and parody come into play. The performer might comically sip from a prop cocktail glass, pretending to become increasingly intoxicated. Her dance becomes more exaggerated and playful, with playful gestures and facial expressions.

Midway through the performance, she begins a striptease, removing her gloves with a playful wink to the audience. However, instead of revealing her bare skin, she unveils another layer of clothing, such as a sparkling leotard underneath her dress. This subversion of expectations adds a humorous twist to the striptease element.

As the performance reaches its climax, she may perform a surprise act like producing a prop toy saxophone and playfully miming a jazzy solo, all while maintaining the flirty and exaggerated persona.

Explanation: In this burlesque performance, several key elements of burlesque are at play:

Exaggeration: The performer exaggerates the characteristics and behaviors associated with a 1920s flapper, such as the exaggerated dance moves and playful mannerisms. This adds humor to the performance.

Parody: The act parodies the glamorous and seductive image of the flapper, poking fun at the era's fascination with speakeasies and cocktails during Prohibition.

Tease and Striptease: While there is a striptease element, it doesn't follow the traditional pattern of complete nudity. Instead, it plays with audience expectations, adding surprise and humor.

Comedy: The performer's playful interactions with props, like the cocktail glass and toy saxophone, inject humor into the act, making the audience laugh.

Glamorous Costumes: The performer's costume, with its fringed dress and accessories, adds a touch of glamour and extravagance, which is a hallmark of burlesque.

This example showcases how burlesque combines humor, parody, and theatricality to create an entertaining and often satirical performance that both celebrates and pokes fun at cultural elements from a specific era or context. It's a form of entertainment that thrives on the unexpected and the exaggerated, keeping the audience engaged and amused throughout the show.

RAPE OF THE LOCK   EXAMPLE OF BURLESQUE

"Rape of the Lock" by Alexander Pope is a classic example of a burlesque poem. This mock-heroic poem was written in the 18th century and uses the style and conventions of an epic poem to satirize trivial social customs and conflicts. Here's an example from "Rape of the Lock" that illustrates its burlesque elements:
Example:
"Whether the Nymph shall break Diana's Law,
Or some frail China Jar receive a Flaw,
Or stain her Honour, or her new Brocade,
Forget her Pray'rs, or miss a Masquerade,
Or lose her Heart, or Necklace, at a Ball;
Or whether Heav'n has doom'd that Shock must fall."

Explanation: In this passage, Pope humorously elevates trivial and mundane events, such as a woman breaking Diana's law (a reference to chastity), damaging a porcelain jar, or losing a piece of jewelry, to the same level of importance as epic events in traditional heroic poetry. He uses grandiose language and epic structure to emphasize the absurdity of these concerns in the context of the poem.

"Rape of the Lock" centers around the theft of a lock of Belinda's hair and the ensuing social turmoil. Pope uses the poem to satirize the shallowness and extravagance of 18th-century society, particularly among the aristocracy. The poem is a burlesque of the epic genre, as it takes a trivial event and treats it with all the seriousness and pomp of traditional epic poetry. This blending of the trivial and the grandiose is a hallmark of burlesque, as it uses exaggeration and parody to create humor and social commentary.

METAPHYSICAL CONCEIT

Metaphysical conceit is a specific type of conceit found in metaphysical poetry, which was popular in the 17th century, particularly in the works of poets like John Donne, George Herbert, and Andrew Marvell. Metaphysical conceits are characterised by their intellectual and often elaborate comparisons that explore complex and abstract ideas. These conceits are typically extended metaphors that delve deeply into the subject matter.

Characteristics of Metaphysical Conceits:

Intellectual Complexity: Metaphysical conceits are known for their intricate and intellectually challenging nature. They often involve unusual and surprising comparisons between seemingly unrelated concepts.

Exploration of Abstract Ideas: These conceits are used to explore abstract concepts, such as the nature of love, the relationship between the physical and spiritual worlds, or the complexities of human emotions and relationships.

Extended Metaphors: Metaphysical conceits are extended metaphors that can span multiple lines or even entire poems. They are not limited to a single word or phrase.

Paradoxical Nature: Many metaphysical conceits contain paradoxes or contradictions that add depth and complexity to the comparison. These paradoxes often challenge conventional thinking.

Types of Metaphysical Conceits:

Love as Exploration: Metaphysical poets often used conceits to explore the nature of love. For example, John Donne's "A Valediction: Forbidding Mourning" uses the conceit of a compass to describe the constancy of love.

Nature and Science: Some metaphysical conceits draw parallels between human experiences and elements of the natural world or scientific concepts. George Herbert's "The Pulley" compares God's gift of restlessness to a pulley that lifts the soul toward Him.

Religious and Spiritual Themes: Metaphysical poets frequently employed conceits to delve into religious and spiritual matters. Andrew Marvell's "To His Coy Mistress" uses the conceit of time as a wingèd chariot to urge the speaker's beloved to seize the moment.

Example of a Metaphysical Conceit:
In John Donne's poem "The Flea," the speaker uses the conceit of a flea to persuade his beloved to engage in a physical relationship. The flea becomes a symbol of their union, and the speaker argues that the flea's act of mingling their blood is a more innocent and insignificant act than their potential union. Here, the conceit of the flea allows Donne to explore themes of love, physicality, and morality in a provocative and intellectual manner.
Key Line from "The Flea" by John Donne:
"And in this flea our two bloods mingled be."
Metaphysical conceits, with their intellectual depth and intricate comparisons, are a defining feature of metaphysical poetry. They challenge readers to engage with complex ideas and imagery while exploring the depths of human experience and emotion.

More examples of metaphysical conceits from the works of various metaphysical poets:
George Herbert's "The Collar": In this poem, Herbert uses the conceit of a collar (an article of clothing) to explore the idea of divine obedience. He likens the constraints of the collar to the guidance and structure provided by his faith in God.

John Donne's "The Good-Morrow": In this poem, Donne employs the conceit of a compass to describe the spiritual connection between two lovers. He suggests that their souls are like the legs of a compass, always connected even when physically apart.

Andrew Marvell's "Bermudas": Marvell's poem "Bermudas" uses the conceit of an idyllic island paradise to symbolize the idea of heavenly bliss. He describes the Bermudas as a place where nature and divinity coexist in harmony.

John Donne's "The Ecstasy": In this poem, Donne uses the conceit of two souls merging and becoming one as a result of intense spiritual and physical love. He compares this union to the joining of two celestial bodies in the sky.

George Herbert's "The Flower": Herbert employs the conceit of a flower to explore the themes of human frailty and God's grace. He likens the flower's fleeting beauty to the transitory nature of human life.

John Milton's "Paradise Lost": In his epic poem "Paradise Lost," Milton uses the conceit of a celestial battle between angels and demons to explore profound theological and philosophical ideas, including the concept of free will.

Andrew Marvell's "The Definition of Love": Marvell's poem uses the conceit of a ship sailing toward an iceberg to symbolize a doomed love affair. The ship's collision with the iceberg represents the inevitable failure of the relationship.

John Donne's "A Valediction: Of Weeping": In this poem, Donne employs the conceit of a compass once again, but this time to describe the parting of two lovers. He compares their separation to the compass's movement, emphasizing the stability of their love despite physical distance.

These examples showcase the diverse and imaginative ways in which metaphysical conceits were used by poets to explore complex and abstract themes in their works. The conceits often require careful consideration and reflection to fully appreciate the depth of their meaning and symbolism.

CONCEIT

The term "conceit" in literature can refer to two different concepts: metaphysical conceit and regular conceit. Here's the difference between the two:

1. Metaphysical Conceit:
Definition: Metaphysical conceit is a specific type of conceit that was popular in metaphysical poetry during the 17th century. It involves an extended and elaborate metaphor or comparison between two seemingly unrelated things, often exploring complex and abstract ideas.
Characteristics: Metaphysical conceits are known for their intellectual complexity, exploration of abstract concepts, use of paradoxes, and extended metaphorical comparisons. They are typically found in the works of metaphysical poets like John Donne and George Herbert.
Example: In John Donne's "A Valediction: Forbidding Mourning," the conceit of a compass is used to compare and symbolize the constancy of love between two individuals.

2. Regular Conceit:
Definition: A regular conceit, also known as a simple conceit, is a more common literary device where a comparison is made between two dissimilar things, often using the words "like" or "as" to draw the comparison. It is a straightforward and concise form of figurative language.
Characteristics: Regular conceits are typically shorter and less complex than metaphysical conceits. They provide a clear and direct comparison between two elements to create vivid imagery or enhance understanding.
Example: In William Shakespeare's Sonnet 18, the line "Shall I compare thee to a summer's day?" is a regular conceit. It compares the beauty of the subject to that of a summer's day using a direct and simple comparison.

In summary, the key difference between metaphysical conceit and regular conceit lies in their complexity and depth. Metaphysical conceits are intricate and intellectually challenging, often exploring abstract concepts, while regular conceits are more straightforward and use simple comparisons to create imagery or convey meaning. Both types of conceit are forms of figurative language used by poets and writers to add depth and creativity to their works.

PARADOX

A paradox is a literary device that involves a statement or situation that appears contradictory or goes against common sense, but upon closer examination, may reveal an underlying truth or complexity. Paradoxes are often used in literature to provoke thought, create dramatic tension, or highlight the complexities of human experience.

Characteristics of Paradoxes:
Apparent Contradiction: Paradoxes present an initial contradiction or conflict between ideas or elements within a statement or situation.

Resolution: Upon deeper consideration, a paradox may reveal a resolution or underlying truth that reconciles the apparent contradiction.

Provocative: Paradoxes are thought-provoking and challenge the reader's or listener's understanding of reality.

Examples of Paradoxes:
"Less is more." This paradox suggests that simplicity and minimalism can sometimes be more effective and powerful than complexity.

"I can resist anything except temptation." This paradox by Oscar Wilde humorously highlights the human struggle with self-control and temptation.

"This statement is false." Known as the "liar paradox," this statement creates a self-referential contradiction. If the statement is true, then it must be false, but if it's false, then it must be true.

"The only constant is change." This paradox suggests that change is the one consistent element in life, even though change itself implies inconsistency.

"You have to be cruel to be kind." This paradox points out that sometimes, taking harsh actions or making tough decisions can ultimately lead to a better outcome or show genuine concern.

"It was the best of times, it was the worst of times." This famous opening line from Charles Dickens' "A Tale of Two Cities" presents a paradox by juxtaposing extreme opposites to set the historical and emotional context of the novel.

"War is peace, freedom is slavery, ignorance is strength." These paradoxical slogans from George Orwell's "1984" highlight the manipulation of language and thought by the totalitarian regime in the novel.

Paradoxes are a valuable literary tool for writers to create depth, provoke thought, and convey complex ideas. They challenge readers to think critically and engage with the text on a deeper level by exploring the tension between contradictory elements.

Examples of paradoxes in literature along with explanations:
"Jumbo shrimp."

> Explanation: This paradox combines the contradictory ideas of something being "jumbo" or large and "shrimp" which are typically small. It highlights the idea of unexpected contrasts and is often used humorously.

"Cruel kindness."

> Explanation: This paradox suggests that kindness, when delivered in a harsh or tough manner, can be perceived as cruelty. It reflects the complexity of human emotions and actions.

"Bittersweet."

Explanation: This paradox combines the contradictory tastes of bitterness and sweetness. It is often used to describe experiences that are both pleasurable and painful, such as nostalgia.

"Living dead."

Explanation: This paradox refers to someone who is physically alive but emotionally or spiritually detached, as if they are not fully experiencing life. It highlights the contrast between existence and vitality.

"Deafening silence."

Explanation: This paradox describes a situation where there is absolute silence, but it feels so loud and overwhelming that it's as if it deafens the senses. It underscores the power of silence in certain moments.

"A fine mess."

Explanation: This paradox refers to a situation that is chaotic, disorderly, or problematic, but it uses the word "fine" to create irony. It suggests that even amidst disorder, there can be a peculiar kind of order or value.

"Act naturally."

Explanation: This paradox instructs someone to behave in a natural, unscripted manner, but the act of being told to "act" implies an artificial performance. It underscores the challenge of being authentic in a contrived situation.

"Same difference."

Explanation: This paradox acknowledges that two things may appear different but have an equivalent outcome or result. It often serves as a casual way of dismissing minor distinctions.

"Only choice."

Explanation: This paradox suggests that when there's no alternative or freedom to choose, the absence of choice becomes the only option. It highlights the sense of constraint or inevitability.

"Awfully good."

     Explanation: This paradox combines opposing adjectives to create a nuanced description. It implies that something is both exceptionally good and carries a sense of awe or surprise.

Paradoxes, with their inherent contradictions, add depth and complexity to language and literature. They challenge conventional thinking and encourage readers to explore the nuances and subtleties of ideas and emotions.

Oxymoron and Paradox are both figures of speech that involve the use of seemingly contradictory or conflicting elements, but they differ in their structure and how they create meaning:

Oxymoron:

Definition: An oxymoron is a figure of speech in which two contradictory or opposing words or ideas are combined to create a new and meaningful expression.

Structure: Oxymorons typically consist of two words placed next to each other in a phrase, and they are often connected by "and" or "but." For example, "jumbo shrimp" or "bittersweet."

Purpose: Oxymorons are used to create a striking or thought-provoking effect, often by highlighting a paradoxical or ironic aspect of the situation or concept being described.

Paradox:

Definition: A paradox is a statement, situation, or concept that appears self-contradictory or logically absurd but may reveal an underlying truth, complexity, or unexpected insight upon closer examination.

Structure: Paradoxes can be longer and more complex than oxymorons. They often involve a statement or idea that presents an apparent contradiction, such as "less is more" or "the beginning of the end."

Purpose: Paradoxes are used to challenge conventional thinking, provoke thought, or emphasize the complexity of a subject. They often encourage deeper reflection and may have profound implications.

Key Differences:

Structure: Oxymorons are typically composed of two juxtaposed words, while paradoxes can be longer statements or ideas that appear self-contradictory.

Complexity: Oxymorons are usually simpler and more straightforward in their contradiction, whereas paradoxes often involve deeper and more intricate contradictions.

Usage: Oxymorons are often used for humor, irony, or wordplay and may be found in everyday language. Paradoxes are more likely to be used in philosophical, literary, or rhetorical contexts to explore profound or abstract concepts.

While both oxymorons and paradoxes involve contradictory elements, oxymorons are shorter, simpler, and often used for humorous or ironic effect, while paradoxes are more complex, thought-provoking, and used to challenge conventional understanding or explore deeper truths.

PUN

A pun is a form of wordplay that involves using a word or phrase in a way that exploits multiple meanings, or it involves words that sound similar but have different meanings. Puns are often used for humor, creating double entendres, and adding cleverness to language. They can be found in various forms of writing, including literature, jokes, and everyday conversation.

Characteristics of Puns:
Double Meaning: Puns rely on the double meanings of words or phrases to create humor or a play on words.

Word Sound: Puns may involve words that sound similar but have different meanings (homophonic puns) or words that have multiple meanings (homographic puns).

Surprise or Wit: Puns often surprise the reader or listener with an unexpected twist or clever use of language.

Examples of Puns:
Homophonic Pun: "I used to be a baker, but I couldn't make enough dough." In this pun, "dough" refers to both money

(figuratively) and the ingredient used in baking.

Homographic Pun: "Time flies like an arrow; fruit flies like a banana." In this pun, "flies" can mean both the passage of time and insects.

Double Meaning: "I'm reading a book on anti-gravity. It's impossible to put down!" Here, "put down" has both a literal meaning (placing something on a surface) and a figurative meaning (unable to stop reading).

Clever Wordplay: "I'm on a seafood diet. I see food, and I eat it." This pun plays on the phrase "I see food" as if the person eats everything they see.

Brand Names: "I'm friends with all electricians; we have such good current connections." This pun uses "current" to refer to both electrical current and social connections.

Names and Titles: "I used to be a baker, and I loafed it." In this pun, "loafed" sounds like "loved," creating a wordplay on the person's enjoyment of baking.

Literary Puns: In Shakespeare's "Much Ado About Nothing," the character Benedick says, "A man loves the meat in his youth that he cannot endure in his age." The pun here is on "meat" (food) and "meet" (encounter or marry).

Puns are a versatile form of wordplay that can add humor, wit, and cleverness to language. They are often appreciated for their ability to create humor through linguistic creativity and clever connections between words and meanings.

Examples of puns along with explanations:

Homophonic Pun: "I used to be a baker because I kneaded dough." In this pun, "kneaded" sounds like "needed," creating a humorous play on words. It suggests that the person became a baker because they "needed" (kneaded) dough for baking, but it also sounds like they "needed" (required) a job.

Homographic Pun: "The bass was so heavy; it left me bass-ically speechless." Here, "bass" refers to both a type of fish (pronounced like "base") and the low-frequency sound (pronounced like "bays"). The pun adds humor by combining the two meanings.

Double Meaning: "I told my computer I needed a break, and now it won't stop giving me Kit Kats." In this pun, "break" can mean both a pause from work and "breaks" (Kit Kat chocolate bars). The computer humorously responds to the request by giving Kit Kats.

Clever Wordplay: "Time flies like an arrow; fruit flies like a banana." This classic pun uses the word "flies" to create humor by comparing the movement of time with the behavior of fruit flies, highlighting the unexpected comparison.

Names and Titles: "I couldn't figure out how lightning works, but then it struck me." This pun plays on the two meanings of "struck." It initially suggests the person couldn't understand lightning, but then they were physically "struck" by it, providing an amusing twist.

Literary Puns: In Lewis Carroll's "Alice's Adventures in Wonderland," the Cheshire Cat says, "We're all mad here." The pun lies in the word "mad," which can mean both insane and enthusiastic. In Wonderland, the characters are known for their whimsical behavior.

Brand Names: "I couldn't make a reservation at the Italian restaurant because it was pasta point of no return." This pun combines the idea of reaching a point of no return with "pasta," humorously suggesting that once you enter the Italian restaurant, there's no turning back.

Visual Puns: A sign in a library might say, "Please do not book the librarian's time; they're always checked out." This pun uses book-related terminology to humorously convey that the librarian is busy.

Animal Puns: "I'm trying to find a leopard that lost its spots. It's been spotted in the area." This pun combines the idea of a leopard losing its spots with the notion of someone spotting it (seeing it).

Geography Puns: "I used to be a baker in Paris, but I couldn't make enough 'cents' there." Here, "cents" sounds like "sense," creating a play on words related to financial success.

Puns are versatile and can be found in various contexts, from everyday conversations to literature and advertising. They rely on the dual meanings or sounds of words to create humor, surprise, or clever wordplay, making them a popular form of linguistic entertainment.

REPETITION

Repetition is a literary device that involves the repeated use of a word, phrase, sound, or element within a text. It is a deliberate and purposeful technique employed by writers to create various effects and emphasize key points or ideas. Repetition can serve both aesthetic and rhetorical purposes in literature.

Repetition in Literature: Types and Examples

Emphasis: Repetition is often used to emphasize a particular word, phrase, or idea, making it stand out and drawing the reader's attention to its importance. For example, in Martin Luther King Jr.'s "I Have a Dream" speech, he repeats the phrase "I have a dream" to emphasize his vision for a future of racial equality.

Rhythm and Musicality: Repetition can contribute to the rhythm and musicality of a piece of writing, creating a pattern that can be pleasing to the ear. In Edgar Allan Poe's poem "The Raven," the repetition of the word "nevermore" creates a haunting and rhythmic quality that adds to the poem's eerie atmosphere.

Amplification: Repetition can be used to amplify or intensify an idea or emotion. Repeating a word or phrase can make it more powerful and emotionally resonant. In Shakespeare's "Macbeth," the character Macbeth repeats the word "tomorrow" in the soliloquy, "Tomorrow, and tomorrow, and tomorrow," to emphasize the relentless passage of time and the futility of life.

Parallelism: Repetition can establish parallel structures in a text, creating balance and symmetry. This can be particularly effective in speeches and persuasive writing, where it helps organize and clarify ideas. In the Gettysburg Address, Abraham Lincoln uses repetition of the phrase "we cannot" to create parallelism and emphasize the nation's dedication to the principles of freedom and equality.

Symbolism: Repetition can imbue certain words or phrases with symbolic significance, giving them deeper meaning and resonance throughout the text. In George Orwell's "Animal Farm," the repeated chant "Four legs good, two legs bad" symbolizes the principles of the animal rebellion and the corruption of power. Unity and Cohesion: Repetition can help unify a text and provide cohesion by connecting different parts of a narrative or argument. It can serve as a thread that ties the text together. In F. Scott Fitzgerald's "The Great Gatsby," the green light at the end of Daisy's dock is repeatedly mentioned, symbolizing Gatsby's unattainable dreams and providing unity throughout the novel.

STYLE

In literature, style refers to the distinctive way in which an author uses language to express their thoughts, ideas, and emotions in a written work. It encompasses a writer's unique voice, tone, and choice of words, sentence structure, and literary devices. An author's style can greatly influence the overall mood and impact of a literary work. Here are some key elements and characteristics of literary style:
Voice: A writer's voice is their unique way of expressing themselves through words. It reflects their personality, perspective, and attitude. Voice can be authoritative, conversational, formal, humorous, or any other quality that distinguishes the writer's tone.

Tone: Tone refers to the author's attitude or emotional stance towards the subject matter. It can range from serious and somber to light-hearted and humorous. The tone can greatly affect the reader's emotional response to a work.

Diction: Diction refers to the author's choice of words. It includes vocabulary, word usage, and the level of formality or informality. A writer's diction can be precise and descriptive or abstract and figurative, depending on their intended effect.

Sentence Structure: The way sentences are structured, including their length, complexity, and rhythm, contributes to a writer's style. Some authors prefer long, intricate sentences, while others use short, punchy ones.

Imagery and Figurative Language: The use of imagery, metaphors, similes, and other figurative language can be a distinctive feature of an author's style. These devices add depth and vividness to the writing.

Repetition: Repetition of words, phrases, or themes can reinforce key ideas and contribute to the overall style. It can create emphasis or establish patterns in the text.

Narrative Perspective: The choice of a first-person, third-person, or omniscient narrator can influence the style of a narrative. Each perspective offers a unique way of presenting the story.

Dialogue: The way characters speak in dialogue can be an important aspect of an author's style. It can reveal their personalities, backgrounds, and relationships.

Punctuation and Grammar: Authors may use punctuation marks and grammatical structures creatively to shape their style. For example, the use of ellipses (...) can create a sense of pause or hesitation.

Sentence Variation: Varying sentence structures, from simple to complex, can contribute to the overall flow and rhythm of a piece.

Allusion and Intertextuality: Authors may reference other works of literature, history, or culture through allusions, intertextual references, or quotes, adding layers of meaning to their writing.

Context and Genre: An author's style may vary depending on the genre of their work and the cultural or historical context in which it was written. For example, a novel written in the 19th century may have a different style than a contemporary work of science fiction.

Consistency: A consistent style throughout a work or a body of an author's work can create a sense of coherence and authorial identity.

Authors develop their style over time, and it becomes a signature element of their literary identity. Recognizing and analyzing an author's style can enhance the understanding and appreciation of their work and how it contributes to the overall meaning and impact of a literary piece.

An example that illustrates different elements of an author's style:
Author: Jane Austen
Novel: "Pride and Prejudice"
In Jane Austen's "Pride and Prejudice," her style is characterised by a witty and satirical tone, precise diction, and a focus on social manners and relationships in 19th-century English society.

Here's an excerpt that showcases her style:

"It is a truth universally acknowledged, that a single man in possession of a good fortune, must be in want of a wife."
In this famous opening line, Austen immediately establishes her ironic and satirical tone by presenting a supposedly "universal truth" about marriage, while subtly critiquing the social expectations of her time. Her choice of words and phrasing, such as "universally acknowledged" and "in possession of a good fortune," adds a touch of humor and commentary on the societal pressures regarding marriage and wealth.

Throughout the novel, Austen's style includes sharp and clever dialogue that reveals the personalities and social dynamics of her characters. Her use of polite and formal language reflects the manners of the Regency era, and she employs irony and wit to comment on the limitations and prejudices faced by women in that society.

This excerpt demonstrates how an author's style encompasses elements like tone, diction, irony, and the portrayal of social norms. Jane Austen's distinct style has made her novels enduring classics, known for their incisive social commentary and engaging storytelling.

UNDERSTATEMENT

Understatement is a rhetorical device used in literature and language to downplay or minimise the significance of something, often for comedic, ironic, or dramatic effect. It involves the deliberate use of understated language to make a situation, event, or idea appear less important, intense, or serious than it truly is. Understatement is the opposite of exaggeration or hyperbole.

Examples of understatement:

A Titanic Description: Describing the Titanic, one of the most famous ships in history, as "a bit of a disappointment" after it sank tragically in 1912 is a stark example of understatement. The magnitude of the disaster is far greater than the words used to describe it.

Facing a Hurricane: When someone says, "It's a little windy outside," during a powerful hurricane, they are using understatement to downplay the dangerous weather conditions.

A Massive Mess: If a room is in complete disarray with items scattered everywhere, and someone remarks, "We might need to tidy up a bit," it's an understated way of acknowledging the chaotic state of the room.

A Challenging Task: When faced with a difficult assignment or project, saying, "This might take a little effort," is a classic understatement. The word "little" belies the true level of effort required.

A Minor Mistake: If someone accidentally spills coffee on their shirt and casually comments, "Oops, I made a small mess," they are using understatement to describe a situation that might be more embarrassing or frustrating than they're letting on.

Understatement is a versatile literary and rhetorical device used to create humor, irony, or a sense of detachment from intense or serious situations. It can also be a subtle form of commentary or criticism. By minimizing the impact or significance of something, authors and speakers can engage their audience's imagination and invite them to read between the lines, which adds depth and complexity to the text.

An example of understatement along with an explanation:
Example: Imagine a scenario in which a person arrives at work completely soaked from head to toe due to heavy rain. They casually say, "I got a little wet on my way here."
Explanation: In this example, the person uses understatement to describe the situation of being drenched in rainwater. By saying they "got a little wet," they downplay the severity of their condition. In reality, being completely soaked is far more significant than the mild expression suggests. This understatement can serve various purposes:
Humor: The understatement in this context adds a touch of humor. It's comical because the situation is clearly much more extreme than the words used to describe it.

Modesty: The speaker might use understatement to avoid drawing excessive attention to themselves or to avoid complaining about a common inconvenience like rain.

Tone of Nonchalance: The speaker's tone appears relaxed and unfazed, as if being soaked is a minor inconvenience rather than a major disruption.

Emphasis: By understating the situation, the speaker indirectly highlights the absurdity of the contrast between the words and the reality, drawing the listener's attention to the exaggeration in a humorous way.

In literature, understatement can be a valuable tool for creating humor, irony, or commentary, and it often relies on the reader's ability to recognize the gap between what is stated and what is actually meant.

SUBLIME

The term "sublime" in literature and aesthetics refers to a quality of greatness, grandeur, or beauty that inspires a sense of awe, wonder, or admiration in the observer or reader. It represents an experience that transcends the ordinary and touches upon the extraordinary. The concept of the sublime has been explored in various forms of art, including literature, painting, and philosophy.
Here are key aspects of the sublime in literature:
Vastness and Grandeur: The sublime often involves elements of vastness, such as the grandeur of nature or the cosmos. It can be associated with immense landscapes, towering mountains, expansive oceans, or celestial bodies. These elements evoke a feeling of insignificance in the face of the sublime, emphasizing the power and magnitude of the subject.

Emotion and Awe: Experiencing the sublime often elicits strong emotions, particularly a sense of awe, wonder, or even terror. It goes beyond mere beauty and touches on the profound and overwhelming. The sublime can evoke both positive and negative emotions, as it encompasses both the breathtaking and the fearsome.

Transcendence: The sublime is often associated with a sense of transcendence or going beyond the ordinary. It can lead to moments of self-reflection, spiritual contemplation, or a feeling of being connected to something greater than oneself.

Artistic Representation: Writers and artists use various techniques to evoke the sublime in their works. Detailed descriptions of majestic landscapes, vivid imagery, and the use of metaphors and symbols can help convey the idea of the sublime. Additionally, the sublime is often explored in poetry and prose to convey the overwhelming beauty and power of nature.

Literary Examples: The concept of the sublime has been explored in literature for centuries. For example, Romantic poets like William Wordsworth and Samuel Taylor Coleridge often wrote about the sublime in their nature poems. In Mary Shelley's "Frankenstein," the character Victor Frankenstein grapples with the sublime as he pursues his scientific ambitions.

Philosophical Exploration: The sublime has also been a subject of philosophical inquiry, particularly in the works of Edmund Burke and Immanuel Kant. Kant, for instance, distinguished between the "mathematical sublime" (related to vastness and magnitude) and the "dynamic sublime" (related to overpowering forces and threats), providing philosophical frameworks for understanding the concept.

In literature, the sublime serves to provoke deep emotional and intellectual responses in readers, challenging them to confront the vastness and complexity of the world and their place within it. It can be a source of inspiration, reflection, and contemplation, making it a powerful and enduring theme in literary and artistic expression.

Example: In Mary Shelley's novel "Frankenstein," the character Victor Frankenstein encounters the sublime when he ascends Montanvert, a glacier-covered mountain in the Swiss Alps. Here is an excerpt from the novel:
"A tingling long-lost sense of pleasure often came across me during this journey. Some turn in the road, some new object suddenly perceived and recognized, reminded me of days gone by, and were associated with the lighthearted gaiety of boyhood. The very winds whispered in soothing accents, and maternal Nature bade me weep no more."

Explanation: In this passage, Victor Frankenstein is describing his ascent of Montanvert, which is depicted as a sublime natural landscape. The description captures several aspects of the sublime: Vastness and Grandeur: Montanvert is a magnificent, glacier-covered mountain in the Swiss Alps, representing the vastness and grandeur of nature. The towering mountains and awe-inspiring scenery evoke a sense of the sublime.

Emotion and Awe: As Victor ascends the mountain, he experiences a range of emotions. He mentions a tingling sense of pleasure and a connection to his childhood joy. However, the sublime is not limited to positive emotions. It also includes a sense of awe, and Victor's journey through the sublime landscape is a mix of both pleasure and profound emotional experiences.

Transcendence: Victor's journey through the sublime landscape has a transcendent quality. He is transported back to his youth, and the sublime scenery seems to have a maternal and soothing effect on him. It is as if he is connecting with something greater than himself.
This passage exemplifies how the sublime is used in literature to convey the overwhelming beauty and power of nature and the profound emotional impact it can have on characters. It also highlights the dual nature of the sublime, encompassing both moments of joy and moments of awe and introspection. In "Frankenstein," the sublime landscape serves as a backdrop to Victor's scientific ambitions and inner struggles, adding depth and complexity to the narrative.

COLLOQUIALISM

Colloquialism is a linguistic and literary device characterised by the use of informal or everyday language, expressions, slang, and regionalisms. It reflects the way people speak in everyday conversation, making it more relatable and authentic in written or spoken communication. Colloquial language varies by region, culture, and social context, and it is often used to establish a casual or conversational tone.

Some key aspects of colloquialism:

Everyday Language: Colloquial expressions are commonly used in everyday conversation among native speakers. They may include informal vocabulary, contractions, and idiomatic phrases that may not be considered standard in formal writing.

Regional Variations: Colloquialisms can vary by region or dialect, reflecting the unique linguistic characteristics of a particular area. For example, the colloquial language used in the southern United States may differ from that used in the northern states.

Slang: Slang terms are a type of colloquialism characterized by unconventional and often temporary language used by specific groups or subcultures. Slang can quickly change and evolve, making it a dynamic aspect of colloquial language.

Conversational Tone: The use of colloquial language creates a conversational and informal tone in writing or speech. This tone can be effective for engaging the audience, making the content more relatable.

Character Development: In literature, authors may use colloquialism to develop characters and convey their backgrounds, personalities, or social statuses. A character's use of colloquial language can provide insights into their identity and upbringing.

Authenticity: Colloquialism is often used to capture the authenticity and realism of dialogue in fiction, drama, or dialogue-driven narratives. It helps make characters sound genuine and relatable to readers or viewers.

Effect on Style: The use of colloquialism can significantly affect the style of a literary work. Authors may employ it to create a specific atmosphere, such as a folksy or regional feel, or to juxtapose it with more formal language for stylistic contrast.

Examples of Colloquialism:
"Wanna" instead of "want to."
        Example: "I wanna go to the movies tonight."
"Y'all" as a regional plural form of "you."
        Example: "Y'all should come over for dinner sometime."
"Gonna" instead of "going to."
        Example: "I'm gonna meet up with my friends later."
"Ain't" as a contraction for "am not," "is not," or "are not."
        Example: "I ain't going to that party."
"Kid" as a colloquial term for a child or young person.
        Example: "The kids are playing in the park."
"Couch potato" as an idiomatic expression for someone who spends a lot of time watching television.
        Example: "My brother is such a couch potato; he never
        leaves the living room."
Colloquialism serves to capture the richness and diversity of language as it is spoken and used by people in various contexts. It adds depth and authenticity to both spoken dialogue and written narratives, enhancing the overall impact of literary works and communication.

EPIGRRAPH

An Epigraph is a literary device often used at the beginning of a book, chapter, or section to provide a brief quotation, phrase, or passage that sets the tone, theme, or context for the work that follows. Epigraphs can come from various sources, including other literary works, historical texts, poems, songs, or even the Bible. They serve to introduce key themes, ideas, or moods and can provide readers with valuable insights into the text.
Main aspects of epigraphs:
Quotation or Passage: An epigraph typically consists of a quotation, a short excerpt, or a passage from another source. This external text is presented before the main body of the work.

Attribution: Epigraphs usually include attribution to the source of the quotation or passage, such as the author's name, the title of the work, and sometimes additional context.

Relevance: Epigraphs are carefully selected to relate to the themes, motifs, or ideas explored within the main text. They can foreshadow events, provide commentary, or offer a different perspective on the subject matter.

Atmosphere and Tone: Epigraphs can set the atmosphere and tone for the work, helping readers anticipate the emotional or intellectual journey they are about to embark upon.

Cultural References: They may include references to literature, philosophy, history, or culture, inviting readers to engage with the broader context of the text.

Interpretation: Epigraphs often require readers to interpret their significance in relation to the main text. They can be a source of reflection and discussion.

Examples of Epigraphs:

Charles Dickens, "A Tale of Two Cities":

> Epigraph: *"It was the best of times, it was the worst of times..."*
>
> Attribution: Charles Dickens, "A Tale of Two Cities"

In this epigraph, Dickens sets the tone for his novel by juxtaposing opposites and introducing the theme of duality.

F. Scott Fitzgerald, "The Great Gatsby":

> Epigraph: *"So we beat on, boats against the current, borne back ceaselessly into the past."*
>
> Attribution: F. Scott Fitzgerald, "The Great Gatsby"

Fitzgerald's epigraph encapsulates the novel's themes of nostalgia and the inexorable passage of time.

Harper Lee, "To Kill a Mockingbird":

> Epigraph: *"Lawyers, I suppose, were children once."*
>
> Attribution: Charles Lamb

Lee's choice of this epigraph prompts readers to consider the human experiences and backgrounds of the legal professionals in the story.

J.D. Salinger, "The Catcher in the Rye":

> Epigraph: *"Among other things, you'll find that you're not the first person who was ever confused and frightened and even sickened by human behaviour."*
>
> Attribution: J.D. Salinger

Salinger's epigraph foreshadows the protagonist Holden Caulfield's disillusionment with society and his struggles with human behavior.

Ernest Hemingway, "The Sun Also Rises":
>	Epigraph: *"You are all a lost generation."*
>	Attribution: Gertrude Stein

Hemingway's epigraph, attributed to Stein, encapsulates the sense of disillusionment and aimlessness that characterizes the "Lost Generation" of the post-World War I era.

Epigraphs serve as literary devices that enrich the reading experience by providing context, thematic cues, or thought-provoking quotes that invite readers to delve deeper into the text. They can enhance the overall meaning and resonance of a literary work.

EPITAPH

An epitaph is a brief inscription or written tribute that is often found on a tombstone or monument to honor a deceased person. It typically includes the person's name, dates of birth and death, and a short message or statement. Epitaphs can vary widely in tone, style, and content, reflecting the personality, achievements, or sentiments associated with the individual.

Here are some key aspects of epitaphs:

Inscription on a Tombstone: Epitaphs are primarily associated with gravestones, mausoleums, and other memorial markers. They provide a way to commemorate and remember the deceased.

Personalized Messages: Epitaphs can be highly personalized and may include a variety of elements, such as the person's accomplishments, virtues, beliefs, or even a favorite quote or verse.

Emotional Expressions: Epitaphs often convey emotions, ranging from sorrow and grief to love, admiration, and even humor. They serve as a way for loved ones to express their feelings and pay tribute to the departed.

Historical Significance: In some cases, epitaphs can have historical or cultural significance, providing insights into the time period, societal norms, or values of the era in which the person lived.

Religious and Spiritual Themes: Many epitaphs contain religious or spiritual references, such as Bible verses, prayers, or references to the afterlife. These elements reflect the deceased's faith and beliefs.

Literary or Poetic Style: Some epitaphs are crafted in a literary or poetic style, using figurative language, metaphors, or symbolism to create a memorable and meaningful tribute.

Famous Epitaphs: Throughout history, there have been notable epitaphs associated with famous individuals. For example, the epitaph on William Shakespeare's tombstone reads, "Good friend, for Jesus' sake forbear, / To dig the dust enclosed here. / Blessed be the man that spares these stones, / And cursed be he that moves my bones."

Legacy and Remembrance: Epitaphs play a role in preserving the memory of the deceased. They serve as a lasting testament to the person's life, character, and contributions.

EPITAPHS OF FAMOUS POETS

Here are epitaphs for some famous poets:

William Shakespeare (1564-1616):

> Epitaph: *"Good friend, for Jesus' sake forbeare, To digg the dust encloased heare; Bleste be ye man yt spares thes stones, And curst be he yt moves my bones."*

Explanation: Shakespeare's epitaph, found on his gravestone at Holy Trinity Church in Stratford-upon-Avon, is a warning against disturbing his final resting place. It reflects the superstitions of the time, where it was believed that disturbing the dead could bring bad luck.

John Keats (1795-1821):

> Epitaph: *"Here lies one whose name was writ in water."*

Explanation: This epitaph, which Keats wrote for himself shortly before his death from tuberculosis, reflects the idea that his work would not be recognized or appreciated during his lifetime but would endure and be celebrated long after his passing.

Percy Bysshe Shelley (1792-1822):

> Epitaph: *"Nothing of him that doth fade, But doth suffer a sea-change Into something rich and strange."*

Explanation: Shelley's epitaph, from his poem "The Tempest," suggests a transformation after death, with the fading of the

physical body leading to a mystical change into something otherworldly and remarkable.
Emily Dickinson (1830-1886):
> Epitaph: "Called Back."

Explanation: Emily Dickinson's epitaph is simple and enigmatic, much like her poetry. *"Called Back" suggests the idea of a spiritual return or a calling back to the divine.*
Walt Whitman (1819-1892):
> Epitaph: *"This is what you shall do; Love the earth and sun and the animals, despise riches, give alms to every one that asks, stand up for the stupid and crazy, devote your income and labor to others, hate tyrants, argue not concerning God, … …*

> Explanation: This passage from Whitman's "Leaves of Grass" serves as a poetic epitaph in which he imparts his wisdom and philosophy of life, encouraging readers to embrace the beauty of the world, reject societal constraints, and strive for a life filled with compassion and purpose.

These epitaphs capture the essence of these famous poets and often reflect their views on life, death, and the enduring power of their words. Each epitaph is a reflection of the poet's unique perspective and contribution to the world of literature.

Robert Frost (1874-1963):
> Epitaph: *"I had a lover's quarrel with the world."*

Explanation: This epitaph, from Frost's poem "The Lesson for Today," expresses his complex relationship with the world and his role as a poet who often grappled with its challenges.
Edgar Allan Poe (1809-1849):
> Epitaph: *"Quoth the Raven, 'Nevermore.'"*

Explanation: Poe's epitaph is a reference to his famous poem "The Raven," in which the titular bird repeats the word "Nevermore." It adds an eerie and mysterious touch to his grave.
Langston Hughes (1902-1967):

Epitaph: *"The Negro Speaks of Rivers."*

Explanation: This epitaph references Hughes' iconic poem "The Negro Speaks of Rivers," which explores the deep historical and cultural connections between African Americans and the world's great rivers.

William Wordsworth (1770-1850):

Epitaph: *"To the poet, to the philosopher, to the saint, all things are friendly and sacred, all events profitable, all days holy, all men divine."*

Explanation: This epitaph reflects Wordsworth's Romantic philosophy, which celebrated the beauty of nature, the importance of the individual, and the divine presence in all aspects of life.

Sylvia Plath (1932-1963):

Epitaph: *"Even amidst fierce flames, the golden lotus can be planted."*

Explanation: Plath's epitaph is a reference to the lotus flower, which symbolises beauty and resilience emerging from challenging circumstances. It speaks to her enduring legacy as a poet.

Robert Burns (1759-1796):

Epitaph: *"An honest man's the noblest work of God."*

Explanation: Burns' epitaph reflects his belief in the intrinsic worth and virtue of an honest person, emphasizing the importance of moral character.

John Milton (1608-1674):

Epitaph: *"Here at last I shall rest with thee."*

Explanation: This simple epitaph, found on Milton's grave, suggests a sense of final peace and reunion with a loved one, likely referring to his deceased wife, Mary Powell Milton.

Emily Brontë (1818-1848):

Epitaph: *"No coward soul is mine."*

Explanation: This epitaph, taken from one of Emily Brontë's poems, conveys her defiant and resolute spirit, emphasizing her strength and courage.

Dylan Thomas (1914-1953):

Epitaph: *"After the first death, there is no other."*

Explanation: This epitaph, from Thomas's poem "A Refusal to Mourn the Death, by Fire, of a Child in London," explores the idea that death, once experienced, changes our perspective on mortality.

E. E. Cummings (1894-1962):

Epitaph: *"I thank You God for most this amazing day."*

Explanation: Cummings' epitaph reflects his celebration of life and the beauty of the world, which is a recurring theme in his poetry.

Lord Byron (1788-1824):

Epitaph: *"Here lies the friend most loved, the son most dear."*

Explanation: This epitaph, written by Byron himself, is inscribed on the monument marking his final resting place in the family vault at Hucknall Torkard Church. It expresses the deep love and affection for his mother, Catherine Gordon Byron.

Ralph Waldo Emerson (1803-1882):

Epitaph: *"The passive master lent his hand, To the vast soul that o'er him planned."*

Explanation: This epitaph, from Emerson's poem "The Problem," conveys the idea that a person's life is guided by a greater spiritual force or destiny.

Anne Brontë (1820-1849):

Epitaph: *"And when the sun begins to fling His flaring beams, me, goddess, bring To arched walks of twilight groves, And shadows brown that Sylvan loves Of pine or monumental oak, Where the rude axe with heaved stroke Was never heard the nymphs to daunt, Or fright them from their hallowed haunt."*

Explanation: Anne Brontë's epitaph, from her poem "Music on Christmas Morning," evokes a sense of peace and natural beauty, reflecting her love for the outdoors and the tranquility of nature.

Pablo Neruda (1904-1973):

Epitaph: *"Tonight I can write the saddest lines."*

Explanation: This epitaph, taken from Neruda's famous poem "Tonight I Can Write," speaks to the themes of love, loss, and nostalgia that permeate much of his work.

William Blake (1757-1827):

> Epitaph: *"I give you the end of a golden string,*
> Only wind it into a ball:
> It will lead you in at Heaven's gate,
> Built in Jerusalem's wall."

Rumi (1207-1273):

> Epitaph: *"Do not be satisfied with the stories that come before you. Unfold your own myth."*

W. B. Yeats (1865-1939):

> Epitaph: *"Cast a cold Eye*
> *On Life, on Death.*
> *Horseman, pass by!"*

Seamus Heaney (1939-2013):

> Epitaph: *"Walk on air against your better judgment."*

Maya Angelou (1928-2014):

> Epitaph: *"A bird doesn't sing because it has an answer, it sings because it has a song."*

T. S. Eliot (1888-1965):

> Epitaph: *"In my beginning is my end."*

Dante Alighieri (1265-1321):

> Epitaph: *"In His will is our peace."*

Matsuo Basho (1644-1694):

> Epitaph: *"Sick on a journey, / Over parched fields, / Dreams wander on."*

Edna St. Vincent Millay (1892-1950):

> Epitaph: *"My candle burns at both ends; / It will not last the night; / But ah, my foes, and oh, my friends— / It gives a lovely light."*

These epitaphs capture the essence of these poets' philosophies, perspectives, and legacies, adding depth and meaning to their final resting places.

JUXTAPOSITION

Juxtaposition is a literary and rhetorical device that involves placing two or more contrasting elements side by side in order to highlight their differences or create a specific effect. It is a technique commonly used in literature, art, and everyday language to draw attention to contrasts, provoke thought, or create a vivid and memorable impression. Juxtaposition can involve contrasting ideas, characters, settings, themes, or images, and it is often employed to achieve various literary and artistic purposes.
Here are some key aspects of juxtaposition:
Highlighting Contrast: Juxtaposition serves to emphasize the differences between the juxtaposed elements. By placing them side by side, the contrasts become more apparent, allowing the audience to compare and contrast them directly.

Creating Tension: Juxtaposition can generate tension or conflict within a narrative, artwork, or argument. When opposing elements are juxtaposed, they can create a sense of tension or contradiction that engages the audience.

Enhancing Meaning: Juxtaposition can deepen the meaning of a literary work by juxtaposing complementary or opposing ideas, themes, or symbols. This can lead to new insights and interpretations.

Affecting Mood and Tone: Depending on the juxtaposed elements, this device can evoke different emotional responses from the audience. It can be used to create humor, drama, irony, or other emotional effects.

Drawing Attention: Juxtaposition can be used to draw attention to a particular element or concept in a work, making it stand out more prominently.

Symbolism and Imagery: Juxtaposing certain symbols or images can convey deeper symbolic meanings or create powerful visual effects. For example, contrasting light and darkness in a painting can symbolize the struggle between good and evil.

Examples of Juxtaposition:
Good vs. Evil: Juxtaposing morally upright characters with morally corrupt ones is a common theme in literature. In Shakespeare's "Macbeth," the virtuous King Duncan is juxtaposed with the villainous Macbeth.

Youth vs. Old Age: Contrasting youthful characters with elderly characters can highlight differences in outlook, energy, and experience. This is seen in Shakespeare's "Romeo and Juliet," where the young lovers are juxtaposed with the older generation.

Rich vs. Poor: Juxtaposing characters from different socioeconomic backgrounds can explore themes of wealth and poverty. In Charles Dickens' "A Tale of Two Cities," the opulent lives of the aristocracy are juxtaposed with the impoverished conditions of the working class.

Nature vs. Technology: Juxtaposing the natural world with technological advancements is a recurring theme. In the film "Blade Runner," futuristic technology is juxtaposed with the natural world to comment on the consequences of unchecked progress.

Light vs. Darkness: Contrasting light and darkness is a common visual juxtaposition used in literature and art to symbolize various themes, such as good vs. evil or knowledge vs. ignorance.

War vs. Peace: Juxtaposing scenes of war and scenes of peace can create a powerful contrast. The juxtaposition of battlefield scenes with moments of tranquility in Erich Maria Remarque's "All Quiet on the Western Front" underscores the horrors of war.

Juxtaposition is a versatile literary and artistic device that can be used in various forms and contexts to convey complex ideas, evoke emotions, and engage the audience in meaningful ways. It adds depth and complexity to creative works by inviting readers or viewers to explore the relationships between contrasting elements.

APHORISM

An aphorism is a concise, terse, and often witty statement expressing a general truth or observation about life. It's a type of saying that packs a lot of meaning into a few words, making it memorable and thought-provoking. Aphorisms are often philosophical or moral in nature and are designed to make the reader or listener reflect on deeper truths and insights.
Some famous examples of aphorisms include:
"Actions speak louder than words."
"If it ain't broke, don't fix it."
"Power tends to corrupt, and absolute power corrupts absolutely." - Lord Acton
"The only thing necessary for the triumph of evil is for good men to do nothing." - Edmund Burke
"Life is short, art is long." - Hippocrates
"Man is the measure of all things." - Protagoras
"To be or not to be, that is the question." - William Shakespeare
Aphorisms are found in many cultures and traditions and can be traced back to ancient times. They have been used by philosophers, writers, political leaders, and everyday people to convey insights and truths about human nature, society, and the world at large.

Francis Bacon, one of the pioneers of English essay writing, made extensive use of aphorisms in his essays. These aphoristic sentences are sharp, concise, and filled with wit, often conveying profound insights about human behavior and natural phenomena. Bacon's unique style involved juxtaposing contrasting thoughts in balanced structures, thereby engaging the reader in active contemplation.
For instance, in his essay "Of Studies," Bacon writes:
"Reading maketh a full man; conference a ready man; and writing an exact man."
Here, Bacon provides a balanced view of the benefits of three activities: reading, conversing, and writing. Each part of the

aphorism complements the other, and together, they provide a holistic view of personal development.

Another example from "Of Truth" is:

"A mixture of a lie doth ever add pleasure."

This aphorism conveys the idea that people sometimes derive pleasure from lies, perhaps because they paint a more favorable picture than reality. The balance in the sentence lies in the contrast between the concepts of "mixture" and "pleasure," suggesting that a dose of falsehood can be enjoyable.

Through such balanced aphorisms, Bacon forces readers to weigh both sides of an idea, prompting deep reflection and a broader understanding of th

MUSICAL DEVICES IN POETRY

Musical devices in poetry are techniques and elements that poets use to create a musical quality or rhythm in their poems. These devices enhance the auditory experience of the poem and can add emotional resonance.

Some common musical devices in poetry include:
Rhyme: The repetition of similar sounds at the end of lines or within lines. Rhyme can create a pleasing musical effect and emphasize certain words or ideas. Examples include end rhyme, internal rhyme, and slant rhyme.

Rhythm: The pattern of stressed and unstressed syllables in a line of poetry. Rhythm creates a musical flow in the poem and can be regular (e.g., iambic pentameter) or irregular.

Meter: A regular pattern of stressed and unstressed syllables in a line of poetry. Common meters include iambic, trochaic, anapestic, and dactylic. Meter contributes to the poem's musicality and structure.

Alliteration: The repetition of consonant sounds at the beginning of words in close proximity. Alliteration can create a pleasing sound and rhythm, as well as emphasize specific words or phrases.

Assonance: The repetition of vowel sounds within words in close proximity. Assonance adds musicality to the poem and can create subtle patterns and connections.

Consonance: The repetition of consonant sounds within words in close proximity. Consonance can create a musical effect and contribute to the poem's sound and meaning.

Onomatopoeia: Words that imitate the sound they represent. Onomatopoeic words create a direct connection between the poem's language and the sensory experience it describes.

Euphony: The use of pleasant, melodious, and harmonious sounds in poetry. Euphony creates a soothing and pleasing auditory experience.

Cacophony: The deliberate use of harsh or discordant sounds in poetry. Cacophony can create tension, dissonance, or emphasize a chaotic or unsettling theme.

Refrain: A repeated line or phrase in a poem, typically at the end of stanzas or throughout the poem. Refrains contribute to the poem's musical structure and can reinforce its theme or message.

Anaphora: The repetition of a word or phrase at the beginning of successive lines or clauses. Anaphora can create a rhythmic and emphatic effect.

Cesura: A pause or break in the middle of a line of poetry, often indicated by punctuation. Cesuras can influence the poem's rhythm and pacing.

Parallelism: The repetition of similar grammatical structures or patterns in successive lines or phrases. Parallelism can create a sense of balance and rhythm in the poem.

Diction: The poet's choice of words and their arrangement. Careful selection of words with pleasing sounds can enhance the poem's musicality.
These musical devices work together to create the overall sonic experience of a poem, making it not only a vehicle for conveying meaning but also a work of art that engages the reader's sense of hearing and emotion.

RHYME

Rhyme is a common musical device in poetry characterised by the repetition of similar or identical sounds at the end of words or within words. Rhyme is used to create rhythm, enhance the musicality of a poem, and often emphasise certain words or ideas. There are various types of rhyme, including:

End Rhyme: This occurs when the rhyming words appear at the end of lines of poetry. End rhyme is the most common type of rhyme and is often used in traditional forms of poetry such as sonnets and ballads.

Example:

> *"I wandered lonely as a cloud*
> *That floats on high o'er vales and hills,*
> *When all at once I saw a crowd,*
> *A host, of golden daffodils."*

In this excerpt from William Wordsworth's "I Wandered Lonely as a Cloud," the end rhyme is seen in the words "cloud" and "crowd," "hills" and "daffodils."

Internal Rhyme: Internal rhyme occurs when rhyming words appear within the same line of poetry. Internal rhyme can add complexity and musicality to a poem.

Example:

> "Once upon a midnight dreary, while I pondered, weak and weary..."

In this line from Edgar Allan Poe's "The Raven," the internal rhyme is found in "dreary" and "weary."

Slant Rhyme: Slant rhyme, also known as near rhyme or half rhyme, involves words with similar but not identical sounds. Slant rhyme is often used for subtlety and can create a unique auditory effect.

Example:

"You said you were going to the store, but you never made it to the door."

In this example, "store" and "door" are a slant rhyme because they share similar vowel sounds but are not perfect matches.

Eye Rhyme: Eye rhyme occurs when words look similar in spelling but are pronounced differently. Eye rhyme relies on visual similarity rather than auditory similarity.

Example:

"Love" and "move"

In this case, "love" and "move" are eye rhymes because they look alike but are not pronounced the same way.

Rhyme is an essential component of many poetic forms and can contribute to the overall structure and musicality of a poem. Poets use rhyme to create patterns, establish rhythm, and draw attention to specific words or ideas, enhancing the reader's experience of the poem.

RHYTHM

Rhythm in poetry refers to the pattern of stressed and unstressed syllables in a line of verse. It is a crucial element that contributes to the musicality and flow of a poem. Rhythm can be created through various metrical patterns and can greatly influence the way a poem is read or recited.

Some key aspects of rhythm in poetry along with an example:

Meter: Meter is the regular pattern of stressed (accented) and unstressed (unaccented) syllables in a line of poetry. Different meters can be used to establish a specific rhythm in a poem. Common meters include iambic pentameter, trochaic tetrameter, anapestic trimeter, and dactylic hexameter.

> Iambic Pentameter: In this meter, each line consists of five iambs, which are metrical feet consisting of one unstressed syllable followed by one stressed syllable. This is one of the most common meters in English poetry.
>
> Example (from William Shakespeare's Sonnet 18):
>
> "Shall I compare thee to a summer's day?"

Stanza Structure: The organization of stanzas in a poem can also create rhythm. For example, a poem with regular quatrains (four-line stanzas) may have a steady and predictable rhythm.

Example (from Emily Dickinson's "Because I could not stop for Death"):

> *"Because I could not stop for Death –*
> *He kindly stopped for me –*
> *The Carriage held but just Ourselves –*
> *And Immortality."*

Free Verse: While many poems adhere to specific metrical patterns, some poems, known as free verse, do not have a regular meter. Instead, they rely on other elements like line length, line breaks, and punctuation to create a unique rhythm.

Example (from Walt Whitman's "Song of Myself"):

> *"I celebrate myself, and sing myself,*
> *And what I assume you shall assume,*

For every atom belonging to me as good belongs to you."
Caesura: Caesura is a pause or break within a line of poetry, often indicated by punctuation. Caesuras can affect the rhythm and pacing of a poem, creating natural pauses that contribute to the overall musicality.
Example (from Samuel Taylor Coleridge's "The Rime of the Ancient Mariner"):
"Water, water, everywhere,
Nor any drop to drink."
Rhythm is an essential element in poetry that can enhance the reader's experience by creating a sense of musicality and flow.

METER

Meter in poetry refers to the rhythmic structure created by the arrangement of stressed and unstressed syllables in a line of verse. It is a fundamental element of traditional poetry and serves as a framework for the poet to establish a consistent pattern of accents and syllables within each line. The most common types of metrical patterns in English poetry include:

Iambic Meter: In iambic meter, each metrical foot consists of an unstressed syllable followed by a stressed syllable (da-DUM). It is one of the most prevalent meters in English poetry.

Example (from William Shakespeare's Sonnet 18):

> *"Shall I com-PARE thee TO a SUM-mer's DAY?"*

Trochaic Meter: Trochaic meter is the reverse of iambic meter, with each metrical foot containing a stressed syllable followed by an unstressed syllable (DUM-da).

Example (from Edgar Allan Poe's "The Raven"):

> *"ONCE up-ON a MID-night DREAR-y..."*

Anapestic Meter: Anapestic meter consists of two unstressed syllables followed by a stressed syllable (da-da-DUM).

Example (from Clement Clarke Moore's "A Visit from St. Nicholas"):

> *"T'was the NIGHT be-FORE CHRIST-mas, WHEN all*
> *THROUGH the HOUSE..."*

Dactylic Meter: Dactylic meter is the reverse of anapestic meter, with each metrical foot containing a stressed syllable followed by two unstressed syllables (DUM-da-da). Example (from Henry Wadsworth Longfellow's "The Song of Hiawatha"):

> *"By the SHO-RE of GITCH-ie GUM-ee..."*

Spondaic Meter: In spondaic meter, each metrical foot consists of two stressed syllables (DUM-DUM). Spondaic meter is relatively rare in English poetry and is often used for emphasis or a deliberate slowing of the rhythm.

Example (from William Shakespeare's "The Tempest"):

> *"ALL KNEE-LING ON the COLD, COLD GROUND..."*

Pyrrhic Meter: Pyrrhic meter consists of two unstressed syllables (da-da). It is even less common than spondaic meter and is often used for subtlety and variety in metrical patterns.
Example (from Shakespeare's "Romeo and Juliet"):
"Two HOUSE-HOLDS, BOTH a-LIKE IN DIG-ni-TY..."
These metrical patterns, along with variations and combinations, provide poets with the tools to create structured and rhythmic verse. Meter helps establish the pacing, musicality, and overall structure of a poem, allowing poets to convey their themes and emotions effectively.

ALLITERATION

Alliteration is a literary device characterised by the repetition of the initial consonant sounds in a series of words within close proximity. It is often used in poetry and prose to create rhythm, emphasise certain words or ideas, and add musicality to the language. Alliteration is not dependent on the repetition of vowel sounds but focuses on consonants. Here are some details about alliteration along with examples:

Purpose of Alliteration:

Emphasis: Alliteration can draw attention to specific words or phrases, making them stand out in the text.

Musicality: It creates a pleasant and rhythmic sound in the language, enhancing the overall auditory experience of the writing.

Memorability: The repetition of sounds can make a text more memorable and easier to recall.

Examples of Alliteration:

"Peter Piper picked a peck of pickled peppers." (repetition of the "p" sound)

"She sells seashells by the seashore." (repetition of the "s" sound)

"The slimy snake slithered silently." (repetition of the "s" sound)

"Sally's sunflowers swayed in the summer breeze." (repetition of the "s" sound)

"The wild, windy waves washed the shore." (repetition of the "w" sound)

Types of Alliteration:

Initial Alliteration: This is the most common type, where the initial consonant sounds are repeated at the beginning of words.

Internal Alliteration: In this type, the repeated consonant sounds occur within words rather than at the beginning. This can create subtler effects.

Consonance: While not traditional alliteration, consonance involves the repetition of consonant sounds anywhere within words or at the end of words.

Effect on Poetry:

In poetry, alliteration can be used to establish a specific rhythm or tone. It can contribute to the poem's mood and style.

Alliterative verse is a form of poetry in which alliteration is a key structural element. It is commonly found in Old English and Middle English poetry.

Alliteration in Literature:

Shakespeare's works often contain examples of alliteration to enhance the musicality of his language.

In J.R.R. Tolkien's "The Lord of the Rings," he uses alliteration to create memorable character names, such as "Bilbo Baggins" and "Gollum."

Alliteration is a versatile literary device that can be used to achieve various effects in writing, from adding a playful tone to creating a sense of seriousness or urgency. Its use can vary from subtle to pronounced, depending on the writer's intent and the context of the text.

Some additional examples of alliteration in sentences:

Sheep should sleep in a shed. (repetition of the "sh" sound)

Crazy cats careened around the corner. (repetition of the "c" sound)

Gleaming green grapes glisten in the sun. (repetition of the "g" sound)

He clutched his coffee cup, craving caffeine. (repetition of the "c" sound)

Bobby's big, blue balloon bobbed in the breeze. (repetition of the "b" sound)

Whispering willows waved in the wind. (repetition of the "w" sound)

The rattling, roaring train rushed down the tracks. (repetition of the "r" sound)
Flickering fireflies flitted through the forest. (repetition of the "f" sound)
Sally's silver sandals sparkled in the sunlight. (repetition of the "s" sound)
The tiny turtle tumbled into the pond. (repetition of the "t" sound)

These examples showcase the use of alliteration to create a rhythmic and melodious quality in sentences. Alliteration can be found in various types of writing and is a versatile literary device that adds both auditory and aesthetic appeal to language.

Some examples of alliteration from some famous English poems:
Samuel Taylor Coleridge's "The Rime of the Ancient Mariner":
>*"The fair breeze blew, the white foam flew,*
>*The furrow followed free;"*

Robert Frost's "Mending Wall":
>*"Before I built a wall I'd ask to know*
>*What I was walling in or walling out,"*

Edgar Allan Poe's "The Raven":
>*"While I nodded, nearly napping, suddenly there came a tapping,"*

William Shakespeare's "Sonnet 1":
>*"From fairest creatures we desire increase,"*

William Blake's "The Tyger":
>*"Tyger Tyger, burning bright,*
>*In the forests of the night;"*

Alfred Lord Tennyson's "The Lady of Shalott":
>*"Willows whiten, aspens quiver,*
>*Little breezes dusk and shiver"*

William Wordsworth's "Lines Written in Early Spring":
>*"Through primrose tufts, in that green bower,*
>*The periwinkle trailed its wreaths;"*

Gerard Manley Hopkins' "Pied Beauty":
>*"Glory be to God for dappled things –*
>*For skies of couple-colour as a brinded cow;"*

Lewis Carroll's "Jabberwocky":
>*"Beware the Jabberwock, my son!*
>*The jaws that bite, the claws that catch!"*

These are just a few examples among countless instances of alliteration in English poetry. Alliteration is a beloved device because of its ability to add musicality, rhythm, and emphasis to poetic lines.

ASSONANCE And CONSONANCE

ASSONANCE

Assonance is a literary device that involves the repetition of vowel sounds within words or in close proximity to each other. Unlike rhyme, which involves the repetition of both consonant and vowel sounds, assonance focuses solely on vowel sounds. This device is often used in poetry and prose to create musicality, emphasize certain words or ideas, and contribute to the overall mood or tone of a piece of writing.

Some details about assonance along with examples:

Purpose of Assonance:

> Musicality: Assonance contributes to the musical quality of language by repeating vowel sounds. This repetition can create a pleasing and rhythmic effect in a poem or piece of writing.

> Emphasis: It can draw attention to specific words or phrases by highlighting the vowel sounds within them.

> Mood and Tone: The choice of vowel sounds can influence the mood or tone of a piece. Different vowel sounds can evoke different emotions or atmospheres.

Examples of Assonance:

> "The rain in Spain stays mainly in the plain." (repetition of the long "a" sound)

> "The cat sat on the mat." (repetition of the short "a" sound)

> "Hear the mellow wedding bells." (repetition of the long "e" sound)

> "A land laid waste with all its young men slain." (repetition of the long "a" and "e" sounds)

Types of Assonance:

> Internal Assonance: Involves the repetition of vowel sounds within a single word.

> Near Assonance: Features vowel sounds that are similar but not identical.

Consonantal Assonance: Includes the repetition of vowel sounds along with some consonant sounds.

Effect on Poetry:

Assonance is commonly used in poetry to enhance the auditory experience and create a sense of rhythm.

Poets often use it to convey emotions, establish atmosphere, or emphasize specific words or themes.

Assonance in Literature:

In "The Raven" by Edgar Allan Poe, there is a notable use of assonance with the long "o" sound, as in "Once upon a midnight dreary, while I pondered, weak and weary."

William Wordsworth's "I Wandered Lonely as a Cloud" features assonance in the repetition of the long "o" sound in "Golden daffodils."

Assonance is a versatile literary device that adds depth and beauty to language. Writers use it creatively to craft memorable and evocative passages in their works, enhancing the overall impact of their writing.

CONSONANCE

Consonance is a literary device that involves the repetition of consonant sounds at the end or in the middle of words within close proximity. Unlike rhyme, which typically involves the repetition of both vowel and consonant sounds at the end of words, consonance focuses specifically on the repetition of consonants. It is often used in poetry and prose to create musicality, emphasize certain words or ideas, and add a sense of cohesion to a piece of writing.

Some details about consonance along with examples:

Purpose of Consonance:

Musicality: Consonance contributes to the musical quality of language by repeating consonant sounds. This repetition can create a pleasing and rhythmic effect in a poem or piece of writing.

Emphasis: It can draw attention to specific words or phrases by highlighting the consonant sounds within them.

Cohesion: Consonance can provide structural unity to a passage or work by repeating certain consonant sounds.

Examples of Consonance:

"Mike likes his bike." (repetition of the "k" sound)

"Pitter-patter, raindrops on the rooftop." (repetition of the "t" and "r" sounds)

"The wind whispered in the willows." (repetition of the "w" and "s" sounds)

"Dark and deep, these woods are lovely." (repetition of the "d" and "s" sounds)

Types of Consonance:

End Consonance: Involves the repetition of consonant sounds at the end of words.

Internal Consonance: Features consonant repetition within words, either at the beginning or in the middle.

Effect on Poetry:

Consonance is commonly used in poetry to enhance the auditory experience and create a sense of rhythm.

Poets often use it to convey emotions, establish atmosphere, or emphasize specific words or themes.

Consonance in Literature:

In Robert Frost's poem "Stopping by Woods on a Snowy Evening," there is consonance with the repetition of the "s" sound in "Whose woods these are I think I know."

In Emily Dickinson's poem "Because I could not stop for Death," there is consonance with the repetition of the "p" and "d" sounds in "Because I could not stop for Death – He kindly stopped for me."

Consonance is a versatile literary device that adds depth and musicality to language. It is used creatively by writers to craft memorable and harmonious passages in their works, enhancing the overall impact of their writing.

BLANK VERSE

Blank verse is a type of poetry characterised by unrhymed lines of iambic pentameter. It is one of the most common forms of verse in English literature and is often used in dramatic and narrative poetry.
 Here are some details about blank verse:

Meter: Blank verse consists of lines of iambic pentameter, which means each line has ten syllables with a specific pattern of alternating unstressed and stressed syllables (da-DUM, da-DUM, da-DUM, da-DUM, da-DUM). This rhythmic pattern creates a natural and flowing cadence in the verse.

Unrhymed: Unlike many other forms of verse, blank verse does not rhyme at the end of lines. Instead, it relies on the meter and the inherent musicality of the language to create a pleasing sound.

Versatility: Blank verse is highly versatile and can be used in a wide range of literary forms, including drama, epic poetry, and narrative poetry. It offers a sense of formality and structure while allowing for a more natural and conversational tone compared to traditional rhymed verse.

Shakespearean Use: Perhaps the most famous use of blank verse is found in the works of William Shakespeare. Many of his plays, including "Hamlet," "Macbeth," and "Othello," are written in blank verse. This form allowed Shakespeare to convey complex characters, themes, and emotions while maintaining a poetic and dramatic quality.

Modern Usage: Blank verse continues to be used in modern literature and drama. It is often employed when a poet or playwright desires the elevated and rhythmic qualities of verse without the constraints of rhyme.

Blank Prose: Prose that follows the pattern of iambic pentameter but lacks rhyme is sometimes referred to as "blank prose." While not as common as blank verse, it is occasionally used for its rhythmic and aesthetic qualities.

Narrative and Epic Poetry: Blank verse is also utilized in long narrative poems and epics. John Milton's "Paradise Lost" is a notable example of an epic poem written in blank verse.

Accessibility: Because it lacks rhyme, blank verse can be more accessible to modern readers and audiences who may find traditional rhymed verse to be old-fashioned or artificial.
It has been a prominent feature of English literature for centuries, employed by many notable poets and playwrights to convey both dramatic and narrative content with grace and rhythm.

Example of blank verse from Act 5, Scene 5 of William Shakespeare's play "Macbeth." In this scene, Macbeth reflects on the futility of life and the inevitability of death:
"To-morrow, and to-morrow, and to-morrow,
Creeps in this petty pace from day to day
To the last syllable of recorded time,
And all our yesterdays have lighted fools
The way to dusty death. Out, out, brief candle!
Life's but a walking shadow, a poor player
That struts and frets his hour upon the stage
And then is heard no more. It is a tale
Told by an idiot, full of sound and fury,
Signifying nothing."
In this passage, you can see the unrhymed lines of iambic pentameter, which are characteristic of blank verse. The rhythm and flow of the verse create a sense of solemnity and contemplation, making it a powerful example of this poetic form.

Another example of blank verse from William Wordsworth's poem "Lines Composed a Few Miles Above Tintern Abbey." In this poem, Wordsworth reflects on the beauty of nature and its impact on his life:

"Five years have past; five summers, with the length
Of five long winters! and again I hear
These waters, rolling from their mountain-springs
With a soft inland murmur. – Once again
Do I behold these steep and lofty cliffs,
Which on a wild secluded scene impress
Thoughts of more deep seclusion; and connect
The landscape with the quiet of the sky."

In this excerpt, Wordsworth uses unrhymed lines of iambic pentameter to convey his sense of nostalgia and the enduring beauty of the natural world. Blank verse allows him to express his thoughts and emotions in a structured yet conversational manner.

FREE VERSE

Free verse is a form of poetry that lacks the regular patterns of rhythm and rhyme found in traditional poetic forms like sonnets or blank verse. Unlike structured forms, free verse does not adhere to specific rules regarding meter, rhyme scheme, or line length. Instead, it offers poets greater freedom and flexibility in crafting their poems.

Some details about free verse:
Lack of Formal Structure: Free verse is characterised by its lack of formal structure. It does not rely on a regular meter, rhyme scheme, or other traditional conventions of poetry.

Natural Speech Patterns: Free verse often seeks to mimic the rhythms and patterns of natural speech. It can be more conversational and less constrained by traditional poetic techniques.

Variety in Line Length: In free verse, lines can vary in length, allowing the poet to emphasize certain words or ideas, create visual effects, or control the pacing of the poem.

Emphasis on Imagery and Language: Because free verse does not rely on traditional poetic forms, it often places a strong emphasis on imagery, language, and the poet's unique voice. Poets can experiment with word choice and metaphor to convey their messages.

Modern and Contemporary Usage: Free verse became more popular in the late 19th and early 20th centuries as poets sought to break away from traditional forms. It is often associated with the modernist and contemporary periods of poetry.

Notable Poets: Prominent poets known for their use of free verse include Walt Whitman, who is considered one of the pioneers of this form, as well as poets like T.S. Eliot, Langston Hughes, and Allen Ginsberg.

Freedom of Expression: Free verse provides poets with a platform for self-expression and experimentation. It allows them to explore unconventional themes, narratives, and emotions.

Here's an example of free verse from Walt Whitman's "Song of Myself," which showcases the form's use of natural speech rhythms and freedom from traditional constraints:
"I celebrate myself, and sing myself,
And what I assume you shall assume,
For every atom belonging to me as good belongs to you."
In this excerpt, you can see how Whitman's lines do not follow a strict meter or rhyme scheme, and the poem flows with a conversational tone.
Free verse remains a vibrant and important form in contemporary poetry, offering poets the freedom to explore new modes of expression and engage with a wide range of themes and subjects.

Here's another example of free verse from Langston Hughes, an influential American poet known for his use of this form.
This poem is titled "The Negro Speaks of Rivers":
"I've known rivers:
I've known rivers ancient as the world and older than the
flow of human blood in human veins.
My soul has grown deep like the rivers.
I bathed in the Euphrates when dawns were young.
I built my hut near the Congo and it lulled me to sleep.
I looked upon the Nile and raised the pyramids above it.
I heard the singing of the Mississippi when Abe Lincoln
went down to New Orleans, and I've seen its muddy
bosom turn all golden in the sunset.

I've known rivers:
Ancient, dusky rivers.
My soul has grown deep like the rivers."

In this poem, Langston Hughes celebrates the deep connection between African Americans and the world's great rivers, using free verse to capture the rich history and cultural significance of these rivers. The absence of a strict rhyme scheme or meter allows Hughes to convey his message with a sense of freedom and authenticity.

CAESURA

A caesura (pronounced "si-ZOO-rah") is a pause or break in a line of poetry, often occurring in the middle of a verse. This pause can be created by various means, such as punctuation, a natural pause in speech, or a shift in the rhythm of the poem. Caesuras are used for a variety of purposes in poetry, including emphasising specific words or ideas, creating a sense of rhythm, and conveying emotional depth.

Some details about caesura:

Types of Caesura:

Feminine Caesura: Occurs after a stressed syllable, followed by an unstressed syllable. For example, *"To be or not to be, | that is the question."*

Masculine Caesura: Occurs after a stressed syllable, followed by another stressed syllable. For example, *"It was the best of times, | it was the worst of times."*

Medial Caesura: Occurs in the middle of a line of poetry, often dividing it into two distinct parts. For example, *"It is the star | to every wandering bark."*

Purpose of Caesura:

Emphasis: Caesuras can emphasize certain words or ideas by placing a pause before or after them. This draws the reader's attention and highlights the significance of those words.

Rhythm: Caesuras can contribute to the overall rhythm and musicality of a poem. They create a sense of flow and pacing, similar to the way punctuation marks influence the structure of a sentence.

Dramatic Effect: Caesuras can add dramatic tension or emotional depth to a poem. They allow for a moment of reflection or contemplation within the verse.

Examples of Caesura:

In William Shakespeare's sonnet 18, there is a caesura in the middle of the first line: *"Shall I compare thee to a summer's day? | Thou art more lovely and more temperate."*

In John Milton's epic poem "Paradise Lost," caesuras are used throughout the work to enhance its epic and rhythmic qualities.

Effect on Poetry:

Caesuras are a valuable tool for poets to control the pacing and meaning of their verse. They can shape the reader's experience and interpretation of the poem.

Overall, caesuras play a significant role in the structure and interpretation of poetry. They provide poets with a means to create rhythm, emphasize words or ideas, and add depth to their work, contributing to the overall artistry of the poem.

ONOMATOPOEIA

Onomatopoeia is a literary device in which a word imitates or resembles the sound it represents. It's a way for writers to convey sensory experiences, especially auditory ones, by using words that sound like what they describe. Onomatopoeic words are often used to bring a vivid and immersive quality to a text, allowing readers to hear the sounds being described. Here are some details about onomatopoeia:

Types of Onomatopoeia: Onomatopoeic words can represent a wide range of sounds, including those related to nature (e.g., "buzz," "hiss"), human actions (e.g., "whisper," "slurp"), and mechanical noises (e.g., "clang," "beep").

Purpose of Onomatopoeia:

Sensory Imagery: Onomatopoeia helps create vivid sensory imagery by allowing readers to mentally hear the sounds described in the text.

Immersive Experience: It immerses readers more deeply in the narrative by engaging their senses and making the text more lifelike.

Expressive Emphasis: Onomatopoeic words can add emphasis or emotional resonance to a description, as the sound itself carries meaning or mood.

Examples of Onomatopoeia:

The "sizzle" of bacon frying in a pan.

The "crash" of waves against the shore.

The "whir" of a ceiling fan.

The "thud" of a heavy book hitting the floor.

The "moo" of a cow in the pasture.

The "chirp" of birds in the morning.

Effect in Poetry and Prose: Onomatopoeia is commonly used in both poetry and prose to enhance the sensory experience for readers. Poets often use it to create rhythm and auditory patterns, while prose writers use it to make descriptions more vibrant.

Cultural and Language Variations: Onomatopoeic words can vary between languages and cultures. Different languages may use different sounds to imitate the same phenomenon. For example, the English "buzz" for the sound of bees might be "bzzz" in another language.

Children's Literature: Onomatopoeia is frequently used in children's literature, as it can be both entertaining and educational for young readers who are learning to associate words with sounds.

Overall, onomatopoeia is a versatile and expressive literary device that adds richness and vividness to written language by bridging the gap between words and sensory experiences, particularly the auditory sense.

Examples of onomatopoeia:

"Crackle": The crackle of the campfire provided warmth and comfort on a cold night.

"Rustle": The leaves rustled in the gentle breeze, creating a soothing sound in the forest.

"Hoot": The owl let out a haunting hoot in the darkness, echoing through the woods.

"Swoosh": The basketball swooshed through the net, scoring a perfect three-pointer.

"Ping": The microwave emitted a sharp ping when the popcorn was ready to eat.

"Gurgle": The stream gurgled as it flowed over the smooth stones in the creek.

"Buzz": The alarm clock's incessant buzz jolted him awake on Monday morning.

"Creak": The old wooden floorboards creaked underfoot as she tiptoed through the haunted house.

"Slam": He heard the slam of the door as his angry neighbor stormed out of the house.

"Splash": The children's laughter echoed as they made a big splash in the swimming pool.

These examples illustrate how onomatopoeia can mimic various sounds in the real world, creating a sensory experience for readers and making descriptions more vivid and engaging.

REFRAIN

A refrain is a repeated line, phrase, or group of lines in a poem or song. It serves as a structural element that is repeated at specific intervals, typically at the end of stanzas or between verses. Refrains are often used in poetry and music to create rhythm, emphasise a theme or message, and provide a sense of unity and familiarity within a piece. They can have a powerful impact on the overall emotional and thematic resonance of a work.

Types of Refrains:
> Regular Refrain: Appears at consistent intervals in a poem or song, such as at the end of every stanza.
> Irregular Refrain: Appears at varying intervals or in a less predictable pattern, adding an element of surprise or emphasis.
> Incremental Refrain: Gradually changes or adds to the refrain with each repetition, building on the theme or story.

Purpose of Refrains:
> Rhythm and Musicality: Refrains contribute to the musical quality of a poem or song, creating a pattern that engages the reader or listener.
> Emphasis: They highlight a key message, theme, or emotion, reinforcing its significance.
> Unity: Refrains unify the text, providing cohesion and structure to the piece.
> Emotional Impact: Repeated refrains can intensify the emotional impact by emphasizing a feeling or idea.

Examples of Refrains:
> In the song "Hallelujah" by Leonard Cohen, the refrain "Hallelujah" is repeated at the end of each verse.
> In the poem "The Raven" by Edgar Allan Poe, the refrain "Nevermore" is repeated by the mysterious raven.

In the poem "Do Not Go Gentle into That Good Night" by Dylan Thomas, the refrain "Rage, rage against the dying of the light" appears at the end of each stanza.

Effect in Poetry and Music: Refrains are a common feature in both poetry and music, adding a layer of complexity and meaning to the work. They can create a sense of anticipation and anticipation as the audience awaits the familiar lines.

Variations: Poets and songwriters may use variations of the refrain to create nuance or emphasize different aspects of the theme. This can add depth and complexity to the work.

Refrains are a valuable poetic and musical device used to enhance the rhythm, emphasize key messages, and unify a piece of literature or song. Their repetition can create a memorable and emotional experience for the audience.

An example of a refrain from the poem "The Raven" by Edgar Allan Poe:

Once upon a midnight dreary, while I pondered, weak and weary,
Over many a quaint and curious volume of forgotten lore—
While I nodded, nearly napping, suddenly there came a tapping,
As of some one gently rapping, rapping at my chamber door.
"'Tis some visitor," I muttered, "tapping at my chamber door—
Only this and nothing more."

In this famous poem, the refrain "rapping at my chamber door" is repeated at the end of each stanza, creating a sense of anticipation and building on the eerie atmosphere of the poem. The refrain emphasizes the visitor's persistent tapping and contributes to the poem's haunting and melancholic mood.

"Sweet Thames, run softly till I end my song" is from T.S. Eliot's poem

"The Waste Land." Specifically, it appears in the third section of the poem, titled "The Fire Sermon." This modernist work is known for its complex layers of allusions and its fragmented narrative. The mention of the Thames River recalls both historical and mythological contexts, serving as a conduit to explore themes of decline, disillusionment, and cultural decay that are prevalent throughout "The Waste Land."
In "The Waste Land," this line evokes an image of the Thames River, and its repetition serves to underscore the significance of the river in the poem as well as anchor the reader in the setting and mood of this section. The repetition also connects different parts of the section and echoes the cyclical nature of rivers and life, all of which contribute to the poem's layered meanings.

The repetition of this line throughout the poem adds a sense of continuity and contemplation. It also reflects the theme of seeking solace and spiritual fulfillment, which is a recurring motif in T.S. Eliot's poetry.

RHYME SCHEME

A rhyme scheme is the pattern of rhymes at the end of each line in a poem. It is typically represented using letters to indicate which lines rhyme with each other. Rhyme schemes are a fundamental aspect of poetic structure and are used to create rhythm, musicality, and a sense of order in a poem. Different types of rhyme schemes can be employed to achieve various effects in poetry.

Couplet (AA): In a couplet, two consecutive lines rhyme with each other. The most common rhyme scheme for a couplet is AA. Example:
"The sun is shining bright today (A)
And flowers bloom in colorful array. (A)"

Quatrain (ABAB): In a quatrain, four lines are grouped together, and the first and third lines rhyme with each other (A), while the second and fourth lines rhyme with each other (B). Example:
"The moon is high up in the sky (A)
Casting a silver light. (B)
The stars twinkle, oh so high (A)
On this calm and peaceful night. (B)"

Tercet (ABA): In a tercet, three lines are grouped together, and the first and third lines rhyme with each other (A), while the second line does not rhyme (B). Example:
"The ocean waves crash on the shore (A)
With a mighty and thunderous roar. (B)
As seagulls circle and freely soar. (A)"
***Alternate Rhyme** (ABABCB): In this scheme, the rhymes alternate between lines, creating a pattern that combines couplets (AB) and a tercet (CB).*
Example:

"The river flows so calm and wide (A)
Reflecting the mountains on its side. (B)
The world is filled with beauty and grace (A)
As nature's wonders we embrace. (B)
Beneath the endless sky's embrace (C)
We find our peaceful, quiet space. (B)"

Sonnet (Various): Sonnets follow specific rhyme schemes depending on their type. For example, the Shakespearean or English sonnet typically follows the ABABCDCDEFEFGG rhyme scheme, while the Petrarchan or Italian sonnet often follows ABBAABBACDCDCD or ABBAABBACDECDE.
Example (Shakespearean Sonnet):
"Shall I compare thee to a summer's day? (A)
Thou art more lovely and more temperate: (B)
Rough winds do shake the darling buds of May, (A)
And summer's lease hath all too short a date: (B)"

These are just a few examples of common rhyme schemes in poetry. Different rhyme schemes can be used to create varying effects, emphasize certain lines or ideas, and contribute to the overall structure and musicality of a poem.

COUPLET

A couplet is a pair of consecutive lines of poetry that usually rhyme with each other. Couplets are a common and versatile form in poetry and can be found in various types of poems, from sonnets to limericks. They provide a sense of rhythm and symmetry to a poem and often serve to complete a thought or idea within the two l

Rhyming Pattern: In a couplet, the two lines typically rhyme with each other. The most common rhyme scheme for a couplet is AA, where both lines end with words that sound alike.
Example:
"The sky is clear, the stars are bright (A)
On this serene and tranquil night. (A)"

Independence: Each couplet can stand alone as a complete thought or idea, but they are often used in pairs to convey a larger message or story.
Example:
"The sun is setting in the west (A)
Painting the sky with hues of red. (A)"

Narrative and Emphasis: Couplets can be used to emphasize a particular point or to create a sense of narrative progression in a poem.
Example:
"He journeyed far to distant lands (A)
With dreams of treasures in his hands. (A)"

Structure: Couplets can be found in various forms of poetry, including sonnets, epigrams, and heroic couplets. Heroic couplets, in particular, are a common form in which each line is written in iambic pentameter and the rhyme scheme is AA.
Example (Heroic Couplet):

"To be or not to be, that is the question. (A)
Whether 'tis nobler in the mind to suffer (A)
The slings and arrows of outrageous fortune, (B)
Or to take arms against a sea of troubles (B)"

Humor and Wit: Couplets are often used in humorous and witty poetry, such as limericks and epigrams, where the rhyme and brevity contribute to the humor.
Example (Limerick):
"There once was a man from Peru (A)
Who dreamt he was eating his shoe. (A)
He woke with a fright (B)
In the middle of the night (B)
And found that his dream had come true. (A)"

A couplet is a pair of rhyming lines in poetry that can function as an independent unit or as part of a larger poem. They are a versatile form used to convey various emotions, ideas, and stories in poetry.

QUATRAIN

A quatrain is a four-line stanza or poem, and it is one of the most common and versatile forms in poetry. Quatrains can take on various rhyme schemes and have been used in a wide range of poetic styles and genres. The flexibility of the quatrain makes it a popular choice for poets to convey their thoughts, emotions, and n

Rhyme Scheme: Quatrains can have different rhyme schemes, but some of the most common ones include:

ABAB: In this rhyme scheme, the first and third lines rhyme with each other (A), and the second and fourth lines rhyme with each other (B).

Example (ABAB):

"The sun sets low behind the hills (A)
Painting the sky with shades of gold (B)
As darkness falls, the world grows still (A)
And nature's secrets it does hold (B)."

ABBA: In this rhyme scheme, the first and fourth lines rhyme with each other (A), and the second and third lines rhyme with each other (B).

Example (ABBA):

"The wind blows softly through the trees (A)
Whispers secrets on the breeze (B)
In the quiet of the night (B)
Everything seems just right (A)."

Structure: Quatrains can be found in various forms of poetry, including sonnets, ballads, and many traditional and modern poems.

Independence: Each quatrain often forms a complete thought or idea, making it possible to convey different aspects of a theme or story within the four lines.

Narrative and Emotion: Quatrains are commonly used in narrative poetry to advance a story or convey a series of events. They are also employed to express emotions, reflect on nature, or contemplate various aspects of life.

Variations: While the examples provided have regular and consistent rhyme schemes, poets can play with the structure of quatrains, using slant rhymes or variations in meter to create unique effects.
Example (Variation):
"The moon's pale light shines from afar (A)
A solitary beacon in the night (B)
It guides us with its gentle star (A)
Through darkness to the morning light (B)."

In summary, a quatrain is a four-line stanza or poem with different rhyme schemes that poets use to convey ideas, emotions, stories, and observations. Its versatility allows poets to adapt it to various purposes and styles, making it a fundamental and widely used form in poetry.

TERCET

A tercet is a three-line stanza or poem, and it is a common form in poetry. Tercets can take on various rhyme schemes and have been used in different styles and genres of poetry. The number of lines in a tercet provides poets with an opportunity to convey concise thoughts, emotions, and ideas.

Rhyme Scheme: Tercets can have different rhyme schemes, but one of the most common ones is the terza rima (ABA) rhyme scheme. In terza rima, the first and third lines rhyme with each other (A), and the second line sets up a new rhyme for the following tercet (B).
Example (Terza Rima):
"The sun sets low behind the hills (A)
Painting the sky with shades of gold (B)
As darkness falls, the world grows still (A)."

Structure: Tercets can be found in various forms of poetry, including terza rima, villanelles, and haikus, among others.

Independence: Each tercet often forms a complete thought or idea, making it possible to convey different aspects of a theme or story within the three lines.

Variations: Poets can use variations of tercets to create unique effects. For example, the terza rima structure can be extended into longer sequences, forming terza rima tercets.
Example (Extended Terza Rima Tercets):
"The river flows so calm and wide (A)
Reflecting the mountains on its side (B)
The moon's reflection in its tide (A)
A peaceful scene, there's nowhere to hide (B)."

Emotion and Observation: Tercets are often used to express emotions, reflect on nature, or convey observations succinctly. Example:

"A single rose in the morning light (A)
Unfolds its petals, red and bright (B)
A symbol of love, pure and white (A)."

TERZA RIMA

Terza rima is a specific type of tercet, a three-line stanza used in poetry, known for its unique rhyme scheme and origins in Italian poetry. Terza rima is characterized by its interlocking rhyme scheme, which creates a sense of continuity and progression in a poem.

Rhyme Scheme: Terza rima uses an ABA rhyme scheme, where the first and third lines of each tercet rhyme with each other, and the second line rhymes with the first and third lines of the following tercet. This interlocking pattern continues throughout the poem.

Example of Terza Rima:

The sun sets low behind the hills (A)
Painting the sky with shades of gold (B)
As darkness falls, the world grows still (A).
The stars emerge, a sight to behold (B)
In the tranquil, silent night's embrace (A)
Their twinkling lights, a story to be told (A).
As morning comes with its warm, gentle grace (B)
The world awakens, a new day to face (A).

Origin: Terza rima is closely associated with Italian poet Dante Alighieri, who used it extensively in his epic poem "The Divine Comedy," written in the 14th century. Dante's use of terza rima contributed to its popularity and recognition in the world of poetry.

Continuity: The interlocking rhyme scheme of terza rima creates a sense of continuity and progression in a poem. It allows the poet to move smoothly from one tercet to the next, connecting ideas and themes seamlessly.

Flexibility: While terza rima is often associated with Italian poetry, it has been used by poets writing in other languages as well. It is a versatile form that can be adapted to various themes and styles.

Longer Forms: Terza rima can be used to create longer poems, such as Dante's "The Divine Comedy," which consists of three books: "Inferno," "Purgatorio," and "Paradiso." Each book uses terza rima throughout.

In summary, terza rima is a poetic form characterized by its ABA rhyme scheme and interlocking structure. It is known for its association with Dante's "The Divine Comedy" and its ability to create a sense of continuity and progression in a poem.

SPENSERIAN STANZA

The Spenserian stanza is a verse form named after the English poet Edmund Spenser, who popularised its use in his epic poem "The Faerie Queene."

This stanza consists of nine lines with a specific rhyme and meter scheme, making it a distinctive and structured form in poetry.

The Spenserian stanza is known for its flexibility and ability to convey complex narratives and themes.

Rhyme Scheme: The Spenserian stanza follows the rhyme scheme ABABBCBCC. This means that the first and third lines of each stanza rhyme with each other (A), the second and fourth lines rhyme with each other (B), and the fifth, sixth, eighth, and ninth lines rhyme with each other (C).

Meter: The Spenserian stanza is traditionally written in iambic pentameter, which means each line has ten syllables with a pattern of unstressed and stressed syllables.

Example of a Spenserian Stanza:

A gentle knight was pricking on the plain, (A)
Yclad in mighty arms and silver shield; (B)
Wherein old dints of deep wounds did remain, (A)
The cruel marks of many a bloody field; (B)
Yet arms till that time did he never wield. (B)

His angry steed did chide his foaming bit, ©
As much disdaining to the curb to yield; (B)
Full jolly knight he seemed, and fair did sit, (C)
As one for knightly jousts and fierce encounters fit. (C)

Origin: The Spenserian stanza was popularized by Edmund Spenser in his epic poem "The Faerie Queene," which was published in the late 16th century. Spenser used this stanza to narrate the adventures of knights, allegorical characters, and epic battles.

Flexibility: While the traditional Spenserian stanza consists of nine lines, poets have occasionally used variations of this form, such as a shorter six-line stanza, maintaining the same rhyme scheme and meter. This flexibility allows poets to adapt the form to different purposes.

Narrative Power: The Spenserian stanza is well-suited for conveying intricate narratives, epic tales, and allegorical themes. Its rhyme and meter structure provide a sense of order and musicality while allowing for the development of complex stories and characters.

Elegance: The Spenserian stanza is often associated with a sense of elegance and refinement due to its structured nature and the use of iambic pentameter.

In summary, the Spenserian stanza is a structured verse form consisting of nine lines with the rhyme scheme ABABBCBCC. It was popularized by Edmund Spenser in "The Faerie Queene" and is known for its narrative capabilities and musicality. Its flexibility has allowed poets to adapt it to various poetic styles and themes.

OCTAVA RIMA

Octava rima is a traditional poetic form that consists of eight lines with a specific rhyme scheme and meter. This form is known for its flexibility and has been used in various languages and literary traditions. Octava rima is often associated with epic and narrative poetry, and it allows poets to convey complex stories and themes. Here are the key characteristics and details of octava rima:

Rhyme Scheme: Octava rima follows a consistent rhyme scheme of ABABABCC. This means that the first, second, fourth, fifth, sixth, and seventh lines rhyme with each other (ABABAB), while the third and eighth lines rhyme with each other (CC).
Meter: Traditionally, octava rima is written in iambic pentameter, which means each line consists of ten syllables with a pattern of unstressed and stressed syllables.
Example of Octava Rima:

A hero bold, with sword in hand, did stand (A)
And faced the dragon, fierce and cruel foe. (B)
He fought with valor, courage in command (A)
To free his land from dread and overthrow. (B)
The battle raged, with flames and smoke aglow (A)
But in the end, the dragon met defeat. (B)
The hero's name in legends will now flow (C)
For victory was sweet, and triumph's sweet. (C)

Origin: Octava rima has its roots in Italian literature and was used by Italian poets such as Ludovico Ariosto and Torquato Tasso. It gained popularity in Spanish and Portuguese literature as well.

Narrative Power: Octava rima is particularly well-suited for conveying narratives, epic tales, and stories with multiple plot developments. Its rhyme scheme and structured meter provide a sense of order and musicality, making it ideal for long-form storytelling.

Flexibility: While the traditional octava rima consists of eight lines, poets have occasionally used variations of this form, adjusting the number of lines to suit their purposes while maintaining the ABABABCC rhyme scheme.

Variations: Some poets have experimented with octava rima by using different meter patterns or by adding variations to the rhyme scheme. These variations can create unique effects in poetry. Literary Works: Octava rima has been used in notable literary works, including Ariosto's "Orlando Furioso" and Byron's "Don Juan," demonstrating its versatility in different literary traditions. In summary, octava rima is a structured poetic form consisting of eight lines with the rhyme scheme ABABABCC. It is known for its narrative capabilities and flexibility, making it suitable for conveying epic stories and themes in poetry.

CHORUS

In drama and poetry, a chorus is a group of characters who speak or sing in unison, often providing commentary, insight, or perspective on the events of the play or poem. The concept of a chorus has its origins in ancient Greek drama, particularly in the works of playwrights like Aeschylus, Sophocles, and Euripides. The chorus played a significant role in Greek tragedies and comedies.

Details and characteristics of a chorus in drama and poetry:
Group Dynamics: A chorus typically consists of multiple characters, often representing a collective voice, such as a group of citizens, elders, or participants in a religious ceremony. The chorus members act as a unified entity, sharing thoughts, emotions, and opinions.

Choral Odes: In Greek drama, the chorus would perform choral odes, which were lyrical and rhythmic passages of poetry or song. These odes were interspersed throughout the play and were used to reflect on the events, offer moral lessons, and express emotions.

Commentary and Reflection: The chorus serves as a bridge between the audience and the characters in the play. They provide commentary on the unfolding plot, offer insights into characters' motivations, and reflect on the themes and moral implications of the story.

Symbolism: In some cases, the chorus can symbolize broader societal or cultural attitudes, making their commentary relevant to the audience's own lives and experiences.

Structure: The structure and function of a chorus may vary depending on the play or poem. In ancient Greek drama, the chorus played a central role, while in later forms of drama, such as

Elizabethan theater, the chorus became less prominent.

Modern Usage: While the concept of a traditional chorus is less common in modern drama, it has been adapted and reimagined in various ways. In some contemporary plays, the chorus may be represented by a group of characters who provide commentary or by a single character who serves a similar function.

Musical Elements: In addition to spoken dialogue, choruses in some dramatic works include musical elements, such as songs, chants, or musical accompaniment.

Examples: Some famous examples of choruses in ancient Greek drama include the chorus in Sophocles' "Antigone" and the chorus in Aeschylus' "The Oresteia." In modern theater, examples can be found in works like William Shakespeare's "Henry V," where the chorus addresses the audience directly.

In summary, a chorus in drama and poetry represents a group of characters who offer commentary, insight, and perspective on the events and themes of the work. While it originated in ancient Greek drama, the concept of a chorus has evolved and been adapted in various ways in the history of theater and literature

TONE OF THE POEM

The tone of a poem refers to the poet's attitude or emotional stance toward the subject matter or the audience. Tone can encompass a wide range of emotions and perspectives, and it greatly influences how readers interpret and experience the poem. Poets use various literary devices and language choices to convey tone in their poems.

Here are some common tones found in poetry:

Elegiac: The tone of an elegiac poem is one of sorrow, mourning, or lamentation. It often expresses a sense of loss or longing, as in poems written in memory of someone who has passed away.

Joyful: A joyful tone conveys happiness, celebration, or exuberance. Poems with this tone may express delight, triumph, or a sense of wonder.

Melancholic: A melancholic tone reflects a deep sadness, sorrow, or melancholy. These poems often explore themes of sadness, loss, or the fleeting nature of happiness.

Confident: A confident tone conveys a strong sense of belief or assurance. Poems with this tone may express certainty, conviction, or self-assuredness.

Reflective: A reflective tone suggests introspection and contemplation. These poems often explore thoughts, memories, or philosophical ideas.

Hopeful: A hopeful tone conveys optimism and a positive outlook. Poems with this tone may inspire or uplift the reader, often exploring themes of hope and resilience.

Satirical: A satirical tone is marked by humor, irony, or sarcasm. These poems often critique or mock human behavior, institutions, or social norms.

Romantic: A romantic tone expresses love, passion, or idealized emotions. These poems often explore themes of love, desire, and the beauty of the natural world.

Angry: An angry tone conveys strong resentment, indignation, or outrage. Poems with this tone may express frustration or protest against injustice.

Mysterious: A mysterious tone creates a sense of intrigue, uncertainty, or enigma. These poems often use ambiguity and symbolism to engage the reader's imagination.

Playful: A playful tone is light-hearted, fun, or whimsical. Poems with this tone may use wordplay, humor, or a childlike sense of wonder.

Serious: A serious tone suggests gravity, solemnity, or a sense of importance. These poems often address weighty subjects or moral dilemmas.

It's important to note that a poem can contain multiple tones or shift in tone throughout the text. Understanding the tone of a poem is essential for interpreting its overall meaning and emotional impact. Poets carefully choose their words and imagery to convey the desired tone and evoke specific emotions in the reader.

MOOD OF THE POEM

The mood of a poem refers to the emotional atmosphere or feeling that the poem conveys to the reader. It is the overall emotional tone or ambiance that the poet creates through various elements of the poem, including imagery, language, and subject matter. The mood can evoke a specific emotional response in the reader, such as joy, sadness, fear, or tranquility. Here are some common moods found in poetry:

Joyful: A poem with a joyful mood conveys happiness, contentment, or celebration. It may inspire feelings of delight or positivity in the reader.

Melancholic: A melancholic mood creates a sense of sadness, sorrow, or introspection. Poems with this mood may evoke feelings of longing or nostalgia.

Eerie: An eerie mood produces a feeling of unease, mystery, or discomfort. It often involves elements of the supernatural or the unknown.

Serene: A serene mood conveys a sense of calm, tranquility, or peacefulness. It may evoke feelings of relaxation or inner peace.

Tense: A tense mood generates a feeling of anxiety, suspense, or anticipation. It often keeps the reader on edge and creates a sense of unease.

Hopeful: A hopeful mood inspires optimism and a positive outlook. Poems with this mood may convey a sense of possibility or renewal.

Romantic: A romantic mood is characterized by love, passion, or sensuality. It often evokes emotions related to desire and intimacy.

Mysterious: A mysterious mood creates a sense of intrigue, curiosity, or ambiguity. It invites the reader to explore the unknown.

Reflective: A reflective mood encourages introspection and contemplation. Poems with this mood often invite the reader to ponder life's complexities.

Whimsical: A whimsical mood is playful, light-hearted, and fanciful. It may involve humor or a sense of childlike wonder.

Dark: A dark mood conveys foreboding, gloom, or despair. It often explores themes of loss, tragedy, or existential angst.

Nostalgic: A nostalgic mood evokes feelings of longing for the past or a sense of wistfulness. It often centers on memories and reminiscences.

Uplifting: An uplifting mood inspires feelings of encouragement, motivation, or empowerment. It may convey a sense of triumph over adversity.

Angry: An angry mood expresses strong resentment, indignation, or outrage. Poems with this mood often critique or protest against injustice.

Surreal: A surreal mood creates a dreamlike or fantastical atmosphere. It often involves bizarre or surreal imagery and defies conventional reality.

The mood of a poem can be subtle or intense, and it plays a significant role in how readers connect with and interpret the poem's emotional impact. Poets use various techniques and choices in their writing to establish and manipulate the mood, allowing them to convey specific emotions and themes to their audience.

REPARTEE

Repartee is a form of quick and witty verbal exchange or conversation characterized by clever responses, humor, and sharp wit. It often involves a rapid back-and-forth between individuals who engage in witty and playful banter. Repartee is commonly associated with humor and intelligence, as it requires the ability to think quickly and respond with clever or humorous remarks.
Key features of repartee include:
Quick Thinking: Repartee involves thinking on one's feet and responding swiftly to remarks or comments from others. It often occurs spontaneously in the course of a conversation.

Cleverness: Repartee is marked by clever and witty responses. Participants often use wordplay, puns, double meanings, and irony to create humor and make their point.

Humor: Humor is a central element of repartee. The exchanges are often designed to amuse and entertain, and they may involve self-deprecating humor or playful teasing.

Wordplay: Repartee frequently employs wordplay and linguistic devices to create clever and memorable responses. These may include clever metaphors, similes, and allusions.

Verbal Duel: In some cases, repartee can escalate into a friendly verbal duel, where participants try to outwit each other with their responses.

Context-Dependent: Repartee is often context-dependent and may involve references to the ongoing conversation, current events, or shared knowledge between the participants.

Social Interaction: Repartee is a form of social interaction and can be used to build rapport, establish camaraderie, or engage in playful teasing with others.

Repartee is commonly seen in literature, theater, film, and real-life conversations. It is a valuable skill in comedy, improvisational theater, and witty discourse. Famous literary works and characters, such as Oscar Wilde's comedies and the exchanges between Sherlock Holmes and Dr. Watson, often feature memorable examples of repartee.
Overall, repartee adds an element of humor, wit, and liveliness to conversations and interactions, making it an engaging and enjoyable form of verbal exchange.

CANTO

In literature, a "canto" is a division or section of a long poem or epic. The term is particularly associated with epic poetry and narrative poems. Cantos are used to organize and structure the narrative, making it easier for readers to navigate through the poem's content. The concept of cantos has been employed in various literary traditions, but it is most commonly associated with two famous works: Dante Alighieri's "Divine Comedy" and Edmund Spenser's "The Faerie Queene."
Here are some key points about cantos:
Epic Poetry: Cantos are most frequently used in epic poetry, which is a genre of poetry that tells a long and heroic story. Epic poems often feature grand themes, heroic characters, and adventurous journeys.

Division and Organization: Epic poems can be quite lengthy, and cantos are used to divide them into manageable sections. Each canto typically deals with a specific episode or part of the larger narrative.

Narrative Progression: Cantos often follow a chronological or thematic progression, allowing the poem to unfold in a structured manner. They help readers follow the plot and character developments.

Common in "The Divine Comedy": Dante Alighieri's "The Divine Comedy," which consists of three parts (Inferno, Purgatorio, and Paradiso), is divided into a total of 100 cantos. Each part contains 33 cantos, except for Inferno, which has an additional introductory canto, resulting in 34 cantos.

Common in "The Faerie Queene": Edmund Spenser's "The Faerie Queene" is divided into six books, and each book is further divided into cantos. The poem is known for its intricate allegorical structure and rich use of cantos to advance the narrative.

Variability: The length and structure of cantos can vary from one epic poem to another. Some may consist of only a few stanzas, while others can be quite long.

Versification: The style and form of the verses within a canto can also vary depending on the poet's choice. Some cantos may feature rhyme and meter, while others may use blank verse or other poetic forms.

Overall, cantos serve as a structural element in epic poetry, allowing poets to create a sense of progression and organization within their lengthy narratives. They help readers engage with the epic's complex themes and characters, making it easier to follow the story and its various episodes.

An example of a canto from Dante Alighieri's "Inferno," the first part of his epic poem "The Divine Comedy." This canto is Canto I, the opening canto of "Inferno," and it sets the stage for Dante's journey through the realms of the afterlife:

In the middle of the journey of our life,
I found myself in a dark wood,
For the straight way had been lost.
Ah, how hard it is to tell
What that wood was, wild, rough, and harsh,
The thought of it renews my fear!
It is so bitter that death is hardly more so.
But to treat of the good that I found there,
I will tell of the other things I saw there.
How I got into it, I cannot really say,
I was so full of sleep at that point
That I strayed from the path.
But when I had reached the foot of a hill

Where the valley, that had pierced my heart
With fear, came to an end.

This canto introduces Dante's journey through the dark forest and
sets the tone for the entire epic. It represents his spiritual and
emotional struggle and his quest for redemption. "Inferno" is
divided into a total of 34 cantos, and each canto describes different
circles of Hell, each with its own punishments and inhabitants, as
Dante moves deeper into the afterlife.

DRAMATIC MONOLOGUE

A dramatic monologue is a poetic form in which a single character, typically the speaker, addresses a silent or implied audience, revealing their inner thoughts, emotions, and reflections. The character's speech provides insight into their personality, motivations, and perspective on a particular situation or theme. Dramatic monologues allow poets to create a vivid portrayal of a character's psyche and to explore complex psychological and moral issues. This form of poetry is often used to reveal the speaker's hidden desires, conflicts, and self-awareness. Robert Browning is particularly known for his skillful use of dramatic monologues. Here are some key features of dramatic monologues:
Speaker and Audience: The speaker of a dramatic monologue is a distinct character with their own voice, thoughts, and experiences. The audience is implied or inferred, often representing a listener or reader who receives the speaker's words.

Revelation of Character: The monologue provides an opportunity for the character to reveal their true self, sometimes in a way that contrasts with their outward appearance or actions. The speaker's honesty and self-disclosure contribute to the depth of characterisation.

Psychological Exploration: Dramatic monologues delve into the psychological landscape of the speaker, exposing their inner conflicts, motivations, and emotions. The form allows for a deep exploration of the human mind and psyche.

Unreliable Narrators: Some dramatic monologues feature speakers whose perspectives may be biased, self-serving, or unreliable. This can create tension and intrigue as readers piece together the truth from the speaker's words.

Setting and Context: The monologue is often situated within a specific setting or situation, providing context for the speaker's words. The setting can influence the speaker's tone, emotions, and choices of expression.

Themes and Ideas: Dramatic monologues are a powerful way to explore complex themes, moral dilemmas, and philosophical ideas. The speaker's internal struggles and reflections can offer insight into broader human experiences.

Variety of Subjects: The subjects of dramatic monologues can range from personal relationships and conflicts to societal issues, historical events, and abstract concepts. The form allows for versatility in exploring different topics.

Distinct Narrative Voice: Each dramatic monologue has a unique narrative voice that reflects the character's background, personality, and speech patterns. The language and style of the monologue are crafted to match the speaker's identity.

Notable examples of poets known for their use of dramatic monologues, in addition to Robert Browning, include T.S. Eliot, Alfred Lord Tennyson, and Browning's contemporary, Alfred Lord Tennyson. Dramatic monologues continue to be a popular and effective form for poets to delve into the intricacies of human psychology and offer readers insights into the complexity of human nature.

Mythological References in a poem as a literary device

Using mythological references in poetry is a literary device that helps poets tap into shared cultural narratives, imbue their work with layers of meaning, and create connections between the past and the present. These references can offer readers a rich tapestry of symbolism, themes, and emotional resonances, drawing on stories that have been told and retold for centuries.

Greek Mythology:

Icarus: The story of Icarus, who flew too close to the sun with wax wings and fell to his death, is often invoked to illustrate the dangers of hubris. W.H. Auden's "Musée des Beaux Arts" comments on how tragedies (like Icarus's fall) can be overlooked in the daily grind of life. The poem references Brueghel's painting in which Icarus's dramatic fall is depicted as a minor event in the background.

Narcissus: Narcissus, who fell in love with his reflection and became the namesake for narcissism, is another popular reference. In her poem "Echo," Carol Ann Duffy uses the myth of Narcissus and Echo to explore themes of unrequited love and self-obsession.

Roman Mythology:

Venus and Mars: The love affair between Venus, the goddess of love, and Mars, the god of war, has been a symbolic representation of the intertwining of opposites. In his poem "Venus and Mars," Robert Bridges contrasts the sensual love of Venus with the aggressive nature of Mars.

Janus: The Roman god of beginnings, gates, transitions, time, duality, doorways, and endings is often referenced to represent duality or change. In "January," Alice Meynell uses Janus to symbolize the transition and reflection as one year changes into the next.

Tiresias: T.S. Eliot uses the blind prophet Tiresias, who features in both Greek and Roman myths, as a central figure in "The Waste Land." Tiresias, having lived as both a man and a woman, serves as a symbol of unity, bringing together the poem's various voices and visions.

Leda and the Swan: W.B. Yeats's "Leda and the Swan" is a vivid retelling of Zeus, in the form of a swan, assaulting and impregnating Leda, leading to the birth of Helen of Troy. Yeats uses the story to delve into the interplay of power, innocence, beauty, and historical inevitability.

By integrating these myths into their works, poets create multiple layers of meaning. Readers familiar with the myths can appreciate the nuances and associations the poet intends, while those unfamiliar with them can still appreciate the broader themes and emotions of the poem. Moreover, such references lend the poem a sense of timelessness and universality, connecting modern emotions and situations to ancient tales of love, tragedy, and transformation.

Indian mythology is rich with stories, characters, and teachings that have influenced literature, including poetry, for millennia. Just as Greek and Roman myths are woven into Western literary traditions, Indian myths from the Vedas, Puranas, Mahabharata, Ramayana, and other sources have been invoked by writers to deepen the thematic content and enhance the symbolic resonance of their works. Here are some notable Indian mythological allusions used in literature:

Krishna and Radha: Their divine love story is symbolic of the ultimate love, sometimes representing the relationship between humanity and God. Many classical Indian poems and songs, particularly in the Bhakti tradition, use the love of Radha and

Krishna to convey the depth and intensity of devotional love.

Rama and Sita: The central figures of the Ramayana, their story often represents righteousness, dharma, and the trials of life. The separation of Sita and Rama, due to the actions of the demon king Ravana, has been used metaphorically in literature to depict separation, longing, and eventual reunion.

Shiva and Parvati: Shiva's dance as Nataraja, the cosmic dancer, symbolizes the dynamic forces of creation and destruction. His relationship with Parvati, his consort, exemplifies the divine union of male and female energies. Their stories, including the birth of their son Ganesha, are often used to illustrate the power of devotion, the merging of opposites, and the cyclical nature of life.

Draupadi's Disrobing: A crucial episode from the Mahabharata, where Draupadi, the wife of the Pandavas, is humiliated in the Kaurava court. This incident has been allegorically used in literature to comment on the mistreatment of women, the breakdown of dharma, and the consequences of unchecked power.

Karna's Sacrifice: Another character from the Mahabharata, Karna's life is fraught with tragedy, sacrifice, and questions of identity. His unwavering loyalty and tragic death are symbolic of the complexities of duty, morality, and the human condition.

Ahalya's Transformation: Ahalya, a beautiful woman, was turned into stone due to a curse and was later redeemed by Lord Rama's touch. This story has been used in literature as a metaphor for purity, redemption, and the transformative power of divine grace.

Modern Indian writers in English, like R.K. Narayan, Salman Rushdie, and Chitra Banerjee Divakaruni, have often employed these mythological allusions to bridge the ancient with the contemporary, providing commentary on current societal issues, human relationships, and spiritual quests.

Using Indian mythological allusions allows writers to tap into the collective unconscious of their readers, leveraging centuries of storytelling and moral lessons to enhance the depth and breadth of their own narratives.

Indian poets have frequently employed mythological references in their works to add depth, evoke emotions, or draw parallels with contemporary themes. Here are some examples from poems that utilize Indian mythological allusions:

A.K. Ramanujan's "A River": In this poem, Ramanujan contrasts the ancient poets' grand descriptions of the river Vaigai, with its modern reality. He alludes to the tale of the Pandya king, who supposedly never saw the river in spate, and the story of Siva burning the ancient city of Madurai. These references serve to highlight the gap between the mythic past and the prosaic present.

Jayanta Mahapatra's "Dawn at Puri": The poem refers to Krishna as "Jagannatha, Lord of the World." The atmosphere of the temple town Puri is beautifully interwoven with images that are steeped in Indian mythology and spirituality.

Toru Dutt's "Sita": This poem is a direct exploration of the character of Sita from the Ramayana. Through her retelling, Dutt delves deep into Sita's emotions, making her a symbol of feminine strength and resilience.

Sarojini Naidu's "In the Bazaars of Hyderabad": While the poem primarily describes the vibrant bazaars of Hyderabad, it includes references to the gods and goddesses, such as "Coral and amber" for Vishnu and Lakshmi, or "wristlet and anklet and ring" for Radha.

Kamala Das's "The Dance of the Eunuchs": Though not a direct retelling, the imagery of the eunuchs' dance can be associated with the cosmic dance of Shiva, symbolizing both creation and destruction.

Rabindranath Tagore's various works: Tagore's poems and songs are replete with mythological allusions. In many of his works, he uses Radha and Krishna to symbolize the relationship between humanity and the divine.

When poets employ these mythological allusions, they tap into a shared cultural and spiritual heritage, imbuing their poems with layers of meaning that resonate deeply with those familiar with the tales. The myths provide a rich tapestry of symbols, characters, and narratives that poets can draw upon to enrich their own works.

CRITICAL APPRECIATION OF A POEM

A critical appreciation of a poem involves a detailed analysis and evaluation of its various elements, such as language, imagery, themes, structure, and literary devices. The goal is to deeply understand the poem's meaning, uncover its layers of significance, and discuss its artistic and literary qualities. Here's a step-by-step guide on how to approach a critical appreciation of a poem:
Read the Poem: Begin by reading the poem multiple times to familiarize yourself with its content and overall tone.

Understand the Poet's Background: Research the poet's life, historical context, and any relevant biographical information that might shed light on the poem's themes and motifs.

Analyze the Title: Consider how the title relates to the poem's content. Titles often offer insights into the central themes or ideas.

Examine the Structure and Form:
> Identify the rhyme scheme, if any, and its impact on the poem's rhythm and tone.
> Note the stanza pattern and line length. Does the structure contribute to the poem's meaning?
> Consider the use of punctuation and line breaks. How do they affect the poem's flow and meaning?

Explore Language and Imagery:
> Examine the diction (word choice) and its connotations. Are there words that hold specific meanings or evoke emotions?
> Analyze the use of figurative language, such as metaphors, similes, personification, and symbols. How do they enhance the poem's meaning?
> Identify sensory details and imagery that create vivid mental pictures and evoke emotions.

Identify Themes and Message:

Determine the central themes or messages conveyed by the poem.

Look for recurring motifs or symbols that contribute to the themes.

Consider Tone and Mood:

Analyze the poet's tone, which is their attitude toward the subject matter. Is it joyful, melancholic, critical, etc.?

Discuss the mood the poem creates for the reader. How does the language and imagery contribute to this mood?

Evaluate Literary Devices:

Explore the use of literary devices such as alliteration, assonance, consonance, and onomatopoeia. How do they affect the poem's rhythm and meaning?

Examine the use of enjambment (continuing a sentence or phrase beyond the end of a line) and its impact on the poem's pacing.

Consider Title-Relevance: Reflect on how the title connects to the content, themes, and motifs of the poem. Does it take on new meaning after reading the poem?

Personal Response: Share your personal reaction to the poem. How did it make you feel, and what thoughts or emotions did it evoke?

Contextualize the Poem: Consider the historical, cultural, or social context in which the poem was written. How might these factors influence its meaning?

Compare and Contrast: If relevant, discuss how the poem compares or contrasts with other works by the same poet or within the same genre.

Summarise and Conclude: Sum up your analysis by highlighting the key points you've discussed. Conclude with a statement about the poem's significance, its impact on readers, or its contribution to the poet's body of work.

Remember that critical appreciation involves not just understanding the poem's literal meaning but also delving into its deeper layers of interpretation and aesthetic qualities.

An Example of Critical Appreciation Of a Poem

DAFFODILS BY WILLIAM WORDSWORTH

I wandered lonely as a cloud
That floats on high o'er vales and hills,
When all at once I saw a crowd,
A host, of golden daffodils;
Beside the lake, beneath the trees,
Fluttering and dancing in the breeze.

Continuous as the stars that shine
And twinkle on the milky way,
They stretched in never-ending line
Along the margin of a bay:
Ten thousand saw I at a glance,
Tossing their heads in sprightly dance.

The waves beside them danced; but they
Out-did the sparkling waves in glee:
A poet could not but be gay,
In such a jocund company:
I gazed—and gazed—but little thought
What wealth the show to me had brought:

For oft, when on my couch I lie
In vacant or in pensive mood,
They flash upon that inward eye
Which is the bliss of solitude;
And then my heart with pleasure fills,
And dances with the daffodils.

"Daffodils" by William Wordsworth: A Critical Appreciation and Summary

William Wordsworth, one of the foremost Romantic poets of the 19th century, held a deep reverence for nature. His poetry often explored the relationship between man and the natural world, emphasizing the solace and profound insights nature offers. Written in 1804 and published in 1807, "Daffodils" stands as a quintessential example of Wordsworth's poetic philosophy and his ability to draw deep emotional resonance from simple observations of nature.

The poem unfolds with the poet's portrayal of himself as a solitary figure, wandering "lonely as a cloud" through valleys and hills. This imagery of solitude sets the tone, positioning the poet as a quiet observer. His solitude, however, is soon disrupted by a magnificent sight: a vast field of golden daffodils. Situated beside a tranquil lake and underneath the trees, these daffodils appear to be dancing, fluttering in the wind, a spectacle that captures the poet's imagination instantly.

Wordsworth's use of vivid imagery paints a vibrant landscape in the reader's mind. He likens the continuous stretch of daffodils to the stars that sprawl across the Milky Way, emphasizing their abundance and luminosity. The adjacent lake with its dancing waves, though animated, pales in comparison to the allure of the daffodils. This juxtaposition underlines nature's capacity to evoke wonder in myriad ways.

Beyond the immediate sensory experience, Wordsworth delves into introspection. While the scene delights him, he confesses an initial unawareness of its profound emotional impact. It's only in moments of reflection that he comprehends the depth of tranquility and joy this memory imparts.

Literary devices pepper the poem, enhancing its emotive qualities. The alliteration in "continuous as the stars that shine" lends a musical quality, while the simile of the daffodils' continuous spread being like the stars in the Milky Way amplifies the scene's grandeur.

Musically, the poem's rhythm and rhyme scheme add to its charm, rendering it both melodic and memorable. Wordsworth's language remains simple yet evocative, allowing readers of all backgrounds to connect with his experience. The overall tone, encompassing awe, tranquility, and introspection, invites readers to find joy in nature's everyday spectacles.

In the concluding stanzas, Wordsworth underscores the enduring impact of this experience. The memory of the daffodils becomes a beacon of hope and comfort, a source of perpetual joy that invigorates his spirit in moments of solitude or melancholy.

One of the poem's most renowned lines, "For oft, when on my couch I lie, In vacant or in pensive mood," encapsulates the transformative power of nature's memories. They serve as an emotional reservoir, offering solace and rejuvenation.

In essence, "Daffodils" isn't just a testament to a single experience but resonates as an ode to nature's eternal influence on the human psyche. It exemplifies the Romantic era's emphasis on personal emotion, nature, and individual experience. Through this piece, Wordsworth encourages readers to observe, appreciate, and draw inspiration from the natural world, finding in its beauty a timeless source of joy and reflection.

Critical Appreciation of "Daffodils" by William Wordsworth

About the Poet:
William Wordsworth (1770-1850) was a major English Romantic poet. His love for nature and his emphasis on the simplicity of life and the purity of heart have made him stand out in the history of English literature. He held the view that poetry should be the spontaneous overflow of powerful feelings, which can be observed in much of his work.

About the Poem:
"Daffodils" is one of Wordsworth's most celebrated pieces, depicting the beauty of a field filled with golden daffodils. It captures the essence of the Romantic Period, celebrating the beauty of nature and the lasting emotional and introspective impact it can have on the individual.

When was it Written:
The poem was written in 1804, inspired by an actual walk Wordsworth took with his sister Dorothy in the Lake District. It was published in 1807 in "Poems in Two Volumes".

Background:
Wordsworth was known for drawing inspiration from nature, seeing it as a source of solace, insight, and even transcendence. The daffodils, in this instance, serve as a representation of nature's power to uplift the human spirit, even in moments of solitude and introspection.

Critical Analysis:
The poem presents an intricate balance between the tangible, physical beauty of the daffodils and the profound, emotional reaction they evoke in the poet. By juxtaposing the daffodils with the vastness of the galaxy — "continuous as the stars that shine and twinkle on the Milky Way" — Wordsworth emphasizes the infinite beauty found in the simplicity of nature.

Literary Terms Used:

Imagery: The poem is replete with vibrant images such as "golden daffodils" and "fluttering and dancing in the breeze."
Metaphor: The daffodils are likened to stars in the Milky Way.
Personification: The daffodils are described as "dancing."
Musical Devices Used:
Rhyme: The poem has a rhyme scheme of ABABCC.
Rhythm: The poem utilizes iambic tetrameter, giving it a rhythmic flow.
Language:
Wordsworth uses simple yet evocative language. The choice of words like "lonely," "crowd," and "glee" evokes a range of emotions, from solitude to exuberance.
Mood
Reflective and introspective, with moments of revelation and joy.
Tone:
The tone shifts from a calm recollection to an exuberant celebration of nature's beauty and its everlasting impact on the poet's heart.
Moral:
The poem emphasises the rejuvenating power of nature. It suggests that even a fleeting moment with nature can have a lasting, joyful impact on the human soul.
Famous Lines:
"For oft, when on my couch I lie
In vacant or in pensive mood,
They flash upon that inward eye
Which is the bliss of solitude"

"Daffodils" stands as a testament to Wordsworth's profound love for nature and his keen observation of its myriad wonders. It captures the universality of a personal experience and underscores the timeless value of finding joy in life's simple pleasures.

RHETORICAL DEVICES

A rhetorical device is a technique used by writers or speakers to convey their message more effectively or persuasively to an audience. These tools, rooted in the art of rhetoric, are designed to invoke specific reactions or emotions, emphasize particular points, or provide clarity or eloquence to an argument. Whether used in literature, speeches, advertisements, or everyday conversations, rhetorical devices enhance communication by adding layers of meaning, creating memorable phrases, or appealing to the audience's intellect and emotions.

Rhetorical devices encompass a wide range of strategies, from simple figures of speech like metaphors and similes to more complex constructs like antitheses or syllogisms. While some devices, like alliteration or onomatopoeia, focus on the sound and rhythm of words, others, such as hyperbole or irony, play with meaning and expectation. The artful application of these devices can elevate a text or speech, making it more engaging, persuasive, or memorable.

ANADIPLOSIS

Anadiplosis is a rhetorical device in which a word or phrase from the end of one sentence or clause is repeated at the beginning of the next sentence or clause. This technique creates a chain-like progression where the end and start of successive clauses are linked. It serves various purposes, such as emphasizing a particular point, creating a rhythmic flow, and enhancing the artistry or poetic nature of the prose or verse.

The effect of anadiplosis is often a build-up of emotion or logic, giving the content a compelling and persuasive edge. By creating continuity and a logical progression from one idea to the next, anadiplosis can also make complex ideas easier to follow and more memorable.

Example 1: In Shakespeare's "Hamlet," the titular character says, *"The world is not thy friend, nor the world's law; The world affords no law to make thee rich; Then be not poor, but break it, and take this."*
Example 2: *"Fear leads to anger. Anger leads to hate. Hate leads to suffering."* - Yoda in "Star Wars: The Phantom Menace"

In both examples, the repetition of words at the end and beginning of successive statements lends a sense of urgency, rhythm, and cohesion to the sentiments expressed.

ANTIMETABOLE

Antimetabole is a rhetorical device in which consecutive clauses or phrases are presented in inverse or reverse order to produce a balancing effect. It's a form of chiasmus where the same words are used in the mirrored structure, often to emphasize contrast or to reinforce a particular message or idea. The repetition and inversion can make the message more memorable, and the contrasting structure can add emphasis or clarity to the point being made. The effect of antimetabole is to offer a fresh perspective on a familiar idea or to underscore the inherent contrasts within a concept. It can make statements sound more profound or thought-provoking and can be especially effective in highlighting the dualities or contradictions in life.

Example 1: *"Ask not what your country can do for you, ask what you can do for your country."* - John F. Kennedy
Example 2: *"When the going gets tough, the tough get going."*
Example 3: *"If you fail to plan, you plan to fail."*

In each of these examples, the inversion of the words or phrases provides a striking way to drive home the point. Kennedy's iconic line emphasizes civic duty; the popular proverb about toughness emphasizes resilience in the face of challenges, and the statement about planning underscores the importance of preparation. By using antimetabole, each message is delivered in a way that's both memorable and impactful.

ASYNDETON

Asyndeton is a rhetorical device in which conjunctions are deliberately omitted from a series of related clauses. This absence of conjunctions can accelerate the rhythm of the prose, emphasizing the items in the list or highlighting their significance. By omitting the expected conjunctions, the writer or speaker can create a more concise, rapid, or dramatic effect.

The use of asyndeton can imbue a passage with a sense of urgency or intensity. It can give the impression of spontaneity or unpremeditated thought. Additionally, it often draws more attention to each individual item or idea by removing the "and" or "or" that would typically link them, thereby suggesting that each item is of equal importance.

Example 1: "I came, I saw, I conquered." - Julius Caesar

Example 2: "Without looking, without making a sound, without talking."

Example 3: "He was a soldier, a hero, a leader."

In the first example from Julius Caesar, the asyndeton gives a quick, decisive feel to the statement, emphasizing the swift action taken by Caesar. The second example generates a sense of quiet, secretive movement, and the third emphasizes each of the person's roles with equal weight. In all cases, the use of asyndeton makes the passage more impactful and memorable by stripping away the conjunctions that might otherwise slow down the rhythm or dilute the emphasis.

CHIASMUS

Chiasmus is a rhetorical device in which two or more parallel clauses are inverted or flipped, so that the structure of the first clause is mirrored in the second. This reversal can involve words, grammatical constructs, or ideas, creating a symmetrical or "crossed" structure, which can lend balance, artistry, or emphasis to a statement. The name "chiasmus" is derived from the Greek letter "chi," which is shaped like an "X," representing the crisscross pattern often found in this device.

A primary function of chiasmus is to create a poetic or thought-provoking effect, often driving home a particular point or highlighting a contrast. It encourages readers or listeners to pay closer attention, re-evaluate, or see connections between mirrored elements.

Example 1: *"Ask not what your country can do for you, ask what you can do for your country."* - John F. Kennedy

Example 2: *"By day the frolic, and the dance by night."* - Samuel Butler

Example 3: *"She has all my love; my heart belongs to her."*

In the first example by JFK, the mirrored structure emphasizes the reciprocal relationship between citizens and their country. The second example from Samuel Butler offers a balanced view of the activities of day and night. The third example showcases the synonymous relationship between love and the heart in an artistic manner. In each instance, chiasmus adds an element of elegance and depth, making the sentiment both memorable and impactful.

EPIZEUXIS

Epizeuxis is a rhetorical device where a word or phrase is repeated in immediate succession, typically with no intervening words, for emphasis or to convey strong emotion. This deliberate repetition aims to drive a point home, evoke an emotion, or highlight the importance of the word or idea being repeated. It's often used to express a deep feeling, an urgent appeal, or a profound conviction. The term "epizeuxis" is derived from the Greek word meaning "to fasten together."

The power of epizeuxis lies in its simplicity. By hammering a single word or phrase repeatedly, it draws the listener's or reader's focus sharply to that idea, amplifying its significance. It can be used in poetry, prose, speeches, and everyday conversation.

Example 1: *"Words, words, words."* - Hamlet by William Shakespeare

Example 2: *"Alone, alone, all, all alone,* Alone on a wide wide sea!" - "The Rime of the Ancient Mariner" by Samuel Taylor Coleridge

Example 3: *"Oh horror, horror, horror!"* - "Macbeth" by William Shakespeare

Example 4: *"Location, location, location"* – A common real estate aphorism

In the first example, Hamlet's repeated utterance of "words" underscores his frustration and skepticism towards language's ability to convey genuine emotion or truth. The second example from Coleridge evokes a profound sense of isolation and vastness. The repetition in "Macbeth" amplifies the shock and revulsion of the speaker. The real estate aphorism underscores the importance of a property's position or site as its prime attribute. In each of these examples, epizeuxis serves to heighten the emotion and leave a lasting impact on the audience.

EPANALEPSIS

Epanalepsis is a rhetorical device in which a word or a phrase from the beginning of a sentence is repeated at the end of that same sentence. The repetition often bookends a central idea or theme, emphasizing it, providing structure, or evoking a particular emotion. The use of epanalepsis creates a circle of sorts, wrapping the sentence or clause in a way that draws attention to the repeated phrase or word, and consequently to the idea it encapsulates.

This device can be quite effective in both prose and poetry, highlighting the interconnectedness of the beginning and end, suggesting that everything comes full circle or emphasizing the significance of the repeated notion.
Example 1: "The king is dead, long live the king!"
Example 2: "A man must be something; he must be a man."
Example 3: "Year chases year, decay pursues decay."
Example 4: "Nothing is worse than doing nothing."
In the first example, the phrase emphasizes the continuity of monarchy; even as one king passes away, the institution and the lineage endure. The second example stresses the essence and inherent value of individuality. The third example from poetry speaks to the cyclical nature of time and deterioration. The fourth highlights the idea that inaction is the greatest fault of all. In each instance, epanalepsis serves as a framing device, drawing attention to the central theme while creating a memorable, rhythmic effect

HENDIADYS

Hendiadys is a rhetorical device in which two words, typically connected by a conjunction (often "and"), are used to express a single complex idea, where ordinarily one of the words would modify the other. The term "hendiadys" is derived from the Greek phrase "hen dia dyoin," which translates to "one through two." Instead of using a word and its modifier, hendiadys splits them into two coordinated elements. This deliberate splitting often introduces additional emphasis, nuance, or richness to the expression, making the statement more vivid or emphatic.

The use of hendiadys can imbue a phrase with a more poetic, layered, or expressive quality, amplifying the imagery or the feeling conveyed. It can also be found in everyday speech, where it might be used for emphasis or to capture a certain tone or mood.
Example 1: "Nice and warm" instead of "nicely warm."
Example 2: "Sound and fury" from Shakespeare's Macbeth, rather than "furious sound."
Example 3: "Song and dance" instead of "dancing song."
Example 4: "I came, I saw, and I conquered" might be a twist to express the sentiment more emphatically than "I came, saw, and conquered."
In the first example, "nice and warm" has a more emphatic, drawn-out feel than "nicely warm," emphasizing the comforting nature of the warmth. In the second, Shakespeare's use of hendiadys in the phrase "sound and fury" gives a more vivid portrayal of chaotic, loud emptiness. The third example portrays the idea of a performance or a fuss more than just a song that has dance. The fourth demonstrates how breaking up a series of actions can add emphasis and rhythm to the statement.
In essence, hendiadys is a tool to add flavor to speech or writing, making an expression more memorable or resonant by splitting and emphasizing its components.

HYPOPHORA

Hypophora is a rhetorical device in which a writer or speaker poses a question and then immediately answers it. This technique allows the speaker to introduce a topic by presenting it as a question, guiding the listener's or reader's attention in a specific direction, and then swiftly offering clarity or elaboration. The key feature of hypophora is that the same person both raises and addresses the question, as opposed to merely waiting for someone else to answer.

Using hypophora can serve various purposes: it can pique curiosity, create emphasis, clarify a statement, or guide a discourse in a predetermined direction. Additionally, it provides a structured way of introducing and immediately exploring or dispelling potential objections or misconceptions.

Example 1: *"What is honor? A word. What is in that word 'honor'? What is that 'honor'? Air."* - From Henry IV, Part 1 by William Shakespeare.

Example 2: *"Why should you learn about history? Because understanding the past can help us shape a better future."*

Example 3: *"Why do we write? To communicate, to persuade, to inform, and to express our deepest thoughts and feelings."*

Example 4: *"Is this the new age? Yes, it's an era where technology dominates and traditions evolve."*

In these examples, the hypophora is used to emphasize and then quickly address or explain a particular concept. In Shakespeare's use, the repetition of the question about honor emphasizes its intangible and fleeting nature. The other examples lead the reader through a guided thought process, introducing a topic or idea and then immediately delving into its implications or explanations.

In sum, hypophora is a potent rhetorical tool that engages audiences by posing relevant questions and then immediately delving into their implications or responses, creating a dynamic flow of thought and keeping the listener or reader actively engaged in the discourse.

LITOTES

Litotes is a rhetorical device that involves making an understatement by denying the opposite, often to emphasize a point or convey irony. The essential characteristic of litotes is its double negative formulation. Instead of saying something is good, for instance, one might say it's "not bad" – the double negative construction downplays the compliment, thereby amplifying it through understatement. Litotes often allows a speaker or writer to say less but convey more, drawing attention through subtlety.

This device is effective for imparting a tone of restraint, humility, or tact. It can make a statement or compliment seem less direct, potentially softening its impact or adding layers of meaning.

Example 1: *"He's no rookie" to mean "He's experienced."*

Example 2: *"She is not the brightest bulb in the box" to suggest "She's not very smart."*

Example 3: *"The trip wasn't a total waste of time" to mean "The trip was beneficial or valuable in some ways."*

Example 4: *"Einstein was not a bad mathematician" to imply "Einstein was a great mathematician."*

Example 5: *"That play was not unlike Romeo and Juliet" to suggest similarities without stating them outright.*

In these examples, the litotes downplays the statements' intensity, thereby drawing attention to them. It's a way of making a point while seemingly retreating from it, creating a nuanced, often ironic emphasis. For instance, saying Einstein was "not a bad mathematician" is clearly an understatement, emphasizing his exceptional skills without stating them directly.

In literature, speeches, and everyday language, litotes offers a way to navigate sensitive subjects or emphasize points with grace, wit, and diplomacy. It reminds us that sometimes saying less can convey so much more.

PARALIPSIS (PRAETERITIN)

Paralipsis (or Praeteritio):

Paralipsis, also known as praeteritio or occupatio, is a rhetorical device wherein a speaker or writer brings attention to something by deliberately and ironically mentioning that they won't or shouldn't discuss it. It's a way of emphasizing a point by claiming to pass over it. This tactic can be manipulative, as it lets the speaker introduce a subject without being held accountable for it, often creating an emphasis stronger than a direct statement would.

The genius of paralipsis lies in its irony. By declaring not to mention or discuss a topic, the speaker ensures that the audience's attention is squarely focused on that very topic. It's a form of reverse psychology applied in rhetoric.

Example 1: *"I won't even mention the fact that you forgot my birthday."*

Example 2: *"Without even touching upon the numerous times he's been late, let's discuss his work quality."*

Example 3: *"I don't want to talk about the rumors of his past scandals, we're here to discuss his current policies."*

Example 4: *"It would be unkind to point out that she has changed her stance on the issue several times."*

Example 5: *"I have promised not to say a word about his dishonesty, so I won't."*

In each of these examples, the speaker is doing precisely what they claim they won't — addressing the issue. By saying they won't discuss it, they not only bring it to the forefront but also underscore its importance or relevance.

Authors, politicians, and orators use paralipsis to subtly introduce controversial or sensitive subjects without taking direct responsibility for them. It allows them to plant an idea or sentiment in their audience's mind without overtly saying it, leveraging the power of suggestion and implication to great effect. It's a strategy that is at once clever and cunning, reminding us of the nuances and indirect ways in which language can shape perception and influence thought.

POLYSYNDETON

Polysyndeton is a rhetorical device that involves the deliberate use of multiple conjunctions between coordinate phrases, clauses, or words within a sentence. This technique can amplify the rhythm of the language and can convey a sense of urgency, excess, or even solemnity. By overloading sentences with conjunctions, polysyndeton can also slow down the pacing of a passage or create an overwhelming effect, indicating a rush of details or ideas.

Its name is derived from the Greek words "poly-" (meaning "many") and "syndeton" (meaning "bound together with"). The opposite of polysyndeton is asyndeton, where conjunctions are deliberately omitted from sentences for effect.
Example 1: "I wore a sweater, and a hat, and a scarf, and a pair of gloves, and thick socks."
Example 2: *"He ran and jumped and laughed and shouted and played."*
Example 3: *"It's a bird, and it's a plane, and it's Superman!"*
Example 4: *"We lived and laughed and loved and left."*
Example 5: *"They read and studied and wrote and tested and passed."*

The repeated use of conjunctions in polysyndeton creates a cadence in the text that can evoke various emotions in the reader or listener. For example, it can convey a feeling of excitement, show the continuity or interrelatedness of events or actions, or emphasize the multitude or vastness of something.

Writers and orators often employ polysyndeton to draw emphasis to a list or series of items, to highlight their importance individually rather than as a collective, or to give a more exhaustive feeling to the series. In some contexts, polysyndeton can add a poetic or lyrical quality to prose, and in others, it might add a dramatic emphasis to a series of actions or events. The choice to use polysyndeton can significantly impact the rhythm and mood of a passage, showcasing the power of conjunctions as more than just simple connective words.

ZEUGMA

Zeugma is a rhetorical device where a word—usually a verb or an adjective—applies to multiple parts of the sentence. This literary tool is employed for creating dramatic, comedic, or unexpected effects by linking seemingly unrelated words or phrases together in an uncommon combination. Originating from the Greek word "ζεῦγμα" which translates to "yoking" or "bonding," zeugma effectively "yokes" different ideas together through a shared word. Examples of Zeugma:
"He stole my heart and my wallet." In this example, the verb "stole" is applied both to the emotional "heart" and the tangible "wallet."

"She opened the door and her heart to the orphan." Here, "opened" relates both to the physical action of opening a door and the metaphorical opening of her heart.

"With weeping eyes and hearts." In this instance, "weeping" refers to the literal weeping of eyes and the metaphorical sorrow of hearts.

"He fished for compliments and trout." This showcases a humorous use where "fished" stands for both the literal act of fishing and the figurative act of seeking praise.

"You are free to execute your laws, and your citizens, as you see fit." Here, "execute" has the double meaning of carrying out laws and the grim sense of killing citizens.

The use of zeugma can add flair, wit, and depth to a sentence. By forcing one word to take on dual roles, it challenges readers or listeners to think more deeply about the relationships between the words and the underlying meanings of the sentence. This can produce striking, amusing, or profound effects, making zeugma a favorite tool among writers, poets, and orators to engage their audiences in a dynamic way. When applied well, it not only showcases linguistic creativity but also evokes a strong response from its audience, be it laughter, introspection, or astonishment.

ANAPHORA

Anaphora is a rhetorical device characterized by the repetition of the same word or group of words at the beginning of successive clauses, sentences, or lines. This repetition emphasizes the repeated phrase and evokes strong emotional resonance in the audience. Derived from the Greek term "ἀναφορά" meaning "carrying back" or "referring," anaphora works as a powerful means to emphasize a particular idea and create rhythm in a passage, enhancing its poetic or persuasive qualities.
Examples of Anaphora:
"I have a dream that one day this nation will rise up, live out the true meaning of its creed... I have a dream that one day on the red hills of Georgia... I have a dream that one day even the state of Mississippi..." - Martin Luther King Jr., "I Have a Dream" speech.

"To raise the level of future generations... To better the conditions for all men... To inspire hope in the hearts of many..."
"It was the best of times, it was the worst of times, it was the age of wisdom, it was the age of foolishness..." - Charles Dickens, "A Tale of Two Cities."

"With malice toward none, with charity for all, with firmness in the right..." - Abraham Lincoln, Second Inaugural Address.
"Every day, every night, in every way, I am getting better."

Anaphora can be found extensively in literature, speeches, and religious texts, making passages more memorable and poignant. By repeating words or phrases, the writer or speaker can emphasize their significance and evoke a rhythmic flow. This repetition also serves to build up anticipation in the audience, leading to a climax or resolution. As a result, anaphora often contributes to the emotional intensity of a text, making it a favorite device for poets, novelists, and orators seeking to leave a lasting impact on their audience.

APOSTROPHE

Apostrophe is a rhetorical device in which the speaker or writer breaks off from addressing one party and instead addresses an absent person, an abstract concept, or an inanimate object. This direct address to the absent or non-human adds emotional intensity and is used to convey the speaker's deep feelings, desires, frustrations, or connections with the addressed entity. The term "apostrophe" comes from the Greek word "apostrophos," which means "turning away." In literature, it's often used to give vent to or display intense emotion, which can no longer be held back. Examples of Apostrophe:
"O Romeo, Romeo! Wherefore art thou Romeo?" - In Shakespeare's "Romeo and Juliet," Juliet speaks to an absent Romeo, expressing her anguish over the name of her beloved, which is the only thing keeping them apart.

"Death, be not proud, though some have called thee Mighty and dreadful, for thou art not so." - In this poem, John Donne addresses Death as if it were a person, challenging its power and

omnipotence.

"O Captain! My Captain! our fearful trip is done..." - Walt Whitman's poem addresses the dead Abraham Lincoln, representing him as the captain of the metaphorical ship that is the United States.

"Twinkle, twinkle, little star, How I wonder what you are!" - This nursery rhyme is a direct address to a star, expressing wonder and curiosity.

"Oh, stars and clouds and winds, ye are all about to mock me; if ye really pity me, crush sensation and memory." - Mary Shelley's "Frankenstein."

Apostrophe creates a more direct and intimate connection between the audience and the subject. By addressing objects, abstract ideas, or absent beings as if they were present and capable of understanding, writers evoke a heightened emotional response and a sense of closeness or understanding toward the addressed entity. The use of apostrophe can make abstract concepts more relatable and tangible, allowing the reader or listener to empathize with the speaker's emotional state.

CACOPHONY

Cacophony is a literary device that refers to the use of words with sharp, harsh, and discordant sounds. These sounds can be created by a combination of consonant sounds or a specific arrangement of syllables. The term "cacophony" is derived from the Greek word "kakophonia," where "kakos" means "bad" and "phone" stands for "voice" or "sound." The primary purpose of using cacophony is to create a jarring, unsettling effect, often to mirror or amplify the content of the text.

Examples of Cacophony:

"Beware the Jabberwock, my son! The jaws that bite, the claws that catch!" - from "Jabberwocky" by Lewis Carroll. The harsh sounds in words like "Jabberwock," "jaws," "bite," and "claws" add to the menacing atmosphere of the poem.

"I detest war because cause of war is always trivial." - Nguyen Trai. The hard "t" and "r" sounds emphasize the harshness and triviality of war's causes.

"Or crack'd across, or started lengthways, or stung and stabbed by wasps and hornets, or cut by broken glass in our own beds." - from "Kurtz Discourse" by Joseph Conrad. The use of sharp sounds like "crack'd," "stung," and "stabbed" create a chaotic and painful atmosphere.

"His fingers rapped and pounded the door, and his foot thumped against the yellowing wood." The use of words like "rapped," "pounded," and "thumped" evoke a sense of aggressive urgency.

Cacophony, when employed effectively, can evoke discomfort, tension, or a sense of chaos in the reader or listener. It can create a vivid emotional atmosphere that aligns with the content or theme of the text. This device can be especially effective in poetry or prose that delves into distressing or chaotic situations, setting a tone that resonates with the narrative's content. By introducing discordant sounds, writers can ensure that their descriptions are not only visual but also auditory, providing a more encompassing sensory experience.

EUPHONY

Euphony is a literary device that refers to the use of words and phrases that are distinguished by their melodic and harmonious sound, rather than by their meaning. The sounds created by euphony are pleasing and soothing to the ear. Euphonic words typically possess soft consonants or long vowels that flow together smoothly, creating a sense of calm and beauty in the spoken language. "Euphony" is derived from the Greek word "euphonos," where "eu" means "good" and "phone" means "voice" or "sound." Writers utilize euphony to create a more enjoyable reading experience and to convey serene or pleasant moods.

Examples of Euphony:
"Season of mists and mellow fruitfulness,
Close bosom-friend of the maturing sun;"
> from "To Autumn" by John Keats. The soft sounds in "mists," "mellow," and "maturing" create a calming and soothing auditory effect.

"So long as men can breathe or eyes can see,
So long lives this, and this gives life to thee."
> from Shakespeare's Sonnet 18. The smooth flow of the words, combined with the long vowels and soft consonants, produces a harmonious sound.

"The moon was a ghostly galleon tossed upon cloudy seas."
> from "The Highwayman" by Alfred Noyes. The long "o" sounds create a soft, melodic quality in this line.

"Over the still world, a bird calls, waking the ravine
Behind the empty house."

       from "The Waste Land" by T.S. Eliot. The gentle sibilance in "still" and "calls" and the long "a" sound in "waking" contribute to the overall euphonic quality of the lines. Euphony is often employed to help set a peaceful, tranquil, or romantic tone in a piece of writing. The deliberate choice of mellifluous words and sounds can greatly enhance the beauty and aesthetic appeal of a literary work, making it more inviting and enjoyable to readers or listeners. When contrasted with cacophony, which uses harsh and discordant sounds, euphony can help to underscore themes of harmony versus discord, peace versus conflict, or beauty versus decay in literature.

TMESIS

Tmesis:
Tmesis is a rhetorical device in which a word or phrase is divided into two parts, with other words interrupting between them. This literary technique is primarily employed for emphasis or to create a humorous or dramatic effect. The term "tmesis" originates from the Greek word "tmesis," which means "to cut." Tmesis is relatively uncommon in everyday speech but is often found in literature, poetry, and sometimes in colloquial expressions for added emphasis.

Examples of Tmesis:
"Un-freaking-believable!" - Here, the word "unbelievable" is split by the insertion of the slang term "freaking" to intensify the emotion of disbelief.

"Whatsoever" becomes "what-so-ever." Splitting the word adds emphasis to each individual segment, highlighting the all-encompassing nature of "whatsoever."

In Shakespeare's Julius Caesar, *"This was the most unkindest cut of all."* The insertion of "unkindest" between "un-" and "kind" amplifies the cruelty of the act.

"Absa-bloody-lutely!" - A colloquial and humorous splitting of the word "absolutely" for added emphasis.

In Troilus and Cressida by Shakespeare: *"How the devil Luxury, with his fat rump and potato finger, tickles these together!"* Here, the word "luxury" is split into "lu-" and "-xury" with a descriptive interjection for comedic and descriptive effect.

Tmesis serves as an effective tool to catch the reader's or listener's attention. By breaking up common words or phrases, the writer or speaker forces the audience to consider the term's meaning more deeply or appreciate its enhanced expressive quality. The insertion can also adjust the rhythm or meter of a phrase, particularly useful in poetry.

TRICOLON

Tricolon is a rhetorical device that employs a series of three parallel words, phrases, clauses, or statements. This structure is employed for its rhythmic and symmetrical effect, making it memorable and impactful. The consistent use of groups of three creates emphasis and can enhance the progression of ideas, offering a sense of completeness and wholeness to the audience. The power of three is rooted deeply in many cultures and traditions; hence, tricolons resonate universally.
Examples of Tricolon:
Julius Caesar's famous declaration: "Veni, vidi, vici." (I came, I saw, I conquered.)

"Government of the people, by the people, for the people." - Abraham Lincoln in the Gettysburg Address.

"I require three things in a man: he must be handsome, ruthless, and stupid." - Dorothy Parker.

"Be sincere, be brief, be seated." - Franklin D. Roosevelt.

"With malice toward none, with charity for all, with firmness in the right..." - Abraham Lincoln's Second Inaugural Address.

"Life, liberty, and the pursuit of happiness" - U.S. Declaration of Independence.

"Friends, Romans, countrymen, lend me your ears!" - From Shakespeare's Julius Caesar.

A tricolon becomes particularly effective when each of its elements has a similar length, maintaining rhythm and balance. It's a structure that's frequently used in speeches, literature, and advertising due to its catchy and memorable nature. By employing tricolon, a writer or speaker can produce a statement that leaves a lasting impression on the audience, often becoming a quotable mantra or guiding principle.

SYLLEPSIS

Syllepsis is a rhetorical device wherein a word (often a verb or an adjective) is applied to multiple parts of the sentence, but it is understood differently in relation to each part. This figure of speech often results in a playful ambiguity or pun, as the word in question maintains its grammatical connection but changes in meaning as it relates to the other words it governs. The beauty of syllepsis lies in its clever and often humorous juxtaposition of literal and figurative meanings.
Examples of Syllepsis:
"You held your breath and the door for me." - From Alanis Morissette's song "Head Over Feet." Here, "held" is used both literally (holding the door) and figuratively (holding one's breath).

"He stole my heart and my wallet." In this case, "stole" applies both to the emotional act of winning someone's affection and the literal act of theft.

"We must all hang together, or assuredly we shall all hang separately." - Benjamin Franklin. Here, the first "hang" means to unite or stand together, while the second refers to being executed by hanging.

"She blew my nose and then she blew my mind." - From The Rolling Stones' song "Honky Tonk Women." Here, "blew" first refers to the act of wiping or cleaning, and then to being profoundly affected or impressed.

"Miss Bolo… went straight home, in a flood of tears and a sedan-chair." - Charles Dickens, The Pickwick Papers. "Went" is used to imply both emotional and physical movement.

"He works his work, I mine." - Alfred Lord Tennyson in "Ulysses." The word "work" is used both as a noun (his job) and a verb (I do mine).

Syllepsis often creates a witty or unexpected twist in a sentence, giving readers or listeners a moment of surprise or amusement. It requires careful crafting to ensure that the dual meanings of the governing word are clear and effective. This device is frequently found in literature, poetry, and song lyrics due to its unique ability to convey dual meanings in a concise manner.

PERIPHRASIS

Periphrasis is a rhetorical device that involves the use of a longer expression or multiple words to convey what could have been conveyed with a shorter or more direct expression. It's a way of describing something indirectly or in a roundabout fashion. The purpose of periphrasis can range from achieving a certain poetic or rhythmic quality, to emphasizing a point, to being evasive or polite.

Examples of Periphrasis:
Referring to Shakespeare as "The Bard of Avon" instead of just "Shakespeare."
Saying "the city that never sleeps" instead of "New York."
Using "man's best friend" to refer to a dog.
Saying "the fairer sex" when one means women.
"The feathered inhabitants of the sky" instead of simply saying "birds."

Types of Periphrasis:
Ornamental Periphrasis: Used for poetic or stylistic purposes. For instance, poets might use this to fit a particular rhythm or rhyme scheme.

Functional Periphrasis: Used for reasons other than style, such as being more polite or tactful. For example, saying "passed away" instead of "died."

Usage in Literature and Rhetoric:
Periphrasis can add a touch of elegance or depth to writing, especially in poetry where the poet might wish to draw attention to a particular object or concept by describing it in a roundabout way. However, it can also be used in rhetoric as a way to avoid confronting uncomfortable truths directly or to talk around a subject.
In everyday language, periphrasis might be used for politeness, as in saying "go to the restroom" instead of more direct alternatives.
Overall, while periphrasis can add depth, color, and rhythm to language, it's essential to use it judiciously. Overuse or unnecessary use can make speech or writing seem verbose or evasive.

APORIA

Aporia is a rhetorical device in which the speaker expresses genuine doubt or uncertainty about something, often feigning this doubt for the sake of argument or to encourage the audience to ponder a particular point. Derived from the Greek term "aporein," which means "to be at a loss," aporia showcases the speaker's internal conflict or questioning about a particular matter, making the audience more engaged or prompting them to think critically about the issue at hand.
Examples of Aporia:
"I'm not sure how I can possibly solve this problem. What could be the right approach?"
"To be or not to be—that is the question!" - from Shakespeare's Hamlet.
"I wonder if there is any way to reconcile these two opposing viewpoints."

"Is this the right path for our country, or have we lost our way?"
Usage in Literature and Rhetoric:
In literature, authors often use aporia to reveal a character's internal conflict or moral dilemma. This device provides depth to characters, showing them as introspective and capable of self-doubt. Shakespeare, for instance, frequently employed aporia in his plays, using it to showcase the intricate mental landscapes of his characters.
In rhetorical speeches or arguments, aporia can be a powerful tool. By voicing doubts or asking questions (even if the speaker knows the answer or has a firm belief), the speaker can guide the audience to a particular conclusion or make them more receptive to the following argument.
For instance, a politician might use aporia by saying, "I wonder if this policy will truly benefit our youth?" By voicing this doubt, they invite their audience to consider the potential impacts of the policy more critically.
In essence, aporia serves as a tool to engage, challenge, and invite introspection, making discussions or narratives richer and more layered.

ANTANACLASIS

Antanaclasis is a rhetorical device in which a word is repeated within a sentence or clause, but its meaning changes in each case. This play on words can be used for a variety of purposes including creating emphasis, producing wit, or introducing a play on words. The repetition often results in a form of pun, where the word's shifting meaning offers a clever or insightful observation.
Example 1: Benjamin Franklin's famous saying, "We must all hang together, or assuredly we shall all hang separately." Here, the word "hang" is used first in the sense of "unite" or "come together," and then in the more literal sense of being executed by hanging.
Example 2: "If you aren't fired with enthusiasm, you will be fired, with enthusiasm." In this case, "fired" is first used to mean ignited or inspired, and then in the sense of being terminated from a job.
Example 3: Shakespeare's line from "Julius Caesar" — "But for mine own part, it was Greek to me." The word "Greek" first appears to refer to the language, but it also suggests the idea of something being incomprehensible or not understood.
Antanaclasis often introduces a layer of irony, wit, or humor, and is commonly found in literature, speeches, and everyday language. It requires the listener or reader to be attentive to the context in which the word is used, allowing them to appreciate the nuanced change in meaning. The device can be a powerful tool in the hands of a skilled writer or orator, enabling them to drive home a point or observation with memorable flair.

APOSIOPSIS

Aposiopesis is a rhetorical device in which the speaker or writer deliberately breaks off and leaves a statement unfinished, creating an impression of being too overcome by emotion, or choosing not to say something for fear of saying too much. This intentional trailing off into silence—denoted in writing with an ellipsis or a dash—allows the speaker to let the unsaid words hang in the air, compelling the audience to delve deeper into the possible implications or to supply the ending themselves.

Example 1: In Shakespeare's "Hamlet," the titular character exclaims, "To be, or not to be, that is the question: Whether 'tis nobler in the mind to suffer…" The famous soliloquy sees Hamlet contemplating existence and mortality, and the use of aposiopesis adds weight to his contemplation.

Example 2: In everyday conversation, one might say, "If he doesn't understand now, then I don't know what…" Here, the speaker doesn't finish the sentence, leaving listeners to infer the rest.

Example 3: "I've warned him enough times. If he doesn't heed my advice now, then…"

The power of aposiopesis lies in its strategic use of silence or unsaid words to communicate a deeper, often stronger, sentiment. It can be employed to convey a range of emotions, from frustration to anticipation, fear to hope. In literature, it can be particularly effective in capturing a character's internal turmoil or hesitation.

CATACHRESIS

Catachresis is a rhetorical device wherein writers use mixed metaphors in an inappropriate or an especially unusual way, deliberately flouting rules of analogy, grammar, or logic. The device often results in a strikingly unique expression or helps to convey a sentiment for which there is no set idiom or term. In essence, catachresis can be seen as a misuse or abuse of language to create a dramatic effect.

Example 1: *"I will speak daggers to her."* - Hamlet by William Shakespeare. Here, "speak" and "daggers" are words not naturally paired together, but the combination vividly captures Hamlet's intent to harm with his words.

Example 2: *"Listen, you ear of corn!"* Here, "ear of corn" is used instead of "eavesdropper" or "overhearer," creating a jarring and humorous image.

Example 3: *"The voice of your eyes is deeper than all roses."* - E. E. Cummings. This line combines "voice" and "eyes," two unrelated entities, to craft a poignant description of the depth and expressiveness of a gaze.

Catachresis is a tool that, when used intentionally, can push the boundaries of language, challenging our understanding of conventional metaphors and inviting readers to see common concepts in a fresh light. While it might seem like an error or a mismatch at first, its true purpose is to leave a memorable impression by juxtaposing unrelated or discordant terms.

ENTHYMEME

Enthymeme is a rhetorical device that derives from the broader realm of syllogism in classical logic. An enthymeme is essentially an abbreviated syllogism, where one of the premises (either major or minor) or the conclusion is left unstated, because it is assumed to be self-evident or commonly accepted by the audience. This "incomplete" nature of enthymeme is intentional and often employed in persuasive discourse, relying on the audience's prior knowledge or beliefs to fill in the gap.
Example 1: "He is a US citizen, so he is entitled to vote." In this enthymeme, the major premise "All US citizens are entitled to vote" is omitted because it's generally accepted and understood.
Example 2: "Where there's smoke, there's fire." The underlying reasoning is that smoke is generally a result of fire. The complete syllogism might look like: "All situations with smoke are situations with fire. This is a situation with smoke. Therefore, this is a situation with fire."
Example 3: "She's from California, so she must be a liberal." The unstated premise here might be "Many people from California are liberals."
Enthymemes are powerful tools in rhetoric because they engage the audience actively in the argument. When the audience fills in the missing premise or conclusion on their own, they are more likely to be persuaded, as they feel the argument is partly theirs. However, enthymemes can also be misleading, as they can rely on stereotypes, generalizations, or unverified assumptions, leading to potentially flawed conclusions.

EPISTROPHE

Epistrophe is a rhetorical device where consecutive sentences or phrases end with the same word or group of words. This repeated ending can be used to emphasize a particular point or idea, create a rhythmic effect, or evoke an emotional response from the audience. Epistrophe is the counterpart to anaphora, which involves the repetition of words or phrases at the beginning of successive clauses.

Usage:

Epistrophe is often used in both written and spoken discourse for emphasis. Its repetitive nature drives home the point the speaker or writer is trying to make, making the message more memorable and impactful.

Examples:

From Abraham Lincoln's "Gettysburg Address":

"of the people, by the people, for the people."

Here, the repeated "the people" emphasizes the idea of a democratic nation and reinforces the importance of the people's role in governance.

From Lyndon B. Johnson's speech:

"There is no Negro problem. There is no Southern problem. There is no Northern problem. There is only an American problem."

By using epistrophe, Johnson underscores the idea that America's issues are collective, belonging to the entire nation rather than individual groups or regions.

In literature, George Orwell's "1984":

"The party told you to reject the evidence of your eyes and ears. It was their final, most essential command."

The repetition of the phrase "it was" stresses the oppressive nature of the Party and their control over individual perception and reality.

Function:
Epistrophe serves to underline a sentiment, bringing attention to a particular point. The repetition can create a rhythm in the prose or speech, making the message more compelling and easier to remember. Through this repetition, the speaker or writer can evoke strong emotions and persuade the audience of their perspective.

PLEONASM

Pleonasm is a rhetorical device that involves using more words than necessary to convey a particular meaning, often with the aim of emphasis or clarity. While some might view it as redundancy, pleonasm can also be used deliberately to add a certain weight or rhythm to a sentence, or to clarify an idea.
Usage:
In everyday language, pleonasms can sometimes be seen as tautological or redundant expressions. But in rhetoric, literature, or oratory, they can add emphasis and produce a stylistic effect. They can also help achieve clarity in legal and formal documents where there is a need to ensure no ambiguity.
Examples:
"I saw it with my own eyes."
Here, "with my own eyes" is pleonastic. Saying "I saw it" would be sufficient, but the addition of "with my own eyes" adds emphasis to the personal experience and certainty of the observation.
"Free gift" or "true fact."
Both phrases contain redundant terms since gifts are inherently free, and facts are inherently true. However, they are often used for emphasis in speech and advertising.
"They are both the same."
Here, the word "both" is redundant since "the same" already

implies a comparison of two things.

Pleonasm can serve multiple purposes:

Emphasis: As seen in the examples, it can be used to emphasize a certain point or detail.

Clarity: Especially in legal or formal contexts, pleonasm can be used to leave no room for doubt or ambiguity.

Rhythm and Style: In literature and oratory, the additional words can add a certain rhythm or cadence to a sentence, making it more memorable or pleasing to the ear.

While pleonasm can be effective in specific contexts, it's essential to be aware of its usage, especially in concise writing, where redundancy might detract from the message's clarity.

RHETORICAL QUESTION

A rhetorical question is a figure of speech in the form of a question that is posed for effect rather than in expectation of a reply. The question is not intended to be answered directly; instead, it prompts the reader or listener to consider a point or simply emphasizes a predetermined conclusion. It's a powerful tool in rhetoric, enabling a speaker or writer to make a statement, assert a point, or draw attention to a particular emphasis.

Rhetorical questions can be used in a variety of situations:

To challenge the audience: By posing a rhetorical question, the speaker can make the audience think about their beliefs or assumptions.

To emphasize a point: Rather than just making a statement, turning it into a question can lend it greater emphasis.

To engage the audience: Asking a question, even if no answer is expected, can draw the audience into the discussion more effectively than a mere statement.

Examples:

"Isn't it a bit unnerving that doctors call what they do 'practice'?"

This question highlights an ironic or humorous perspective on the word 'practice' related to medical professionals.

"Who needs enemies when you have friends like that?"
The question emphasizes the point that with such friends, one doesn't need adversaries, implying that the friends might not be very trustworthy or helpful.

"Are we to believe that equality is only a dream?"
This question challenges the audience to reflect upon societal values and ideals.

Function:

Emphasis: It can underscore a point or idea, making it stand out.

Persuasion: By framing a statement as a question, it can lead the audience to a particular conclusion or belief.

Engagement: A rhetorical question involves the audience, making them an active participant in the discussion or thought process.

Dramatic effect: Especially in literature or speeches, a well-placed rhetorical question can heighten the emotional resonance or drama of a passage.

SYNESTHESIA

Synesthesia is a rhetorical device and literary technique where one sense is described using terms from another sense. The term "synesthesia" originates from the Greek words "syn," meaning "together," and "aisthēsis," meaning "sensation." In a broader neurological context, synesthesia is a perceptual phenomenon in which the stimulation of one sensory or cognitive pathway leads to involuntary experiences in a second sensory or cognitive pathway. However, in literature, it's used more metaphorically to blend sensory experiences to create rich imagery.

Usage:

Synesthesia is employed to craft vivid and evocative descriptions that appeal to multiple senses simultaneously. This cross-sensory description can provide a richer, more immersive experience for the reader.

Examples:

"Tasting of Flora and the country green, Dance, and Provençal song, and sunburnt mirth!"

> From John Keats' "Ode to a Nightingale." Here, the poet describes the taste of the scene, blending it with visuals and sounds.

"A loud color" or "a bitter sound."

> These phrases merge the senses of sight with hearing and taste with hearing, respectively.

"Back to the region where the sun is silent."

> From Dante's "Inferno." The blending of sound (or its absence) with the visual imagery of the sun creates a haunting image.

Function:

Evocative Imagery: By blending sensory experiences, writers can create more vibrant and memorable imagery.

Emotional Resonance: Engaging multiple senses can evoke a stronger emotional reaction in the reader, making the scene or description more poignant or impactful.

Enhanced Description: Synesthesia can offer a fresh and unique perspective, making descriptions more intriguing and less conventional.

In literature, synesthesia serves as a tool to break down the barriers between the senses, allowing for a more holistic and interconnected perception of the world. It challenges readers to experience their environment in a new and enriched manner.

EROTEMA

Erotema, more commonly known as a rhetorical question, is a figure of speech in which a question is posed not to seek an answer but rather to emphasize a point or to challenge the audience. The answer to an erotema is typically obvious or implied by the context in which it is asked, making the actual response unnecessary. The primary purpose of this device is not to gain a response but to assert or deny something indirectly, making a point more persuasive or impactful.

Usage:

Erotema is frequently employed in literature, speeches, and everyday discourse as a way of making a statement, drawing attention to a particular issue, or prompting the audience to reflect on a specific topic.

Examples:

"Is the pope Catholic?"

>This is a common rhetorical question where the obvious answer is "yes," used to emphasize the certainty or obviousness of something.

"What business is it of yours?"

>Here, the speaker is not genuinely seeking an answer but rather challenging the addressee's right to know or intervene.

"To be or not to be: that is the question."

>Perhaps one of the most famous lines from Shakespeare's "Hamlet." While it takes the form of a question, its purpose is more to express Hamlet's deep existential reflection.

Function:

Emphasis: Erotema can highlight the importance or obviousness of a particular point or idea.

Engagement: It can serve to engage the audience, prompting them to think or reflect on a specific topic or issue.

Stylistic Variety: As a rhetorical device, it adds variety to the discourse, breaking up statements and assertions with introspective or challenging queries.

Persuasion: When used effectively, erotema can be a powerful tool for persuasion, allowing the speaker or writer to lead the audience to a particular conclusion without directly stating it.

In essence, erotema is a device that enables speakers and writers to make indirect assertions or denials, often with a greater impact than a straightforward statement might have. It's a tool that, when used aptly, can deeply engage and resonate with the audience.

TAUTOLOGY

Tautology is a rhetorical device wherein redundant or repetitive statements are used, often unintentionally, that add no information to the original statement. Essentially, it means saying the same thing twice in different words, within the same context. While sometimes considered a stylistic error in formal writing and speaking, tautology can also be used purposefully for emphasis or clarity.

Usage:

Tautologies appear in various forms of discourse. In some cases, they might be employed for poetic or rhetorical emphasis, while in others, they could be inadvertent, resulting from an oversight in editing or lack of awareness.

Examples:

"Free gift"

> The word "gift" already implies that it's free, so adding "free" is redundant.

"I saw it with my own eyes."

> The phrase "with my own eyes" is tautological because seeing is inherently a personal experience.

"It's déjà vu all over again."

> This humorous phrase, often attributed to baseball legend Yogi Berra, is tautological because "déjà vu" already conveys the idea of experiencing something again.

Function:

Emphasis: When used deliberately, tautology can lay stress on a particular point or idea.

Clarity: Sometimes, it's employed to make sure a point is understood, even if it's repetitive.

Poetic or Rhetorical Effect: In literature or speeches, tautology can sometimes produce a rhythmic or echoing effect, even if redundant.

Unintended Redundancy: Tautologies can sometimes creep into speech or writing without the author or speaker noticing, especially in casual conversation.

While tautology can be criticized when it results from oversight or when it clutters communication, it also has its place in rhetorical strategies when employed with intention. As with many rhetorical devices, context is crucial, and the effectiveness of a tautology will depend on its purpose and the audience's reception.

DEUS EX MACHINA

The term "Deus Ex Machina" originates from the ancient Greek theater and translates as "god from the machine." It refers to a plot device whereby a seemingly unsolvable problem or conflict within a story is suddenly and abruptly resolved by the unexpected and often unexplained intervention of some new event, character, ability, or object. Historically, in Greek plays, this involved a god being lowered onto the stage via a crane (the "machine") to resolve the play's conflict, hence the name.

Usage:

"Deus Ex Machina" is often criticized when it appears as a contrived plot device. It can be seen as a shortcut or a sign that the writer has written themselves into a corner and can't find a more organic solution to the story's problems. When used carelessly, it

can undermine the story's internal logic and disappoint audiences who expect a more coherent or earned resolution.
Examples:
In ancient Greek tragedy, Euripides often used this device. In "Medea," for instance, the titular character escapes her punishment by flying away in a chariot provided by the sun god Helios.

In modern cinema, some critics argue that the sudden appearance of the giant eagles at the end of "The Lord of the Rings: The Return of the King" is a form of Deus Ex Machina, as they unexpectedly save Frodo and Sam from certain doom.
Function:
Surprising Resolution: It offers a sudden and unexpected solution to a seemingly intractable problem.
Divine Intervention: In many classical uses, the Deus Ex Machina literally represents the will of the gods, intervening in human affairs.
Evoking Wonder or the Supernatural: Especially in fantasy or mythological tales, the use of such a device can emphasize the mysterious and wondrous nature of the world.
Potential Pitfall: As mentioned, relying on Deus Ex Machina can be seen as a storytelling crutch. When the audience senses that a resolution hasn't been earned or set up properly, it can lead to dissatisfaction.

While "Deus Ex Machina" has its roots in classical theater, its influence and the critique around its usage persist in modern storytelling across different media. It serves as a reminder of the balance writers must strike between surprising their audience and maintaining narrative integrity.

EXPOSITION

Exposition is a literary and narrative device that provides critical background information to the audience or readers. This information can include settings, previous events in the story world, foundational character traits or backstories, and other context that is essential for understanding the main plot and its developments. Exposition can be presented in various ways, such as through dialogues, flashbacks, character's thoughts, background details, in-world media, or even through the narrator directly.

Usage:
The primary purpose of exposition is to set the scene and provide the reader or viewer with the essential information needed to understand the unfolding narrative. However, it's a delicate tool. Overuse or blatant exposition can feel heavy-handed, taking the reader out of the narrative. On the other hand, too little exposition can leave readers feeling lost or disconnected from the story.

Examples:
In J.R.R. Tolkien's "The Fellowship of the Ring," the "Prologue" and the "Concerning Hobbits" section give readers a foundational understanding of hobbits and the world of Middle-earth before the main story begins.

In the "Star Wars" franchise, the iconic opening crawl provides exposition, setting the stage for the events of the film.

In Shakespeare's "Romeo and Juliet," the Chorus delivers a prologue that summarizes the forthcoming play, informing the audience about the tragic love story between two young individuals from feuding families.

Function:
Setting the Scene: Exposition provides the necessary background to orient readers to the time, place, and mood of the story.

Character Insight: Through exposition, readers can gain an understanding of a character's motivations, history, and relationships.

Avoiding Confusion: Exposition clarifies any potential areas of confusion, ensuring the reader or viewer can follow the plot without being distracted by unanswered questions.

Thematic Foreshadowing: Sometimes, exposition can hint at broader themes or motifs that will become significant later in the narrative.

Writers must be cautious and skillful with exposition, integrating it seamlessly into the narrative. The goal is to inform without overwhelming, ensuring that the audience remains engaged and immersed in the story. Effective exposition is like a foundation to a building – crucial for stability, but not always prominently visible.

ANTHROPOMORPHISM

Anthropomorphism is a literary, artistic, and conceptual device wherein human traits, emotions, or intentions are attributed to non-human entities, such as animals, plants, objects, or even abstract concepts. It's more than just giving a human-like appearance; it's about assigning human behaviors, motivations, or feelings. This device allows authors and creators to bring to life characters or objects in a way that's relatable to human readers or viewers, facilitating deeper emotional connections and understanding.

Anthropomorphism has been used for millennia across various cultures and mediums. From ancient myths where gods take on human forms and emotions to modern animated films where animals talk and behave like humans, anthropomorphism bridges the gap between the familiar and the unfamiliar.

Examples:

Aesop's Fables: Stories like "The Tortoise and the Hare" or "The Ant and the Grasshopper" feature animals that talk, think, and behave like humans, serving as moral lessons.

Winnie-the-Pooh: A.A. Milne's beloved children's stories feature a bear named Pooh, along with his animal friends, who have very human-like emotions, motivations, and relationships.

Disney's "Cars": Vehicles that not only talk and feel but also have friendships, rivalries, and personal growth journeys.
Function:
Relatability: By giving non-human entities human characteristics, authors make them more familiar and relatable to readers or viewers, allowing for deeper emotional connections.
Teaching and Morality: Anthropomorphic characters, especially in fables and children's stories, often serve to teach moral lessons or convey specific values.
Exploration of Humanity: Anthropomorphism can be used as a mirror to reflect human society, behavior, and dilemmas, offering a unique perspective on our own nature.
Creativity and Imagination: It allows creators to craft entirely new worlds, characters, and stories that, while different in form, are still rooted in human experience and emotion.
While anthropomorphism can be a powerful tool in storytelling, it's essential to handle it with care. The key is to ensure that the human traits given to non-human entities serve the narrative and thematic purpose without coming across as forced or contrived. When done right, anthropomorphism can breathe life into characters, making them memorable and impactful.

ARCHETYPE

An archetype is a universal symbol or recurring pattern in literature, art, or mythology that evokes deep responses in readers or viewers across cultures and eras. Developed extensively by psychologist Carl Jung, archetypes are seen as innate and universal prototypes for ideas, emanating from what he termed the "collective unconscious." Essentially, they are recurring themes, situations, characters, or symbols that resonate universally, often serving to drive the narrative forward or impart some deeper wisdom.
Usage:

Archetypes exist in various forms – from characters and themes to situations and symbols. They can be seen across different cultures, despite these cultures having no apparent connection, implying a kind of shared human experience or universal understanding.
Examples:
The Hero: Often the protagonist, this character overcomes great challenges, undertakes quests, and battles evil. Think of King Arthur, Harry Potter, or Luke Skywalker.
The Mentor: A wise, older figure that helps guide the hero. Examples include Merlin for King Arthur, Dumbledore for Harry Potter, and Obi-Wan Kenobi for Luke Skywalker.
The Mother Figure: Representing nurturance, protection, and warmth. This can be the Fairy Godmother type or the Stepmother type.
The Journey: This represents a search, a quest for discovery, or the pursuit of some kind of truth. Many stories, from "The Odyssey" to "The Lord of the Rings," revolve around this theme.
Water and the Sea: Often symbolic of the mystery of the subconscious mind or the unknown.
The Garden: Typically represents paradise or a utopian world.
Function:
Universal Connectivity: Since archetypes resonate universally, they help in creating connections between the reader and the narrative, across diverse cultural and temporal boundaries.
Narrative Depth: Archetypes add layers to the story, providing depth by linking the narrative to universally understood symbols or themes.
Conveying Collective Experience: They allow authors to tap into shared cultural narratives and human experiences, making stories more profound and relatable.
Evoke Emotional Responses: Given their deep-rooted nature, archetypes can evoke strong, innate emotional responses from readers or viewers.
Understanding archetypes is crucial for both writers and readers. For writers, it provides tools to create compelling narratives that

tap into shared human experiences. For readers, recognizing archetypes enriches the reading experience, providing deeper insights into the narrative's themes and characters. However, while archetypes are templates, they should not be restrictive. The best stories often give these archetypes a fresh spin or subvert them in innovative ways.

ARCHAISM

Archaism refers to the use of words, phrases, or styles that are outdated and no longer commonly used in contemporary language or literature. These words or phrases are used deliberately to give a feeling of antiquity or to invoke a period from the past. Archaism can be found in various aspects of language:

Lexical Archaism: This involves the use of old-fashioned words or phrases. For example:

> "Thou" for "You"
> "Whence" for "From where"
> "Methinks" for "I think"

Phonological Archaism: This relates to old pronunciation. Although this is less common in literature, it can be found in some regional dialects or historical reenactments.

Morphological Archaism: This involves the use of old or outdated grammatical forms or inflections. For instance:

> "Spake" as the past tense for "Speak" instead of "Spoke"
> "Wert" as the second person singular past of "Be" instead of "Were"

Syntactical Archaism: This involves using sentence structures or syntax that is no longer common. For example:

> "Happy he who far from business..." instead of "He who is far from business is happy."

Semantic Archaism: This involves words that have changed meaning over time. For example:

"Girl" once meant a young person of either gender, not specifically a female.

Archaism is often employed for various purposes:

Evoke a Specific Time Period: When an author wants to transport readers to a past era, they might use archaic language to make the setting more authentic.

Stylistic Choice: Archaism can give a poetic or lofty tone to a piece of writing. This is particularly common in poetry and religious texts.

Character Development: An author might make a character use archaic language to show they are from a different time or to highlight their antiquated or scholarly nature.

Humor: Sometimes, archaism is used for comedic effect, as the antiquated language can sound funny or out of place in a modern context.

Legal or Ceremonial Use: Some legal, religious, or ceremonial texts retain archaic language due to tradition.

It's worth noting that over-reliance on archaism can make a text difficult for modern readers to understand. However, when used judiciously, it can add depth, atmosphere, and a rich sense of history to a piece.

EUPHEMISM

A euphemism is a figure of speech wherein a milder or less direct word or phrase is used in place of another, which may be considered harsh, blunt, vulgar, or unpleasant. Euphemisms are employed to convey potentially sensitive or offensive subjects in a more delicate or socially acceptable manner. Their use helps to soften the impact of expressions, ensuring communication remains polite, tactful, or less emotionally charged.

Usage:

Euphemisms are widespread in everyday language, particularly in topics that might be uncomfortable, taboo, or emotionally charged, such as death, bodily functions, or sensitive societal issues.

Examples:

Passed away instead of "died."

Between jobs for "unemployed."

Economically disadvantaged instead of "poor."

Senior citizen for an "old person."

Correctional facility instead of "prison."

Letting someone go for "firing someone."

Function:

Avoiding Discomfort: Euphemisms can mitigate the discomfort or offense of discussing taboo or sensitive subjects.

Maintaining Social Decorum: They help maintain politeness in formal or delicate situations, ensuring conversations don't become inappropriate or rude.

Elevating Tone: In some cases, euphemisms can elevate the tone of a conversation, making it sound more refined or sophisticated.

Masking Harsh Realities: They can be used to downplay or obfuscate harsh realities, especially in political or corporate contexts.

Considerations:

While euphemisms can serve to enhance communication by making it more socially acceptable, they can also be criticized for being misleading or evasive. Overreliance on them, especially in situations requiring transparency and clarity, can lead to miscommunication or the perception of deceit.

In literature and other forms of expression, understanding and identifying euphemisms is essential. They provide insight into the societal norms and taboos of the time or the values and sensitivities of characters. On the other hand, writers and speakers must be aware of the potential pitfalls of euphemisms and ensure that their use is appropriate for the intended audience and context.

MOTIF

A motif is a recurring element, concept, or structure in a work of literature. It can be an image, theme, situation, or a particular phrase that appears multiple times throughout a piece. Motifs are used to establish a particular mood or tone, convey underlying messages, reinforce or highlight particular themes, or draw attention to a certain character or event. In essence, motifs provide consistency to the narrative and often serve symbolic functions, emphasizing recurrent and crucial elements of the story.

Motifs are employed in both prose and poetry, helping to create a thread of continuity or a pattern. They can be straightforward or symbolic, appearing explicitly in the text or functioning on a more subtle, metaphorical level.

Examples:

The green light in F. Scott Fitzgerald's "The Great Gatsby" is a recurring motif symbolizing Gatsby's unattainable dreams and desires, particularly his love for Daisy.

The blood in William Shakespeare's "Macbeth" is a powerful motif representing guilt, violence, and the irreversible nature of certain actions.

The road is often used as a motif in literature, symbolizing a journey, whether literal or metaphorical, showcasing life's unpredictability, challenges, and personal growth.

Nature and the seasons frequently appear as motifs, representing

cycles of life, change, decay, or renewal.
Function:
Emphasis on Themes: By continually revisiting certain symbols, images, or scenarios, the author emphasizes the theme or central idea related to the motif, enhancing its importance in the narrative.
Creating Depth: Motifs add layers of meaning, allowing readers to connect different parts of the story and interpret deeper implications.
Establishing Mood: A recurrent motif can establish and sustain a particular mood or atmosphere, from foreboding to joyousness.
Connecting Plot Points: Motifs can tie together disparate events, characters, or themes, creating cohesion within the narrative.

Considerations:
It's crucial to differentiate between a theme and a motif. While they are closely related, a theme is an idea or message underlying the narrative, whereas a motif is a recurrent element emphasizing that theme. Identifying and understanding motifs can enhance a reader's appreciation of a literary work, revealing the intricacies and nuances embedded within the text.

PORTMANTEAU

A portmanteau is a linguistic blend or combination of two (or sometimes more) words, where portions of the words are joined together to form a new, singular word. The term "portmanteau" itself is derived from the French word for a suitcase, suggesting the idea of packing two things into one. This linguistic device is often used to describe something new or to succinctly capture a more complex idea.

Portmanteaus are especially prevalent in modern English, often arising in contexts like technology, business branding, or pop culture. The creation of a portmanteau can be for convenience, humor, or to fill a linguistic gap.

Examples:

Brunch (breakfast + lunch): A meal that is eaten between the times of breakfast and lunch.

Motel (motor + hotel): A roadside hotel designed primarily for motorists, typically having the rooms arranged in a low building with parking directly outside.

Blog (web + log): A regularly updated website or web page, usually run by an individual, that is written in an informal style.

Gerrymandering (Gerry + salamander): The practice of manipulating boundaries of an electoral constituency to favor one party or class. The term originated from a salamander-shaped electoral district created under Governor Elbridge Gerry of Massachusetts.

Smog (smoke + fog): Fog or haze combined with smoke and other pollutants.

Function:

Efficiency: Portmanteaus can condense complex ideas or descriptions into a single, more easily understood term.

Creativity: They often arise from playful or creative engagements with language, offering fresh and memorable ways to describe new or evolving concepts.

Filling Linguistic Gaps: As culture and technology evolve, new

terms are needed. Portmanteaus can swiftly fill these gaps.
Considerations:
While portmanteaus can be inventive and useful, they can also
become outdated or seem forced if they don't naturally integrate
into everyday language. Effective portmanteaus resonate with a
wide audience and aptly capture the essence of what they describe.

MALAPROPISM

A malapropism is a humorous linguistic error where a word is
mistakenly used in place of another word that sounds similar,
resulting in a nonsensical or ludicrous statement. The term
"malapropism" is derived from a character named Mrs. Malaprop
in **Richard Brinsley Sheridan's 1775 play "The Rivals."** Mrs.
Malaprop frequently misspeaks, substituting one word for another,
to comedic effect.
Usage:
Malapropisms are often used deliberately in literature and media to
create comedic situations and to develop humorous characters. In
everyday speech, unintentional malapropisms can be a source of
amusement, confusion, or embarrassment.
Examples:
"He is the pineapple of politeness." (Instead of "pinnacle")
"Texas has a lot of electrical votes." (Instead of "electoral")
"She's the apple of discord in the family." (Instead of "bone")
"He might fade into Bolivian." (Instead of "fade into oblivion")
Function:
Comedic Effect: Malapropisms can be used deliberately to
generate laughter in plays, films, and literature.
Character Development: They can help in portraying a character as
being ignorant, confused, or both, adding depth to their personality.
Highlighting Misunderstandings: They can emphasize a character's
lack of knowledge or their discomfort in a particular situation or
setting.

Considerations:
While deliberate malapropisms can be humorous, unintentional use in serious contexts can be perceived as a lack of knowledge or carelessness on the part of the speaker or writer. It's essential to be aware of context and intention when encountering or employing malapropisms.

ISOCOLON

Isocolon is a rhetorical device that involves the use of successive sentences, clauses, or phrases of roughly equal length and corresponding structure. It can add rhythm, balance, and emphasis to statements and can be particularly effective in persuasive contexts. The term "isocolon" comes from the Greek "iso-", meaning "equal", and "-colon", which refers to a structural segment.

Usage:
Isocolon is often utilized to create a sense of balance and rhythm in speeches, prose, and poetry. By presenting ideas in structurally parallel ways, the speaker or writer can emphasize their importance or interconnectedness.

Examples:
"Veni, vidi, vici." ("I came, I saw, I conquered.") - Julius Caesar
"It's not the size of the dog in the fight, it's the size of the fight in the dog." - Mark Twain
"Ask not what your country can do for you; ask what you can do for your country." - John F. Kennedy
"By failing to prepare, you are preparing to fail." - Benjamin Franklin

Function:
Rhythmic and Memorable: The balanced structure of isocolon can make statements more rhythmic and, therefore, more memorable. This can be particularly effective in speeches and advertising.

Emphasizes Parallelism: By presenting related ideas in a similar structure, isocolon highlights their relationship or contrast.

Persuasive Power: Because of its balanced and rhythmic nature, isocolon can be persuasive, giving the impression that the presented ideas are equally valid or important.

Considerations:
While isocolon can be a powerful tool, it's essential not to overuse it, as doing so can make speech or writing sound formulaic or artificial. Its effectiveness often comes from its ability to surprise or satisfy the listener or reader with its balanced structure.

About The Author

Meet Professor Abha Bhardwaj Sharma, a luminary in the realm of English Language and Literature Education. With an illustrious career spanning over three decades, she has been a guiding light to countless college and university students in the intricate world of language and literature.

Her unwavering dedication to shaping young minds has brought forth a dream realized - the Miracle English Language & Literature Institute, now a venerable institution celebrating its remarkable 25-year journey. Over this quarter-century, Professor Abha's visionary approach to education has transformed lives and ignited a passion for language and literature in generations of students.
Professor Abha's journey is a testament to her boundless compassion and holistic approach to education. Her humility and immense knowledge create an environment where students flourish not only academically, but also as individuals.

In addition to her distinguished career in education, Professor Abha is a prolific writer. She has authored numerous books spanning English, Linguistics, and Literature, contributing significantly to the academic world. Her literary prowess extends beyond the classroom, encompassing diverse genres and subjects.
As a writer, she has penned insightful essays, illuminating literary critiques, and thought-provoking poetry, leaving an indelible mark on the world of letters. Among her literary accomplishments, she has authored a self-help book titled "I am a Miracle," inspiring readers to embrace their inner potential and achieve personal growth.

Professor Abha's legacy as an educator and writer is etched in the hearts and minds of those she has touched, and her influence continues to shape the trajectory of English Language and Literature education and the world of literature itself.